Open Your Eyes

ALSO BY

Alexandra Stoddard

The Decoration of Houses

Living in Love

Gracious Living in a New World

Mothers: A Celebration

The Art of the Possible

Alexandra Stoddard's Tea Celebrations

Alexandra Stoddard's Book of Days

Making Choices

Grace Notes

Creating a Beautiful Home

Daring to Be Yourself

Gift of a Letter

Alexandra Stoddard's Book of Color

Alexandra Stoddard's Living Beautifully Together

Living a Beautiful Life

The Postcard as Art

Reflections on Beauty

A Child's Place

Style for Living

*Put your hand in mine and let us
help one another to see things better.*

—Claude Monet

Quill

A HarperResource Book
An Imprint of HarperCollins*Publishers*

Open Your Eyes

1,000 Simple Ways
TO BRING Beauty INTO YOUR
Home AND Life

EACH DAY

Alexandra Stoddard

The Library of Congress has cataloged the hardcover
edition as follows:
Stoddard, Alexandra.
    Open your eyes : 1,000 simple ways to bring
beauty into your home and life each day / Alexandra
Stoddard.
        p.   cm.
    Includes index.
    ISBN 0-688-15904-4
    1. Interior decoration. 2. Visual perception. I. Title.
NK2115.S6976 1998
747—dc21   98-26953

Printed in the United States of America

First Quill Edition 2000

ISBN 0-380-73144-4 (pbk.)

2   3   4   5   6   7   8   9   10

BOOK DESIGN BY MARYSARAH QUINN

To Roger Mühl

CONTENTS

WHAT IS SEEING?

How well we see and what we see matters because
we are the ones who direct our glances and, by so
doing, determine how vibrantly we will live.

In my work as an interior designer, I've found that most people go
through life half blind. Few really know how to see and as a result are
unaware of the majesty and beauty around them. But seeing can be
learned, and to those who learn to see well, the world becomes an entirely
different place. Life is suddenly rich with promise, full of light, color, texture, and harmony. A trained eye leads to an awareness of beauty and a way
to find pleasure in all things.

Seeing is democratic. We can all do it. My aim is to help teach you to
see. The principles, exercises, and lessons in this book will help you to
open your eyes wider and wider to all possibilities.

Seeing well saves time, energy, and money. You will learn not to be
dependent on other people's eyes. You will avoid costly mistakes while
experiencing the enrichment of all the moments of your life at home or
anywhere else. You will learn to bring more harmony into your home with
better scale, proportion, order, symmetry, and balance. I hope this book
will inspire you to look and really see that your life can become a work of
art, a life of significance.

INTRODUCTION

It might be good to open our eyes and see.

— THOMAS MERTON

Whenever we want to learn to do something well, we have to go into training. Just because we've been given eyesight doesn't mean we know how to use our eyes to look and really see.

We have to train ourselves to look at all things and see things well. We must not be limited by the familiar but must instead look and look again. Seeing well is a process of opening our mind as well as our eyes. We will be intrigued and curious, but in the beginning we also need to discipline our mind and eyes and discern through practice.

Begin where you are now and embark on a seeing journey with me.

Open Your Eyes: 1,000 Simple Ways to Bring Beauty into Your Home and Life Each Day is my attempt to open you up to a whole new way of seeing the world, a whole new way of living your life. As an interior designer, I'm well aware how much you care about the way your surroundings look and feel to you, your family, and loved ones. You want to live in inviting spaces where the energy is positive, where the colors are uplifting, where the scale and proportion are harmonious, where your objects are arranged in attractive compositions. You want to feel elevated by the refinement and artistry of your possessions. Above all, you want to see and feel the rhythms that lead you to a more meaningful life day by day.

In order to see, you require basic tools that will be the keys to the life you want to live. This book gives you all you need to learn in order to look and see well beyond the ordinary. You will be able to train your own eyes to see with a fresh new vision. If I can help you to perceive depth in the space in front of you, you will in turn be able to live with more depth in other areas, because you will see more divine order in the universe.

When I was sixteen, my aunt took me around the world, exposing me to every kind of seeing experience imaginable. I saw poverty, illness, and death, as well as natural beauty and architectural wonders. In order to see well and discover beauty, you have to expose your eye to everything there is to see. With training, you will be discerning, refining what you see toward beauty. Seeing well not only brings more joy and pleasure to every day but also transforms mere existence into the art of living.

Open Your Eyes

ONE

Seeking the Ideal
Proportion and Scale

Beauty and art pervade all the affairs of life like
some friendly genius, and embellish with their
cheer all our surroundings.

— HEGEL

Making the most of our lives, preserving harmony in our
surroundings, and loving what we have and see is the most
satisfactory way to live. Just as the satisfactory relationship
of one person to another results in comfort, peace, and joy,
so does the satisfactory relationship of ideal proportion and
scale. As in relationships, there is stability in proper proportion and scale that leads to pleasure and sensible living,
health and ease. My aim in this chapter is
to transform the way you see everyday life,
as well as what you do and how you live as
a result.

There are none so blind as
those who cannot see.
JONATHAN SWIFT

The difference between living and half living is seeing well, looking for associations between things, seeking the connections, being aware of scale and proportion. If it is true that what you seek you find, then it is also true that what you see you find. When you see well, you enjoy the beauty of the world rather than seeing only half the treasures around you.

Proportion and scale are the tools for achieving this harmonious ideal. Their benevolent effects are all around you. Not too much, not too little. Not too high, not too low. Not too fat, not too thin; not too sweet, not too sour; not too loud, not too faint; not too busy, not too bland; not too garish, not too dull; not too extravagant, not too stingy. We know the world is not perfect. But if we can see ideal proportion—the relationship of things to themselves—and if we can see scale—the size of objects on their own—we will be better equipped to see that a rich life is out there, ours for the seeing and learning. When you seek the ideal, understanding the relationships among people and objects around you, beauty is wherever you are.

Let scale and proportion help you to become a seer, with your eyes and brain answering to your own highest conception of the ideal.

Proportion

Proportion is the part considered in relationship to the whole. The essence of proportion is the connection among objects (or parts of a single object) in regard to size, dimensions, and character. All things, from simple two-dimensional shapes—a room's floor plan or a tabletop—to more complex three-dimensional objects—a carved mantel or a Ming vase—have proportions. If one part varies, the other parts are affected, and the original harmony of the whole is disturbed. Every object has several individual components that come together to make up a whole. The proportions of an object are determined by its distinctive measurements, form, line, curve, and design details. When there is a harmonious relationship among the parts that make up the whole, aesthetically pleasing proportions result, delighting the eye. When something is not in proportion, when there is no integration between the parts, it lacks unity and is jarring, disturbing to the eye. Recognizing ideal proportion and correcting what is awkward is a fundamental skill for seeing well. Mastering it requires training the eye.

The Science of Proportion

Standards for aesthetically pleasing proportions are scientifically logical, achieved by following mathematical rules that date back to the civilization and architecture of ancient Greece. Though the Greek masters of architecture originally resolved proportions visually, they eventually gave architecture total stability through applying precise, unchanging mathematical formulas. When the classical principles of the Greeks are employed, harmony and excellence result.

Do you wish to see clearly and be free?

BASSUI

One of the twentieth-century masters of proportion was my mentor, Eleanor McMillen Brown. Mrs. Brown traveled extensively in Europe, as Edith Wharton did, studying classical architecture. Her sensitivity to line and proportion was a direct result of her exposure to harmonious architecture. All of her architectural designs were subtle and delicate in their proportions.

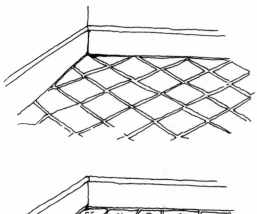

With her discerning eye, Mrs. Brown would look at a drawing, alter the measurement of one element, then redo each of the other elements so that all the measurements were symmetrical. She

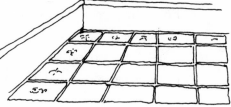

was a genius at adjusting parts of a whole to obtain symmetry. One of her maxims—indelible in the minds of all her protégés—was "When you change one thing, rethink everything." No single unit of a system can be changed without modifying the whole.

During afternoons over tea, I would take my drawings and floor plans to her desk. With tracing paper, Mrs. Brown would fine-tune the proportions, moving elements until they were unquestionably correct. In a drawing where one-quarter inch represented a foot, she would change one inch here, two inches there, and right away I'd see the improvement. Modest about her genius, she'd end the session by saying, "Well, think about it, Sandie." I'd go off to the drafting department and redo the drawings immediately. With her architectural eye, she approached a floor plan as though everything represented in it were marble and couldn't be altered later. And she was essentially right: It is important to establish proper proportion at the beginning when designing a room, because it is very difficult and expensive to change it once the room is executed.

The smallest change in proportion can make a world of difference, and all the remaining parts of

Thinking is more interesting than knowing, but less interesting than looking.

GOETHE

the whole must be altered to the same degree. If the love seat is made longer, for example, the length and width of the coffee table in front of it must also be increased. The end tables should be wider, not longer, to prevent the love seat from looking too long and skinny. Even the size of the throw pillows should be increased for the larger love seat; otherwise, they may look minuscule.

Go into your living room and pretend that your sofa is a two-cushion love seat. How would this alter the appearance of the coffee table, the end tables, and the scale of the chairs? Do this exercise wherever you are. Examine doorways leading from a main hall. If you change the height of one door, you have to change not only the height of all the other doors but their width as well.

Remember to re-see every proportion under changed circumstances. If you purchase a larger sofa, the proportions of the adjacent open-arm chairs might be dwarfed. What is good for plan A is not necessarily appropriate for plan B.

Distorted Proportions

Some artists purposely distort proportions to stretch the boundaries of expression. The twentieth-century literary and artistic movement known as Surrealism uses bizarre imagery and incongruous juxtaposition of objects in an attempt to express visually the fantastical workings of the subconscious. An extra-large head, long face, and other grotesque body configurations with one part out of proportion to the others are examples of distorted proportions. The work of Spanish artist Salvador Dali is a good representation of Surrealist art.

Surrealism, to my eye, is similar to a wavy mirror in an amusement park. Fantastic reality is often weird, making me feel uneasy. I prefer conscious reality to subconscious surrealism.

People see only what they are prepared to see.

EMERSON

The Golden Mean and the Golden Rectangle

The Greeks' definition of good proportion was also their definition of good conduct. Aristotle extolled the virtue of the middle path—moderation between two extremes—as the standard of artistic goodness. He theorized about "the equal being an intermediate between excess and defeat," stating, "By the intermediate in the object I mean that which is equidistant from each of the extremes . . . neither too much or too little." This is how, in essence, you come to see and understand classical proportion.

Let Aristotle teach you about proportion; follow his advice that "every art does its work well—by looking to the intermediate and judging its works by this standard . . . of good works of art it is not possible to take away or to add anything." This theory of correct proportions applies to every aspect of living and leads us to a more significant life.

In architecture, the middle path relates to ideal proportions and shapes. The architects of the Parthenon, the great classical Greek temple in Athens on the Acropolis, used the formula of the golden section to determine the structure's proportions. This formula applies to a one-dimensional line and is related to the golden rectangle and divine proportion. It will give you a solid base for understanding the classical principles of design. A mathematical formula for the ideal proportions of a rectangle, width to length, can be applied to any representation of the rectangle—the most often-used shape—whether a room, building, tabletop, book, index card, notebook, or tray. In its simplest form, the golden rectangle is a rectangle that can be divided in such a way as to make a square and a smaller rectangle, the ratio of the original rectangle's length to its width being equal to the ratio of the smaller rectangle's length to its width.

My particular ability does not lie in mathematical calculation, but rather in visualizing effects, possibilities, and consequences.

ALBERT EINSTEIN

Take a 4 × 6-inch index card, and fold back one third, or two inches, creating a four-inch square. Turn the card over to reveal the two-inch piece. Fold it flat over the four-inch square. Look at the card that is now a square with half of the square covered by the two-inch flap. Now open the flap to display the 4 × 6-inch rectangle.

Remember that this is the simplest formula for the golden rectangle and is not absolutely accurate mathematically. Still, it's important to become familiar with this mathematical rule before moving on to the more subtle relationships of measurements. By mastering this simple method, you will already know more than most seeing people. Your appreciation of the more accurate formula will be greater once you have a firm grasp of this rule.

You can take any square from 4 inches to 4 feet, or from 40 inches to 40 feet, divide the square in half, add the halved part to the end of the square, and thus compose a harmonious rectangle, one that is not too long or too narrow, not too wide or too fat.

You can do these calculations in your head. For example, if you want to build a deck off your kitchen, and you have 18 feet in width and plenty of land, what should be the length of the deck? Divide the 18 feet by 2 and arrive at 9 feet. Add the 9 feet to the 18 feet and you have 27 feet. Therefore, the dimensions of the deck should be 18 × 27 feet. You can create the ideal proportion whether you base the measurement on the length or the width. For example, suppose the length of the deck were 18 feet. What would be the ideal width? It would be 12 feet, because when

you divide 18 by 1.5, it becomes 12; therefore, the ideal dimensions would be 12 × 18 feet. If you want to build a rectangular sunroom, and the established width is 20 feet, the ideal length would be 30 feet. Multiply the width by 1.5 on the calculator to get the ideal length, or divide the length by 1.5 to get the ideal width.

This simple ratio of width to length (multiplying the width by 1.5 to obtain the length) is central not only in architecture but in other design as well. I have used this general formula to help me determine length-to-width relationships for everything from the measurements of gardens, rooms, and swimming pools to desks, coffee tables, and end tables, and even what shape my books should be. You can find this simple golden rectangle formula most useful in everyday life. You'll understand why a rug's dimensions are so satisfying, for example, and why a long hall gives you claustrophobia.

Now, let's advance to the precise formula. If you know the width of something and want to establish the absolute ultimate divine proportion as applied to a golden rectangle, multiply the width by 1.618 (rather than 1.5), and you will have the *perfect* relationship between width and length.

You can let your eye be your guide as to whether you use the simple formula or the more mathematically precise formula. Test both measurements, then use your eye to decide. If you're going to build a rectangular room based on the simple formula, a 16-foot width would have a 24-foot length, a pleasing proportion by any standard. The divine proportion would add 2 feet to the length, making the room 16 × 26 feet. You may prefer the 16 × 24-foot dimensions. In any case, it is always best to know what is considered absolute perfection, then be guided by common sense, intuition, and personal satisfaction. In most cases, I prefer the simple 1.5 formula, because it gives you a generous and, in my opinion, more satisfying rectangle.

A simple way to compare the different formulas and determine what rectangle you prefer is to go back to your original 4 × 6-inch index card. Using the divine proportion formula, the 6 inches would become 6½ inches. Cut a one-half-inch-wide piece of paper, tape it to the length of the index card, and see for yourself. You also have the freedom to select a dimension somewhere between the two formulas.

When you see rectangles that please your eye, measure them and jot the dimensions in your notebook to analyze at your leisure. Find the dimensions that please your unique eye.

There is another method for obtaining the golden rectangle that is most pleasing to my eye. Cut a 4 × 6-inch index card into a 4-inch square. Fold the square on the diagonal, from corner to corner, to form a triangle. Place the triangle on another 4 × 6-inch index card with the point facing down like the flap of an envelope. Make the top left-hand point of the triangle flush with the left-hand edge of the card and tape it in place. Where the top right-hand point of the triangle touches the index card, draw a line from top to bottom. Cut off the excess paper of the index card along that line.

You immediately see that your new index card is slightly smaller than the 4 × 6-inch card. Measure it. You should find that it is a 4 × 5⅝-inch rectangle, the fattest rectangle of the three different formulas. The proportion of this fat rectangle, derived by bisecting a square on the diagonal, is considered by many to be the ideal—even the perfect— measurement of width to length. Play with these different formulas and let your eye be the final judge of your favorite, depending on the function or location of the object or area in question.

The Height Variable

The relationship between the length and width of a space may be ideal, but if the ceiling is too low or too high, the overall feeling of the room will be wrong. In an old New England house, the low ceilings and small rooms were in proper proportion. A typical room was 14 feet square with 8-foot-high ceilings. Higher ceilings were usually ceremonial—to add grandeur and sometimes to inspire awe.

If you have a room that doesn't feel right, measure its length, width, and height. In decades past, builders saved money by making ceilings low, until people admitted they felt squashed and hunched over. Now many new houses have a "great room" with cathedral ceilings. This space is used for many purposes and is in effect an open plan. Where there were once many different rooms, now one large room serves as a gathering place.

If your room is large but has a low ceiling, and if it is a room directly under the roof, consider adding skylights. If you want a ceiling to disappear or feel light emotionally, paint it "atmosphere blue," the color of a beautiful sky. When you look up at the blue sky on a sunny day, you feel a sense of infinite space. A good lighting consultant can light a room in a way that appears to lift a low ceiling, such as by placing a few halogen standing lamps in opposite corners with the light directed at the ceiling to give a heightening effect.

If you have a small room with an extremely high ceiling, you can have a false ceiling installed. Often in apartment buildings, large rooms have been broken up into smaller rooms, causing this awkwardness. In the tiny maid's room of an old apartment, the ceiling may be the same height as that of the much larger living room. To lower the ceiling you can paint it a rich color—bottle green, for example—to match the wall color. This creates a cozy hatbox feeling. The floor will appear lower if it is dark. To lift it up, bleach the wood or install a floor covering that is light in tone.

Look at the four walls of your living room and label them north, south, east, and west. Stand in front of the north wall, or elevation, and visualize it falling forward like a door without hinges. Visually, drop each elevation down. You've now taken a three-dimensional space, the room, and made it two dimensional. What can you see from this exercise? You learn to see the scale and proportion of a rectangle, in this case a wall, by seeing it in a different plane. For example, the antique door surround for our Stonington cottage is 60 inches wide and is ideally proportioned for the front of our house. However, after it was shipped from Colorado to the cottage, and we temporarily stored it in the empty dining room, it looked huge, taking up most of the floor space. I never realized its true scale and proportion until I saw it lying flat on the floor.

Good Proportions Mean Good Bones

Good proportions in a space mean good bone structure, a foundation that gives you a lot to build on. If a house fundamentally has good bones, or good base proportions, you can renovate and decorate it with harmonious results. Our cottage was

Man is capable of an ideal beauty.

IMMANUEL KANT

the ugliest house in America when we bought it, because it was dun-colored—a dull, grayish brown that sapped your energy—on the outside as well as the inside. But the bone structure was good, and I know the magic of white paint. The house had been on the market for four and a half years. We were perhaps the first to see beyond the debilitating, depressing colors.

The sense of proportion as bone structure applies to objects as well. The design has a great deal to do with the charm of a piece of furniture, but without a pleasing relationship of length to width, you won't feel the grace and ease that you do when measurements are ideal.

For the most part, you only see what you train yourself to see.

When you learn how to see ideal proportions, you feel great satisfaction. You can use your knowledge of proportion in every aspect of your life. Although there is a scientific standard for ideal proportions, your eye can be trained to see and envision proper proportion as well as to recognize ill proportion. To the untrained eye, proportion is abstract and complex, yet it is the most pervasive principle of seeing. The ancient Greeks called proportion the soul of what we see.

Finding Our Own Harmonious Proportions

To gaze is to think.

SALVADOR DALI

Each of us has to seek and find harmonious proportions that stir us in emotionally pleasing ways. According to recent studies, neuroscientists can detect chemical changes in the central nervous system of people who are enjoying what they are seeing.

What is your favorite proportion, length to width? Do you prefer rectangles or squares? Here are several rectangle proportions that I find pleasing for tables and benches:

- 29 × 37-inch end table
- 25 × 38-inch end table
- 30 × 44-inch coffee table
- 30 × 50-inch table
- 18 × 23-inch bench
- 17 × 23-inch bench
- 25 × 32-inch small desk

Our building was built in 1925 by Italian craftsmen who were brought here to build a series of fifteen-story apartment houses up Park Avenue to 96th Street. These craftsmen had a masterful grasp of proportion. I find our apartment bedroom to have ideal proportions. When Oprah Winfrey's producer asked me what my favorite room in the apartment was, I immediately answered, "My bedroom." It is a fat rectangle, 15 feet 7½ inches wide × 19 feet 6½ inches long. On the long west wall are two windows. I built a seventeen-inch-deep ledge the entire width of the room, with bookcases underneath on either side, visually bringing the wall forward and making the proportions feel almost square. The ceiling height is a comfortable 9 feet 8 inches. I know this space well, because when we're in New York, not only do I sleep in this room but I do my writing there as well. The bed is near the windows and offers a view of the Brick Presbyterian Church and the sky, leaving half the room for a sitting area. The beautiful proportions of the room allow us freedom to rearrange the furniture. Seasonally, we move the love seat from the east wall, where it sits during the winter, to the foot of the bed during spring and summer, so we have more natural light and can see the ever-changing sky and enjoy fresh air from an open window.

The moments we call life are the moments when we see.

PETER MEGARGEE

BROWN

Walk around your house. What proportions do you find most pleasing? Measure the ones you like. Now measure those you don't feel comfortable with. Study your measurements. You will see that moderate proportions—not too narrow or too wide, not too tall or too short—are those you are intuitively drawn to. Conversely, the proportions that make you uncomfortable are usually not moderate but extreme.

Take time to measure your spaces. By measuring all the proportions you like, you will begin to see the mathematical relationships between length and width. For example, our living room has ideal proportions. It measures 16 feet wide × 24 feet long. If you bisect the width, you have 8 feet. If you add this 8 feet to the width of 16 feet, you arrive at 24 feet, the simple formula of the ideal rectangle. Another example is my writing table in our bedroom. I love its proportions—30 inches deep (or wide) × 48 inches long. The length is perfect for the width. If you bisect the width to get 15 inches, then add 15 inches to the 30-inch width, you get a 45-inch length, very close to the 48-inch length of the table. In fact, this table's dimensions are closer to the *real* golden rectangle where 1.618 rather than 1.5 is the ratio.

The best of men and women are those who have eyes to see.

THE BUDDHA

It is valuable to carry a measuring tape with you as you explore. You probably have a 25-foot-long tape in a tool box, but an inexpensive plastic-cased 6-foot-long tape is especially convenient to have on hand so you become more comfortable with standard proportions. Familiarity with these proportions will help you get a handle on volume, projection, and the impact of objects in your immediate surroundings and how they can work better

Seeing the problem isn't enough. Visual literacy requires knowing how to solve it.

together to create harmony and a cohesive whole. You'll begin to see and understand complementary relationships. You'll begin to see with more nuance, noticing the subtle differences that affect the whole.

Confronting Awkward Proportions of Spaces

In the nineteenth century, to accommodate the many people who could not afford a broad piece of land on the avenues, urban builders put up apartment buildings on long narrow lots. These *To see is to understand.* apartments became known as railroad flats, one room wide and three or four rooms long. To reach the bathroom at one end, you have to go through several other rooms. Though railroad flats are large in terms of square feet, their proportions are extremely awkward—they are much too long for their width. Railroad apartments violate the attributes of human scale and proportion.

When you encounter a space or an object with awkward proportions, whether it's too long for its width or top heavy, you will feel a certain uneasiness. For example, it is never appropriate to cut out a rug around a hearth. The cut-out area violates the proportions of the rug, causing you to feel uneasy. A rug should be a smaller version of the room's dimensions, echoing the overall shape of the room. Always scale down the rug size so you maintain the classic proportions of the rectangle.

Do you see yourself as a visualizer and also a verbalizer? When people see objects that are offensive to their eye due to poor proportion, they often become frustrated and tune out because they don't know how to make it better. They shut their eyes and turn their backs. But flawed proportions *can* be corrected in many instances, and as a decorator I have learned a number of ways to do this.

Using Mirrors to Correct Bad Proportions

Unlike our bedroom, the entrance hall of our apartment does not have gracious proportions. The space measures 8 feet 7½ inches × 23 feet 5½ inches, much too narrow for its length. The ratio of height to width is also a problem: The width of the main hall is less than its height by almost a foot. (Whenever possible, the ceiling should never be higher than the width of the room.) Before I married Peter and moved into the apartment, he told me no one ever used the hall because it looked like a tunnel. It was Mrs. Brown who suggested that we mirror the north wall, visually doubling the width of the space. By multiplying the actual width by 2, the visual measurement becomes 17 feet 3 inches × 23 feet 5½ inches, a fat rectangle satisfying to the eye. When we have receptions in the apartment, everyone likes to gather in the hall because it is pivotal to entering and leaving other areas of the apartment such as the library, living room, kitchen pantry, and bedroom hall. The mirrored wall is a brilliant way to create a golden mean of proportion, fooling the eye to achieve a feeling of harmony.

Here are some other ideas for using mirrors to correct awkward proportions:

Never did eye see the sun unless it had first become sunlike, and never can the Soul have vision of the First beauty unless itself be beautiful.

PLOTINUS

For there is nothing which men love but the good . . . the simple truth is, that men love the good.

PLATO

- ◆ If you have a long narrow hallway, place a mirror at the end of the hall to bring in light and visually widen the space. You can either hang a traditional mirror in a frame or mirror the whole wall from cornice to baseboard.

- ◆ If you have a long dark room, place a mirror or pair of mirrors on the long wall to break up its length. Windowpane mirrors will fool the eye into believing that you have two additional windows, creating more space and light.

◆ If you have a clumsy vertical load-bearing beam that disrupts otherwise ideal proportions, mirror it so it disappears.

Visually Widening a Narrow Space Without the Use of Mirrors

I found our bedroom hallway extremely cramped. The walls are only 39½ inches apart. To make matters worse, the floorboards are laid parallel to the walls, running with the narrowness of the space and making it appear even narrower than it is. We hung botanical watercolors on the walls as well as antique porcelain plates to give the walls vitality and energy. The glass over the watercolors and the surface of the porcelain glow with light.

Develop a searching eye.

What else can you do to visually widen a narrow hall without reverting to mirrors? One solution is to install wall-to-wall carpeting over the floorboards, in effect covering up the directional lines that further narrow the space. But in the case of our bedroom hall, because I love wood, I chose to solve the problem by staining and bleaching the floor in a folk art manner—a chevron pattern from east to west—disrupting the north-south direction of the floorboards. The eye is relieved by the feeling of expanded space.

There are aesthetic standards. You can develop your eye, becoming, in time, an expert on these standards.

Another option is to place area rugs of different shapes and sizes to break up the linear appearance. A hall runner will do the opposite; it will further narrow the space. But a rug that contrasts with the floor looks like an island in the ocean. The eye is drawn to the pattern and color of the rug, making the space around it appear smaller, more broken up. Select rugs with a background color similar to that of the floor.

Square tiles laid on the diagonal widen a space. This principle also applies to squares of sisal carpeting or ceramic tiles.

Flexibility in Proportion

Always trust your eye to detect subtle differences in measurement, because there is a range of ideal proportion depending on location, composition, material, and other circumstances. For example, I wanted the longest and deepest counter possible for our small master bathroom. I lined the ledge up with the tub and made it as deep as the space allowed, ensuring enough space to sit on the toilet on the opposite wall and have access to the bathtub. The dimensions of the counter, $23\frac{1}{2} \times 66\frac{1}{4}$ inches, are not ideal, but with mirrors placed along the entire back wall, the proportions changed character and became harmonious.

If you are going to tile a bathroom counter, the dimensions of the counter and tiles should be taken into consideration in determining how the tiles will look laid out with grouting. Ideally, you don't want to cut tiles to fit. Even if your counter has ideal proportions, if you haven't worked out the execution of the material, the harmony you are seeking will be diminished. When using tiles or when painting a checkerboard pattern on a wooden surface, plan your layout on grid paper, taking into account the dimensions of the area to be tiled and the measurement of the tiles themselves. Whenever possible, try not to use half tiles on the floor or other surfaces. If your tiles don't lay out ideally, you can probably get a border tile that will work out mathematically for a finished look. If you need to use half square tiles, use them on all four sides as a border.

An artist observes, selects, guesses, and synthesizes.

Anton Pavlovich Chekhov

Proportions of Objects

Understanding the proportions of objects is more complicated than understanding the proportions of rooms and other rectangles, because objects have many more lines and curves that can relate in awkward proportions. An object's proportions are also affected by its location.

When you look at an object, examine its various elements. Identify how many different parts make up the whole. Study a favorite open-arm chair. Look at the back, the seat, the arms, and the legs. Don't be distracted by the wood or the pattern on the cushion. Examine it from every angle. The parts come together in a graceful way. Now look at a chair you don't like. If you can't find one in your house, look for an ugly chair at the office. Spot the flaw. Why is the chair not pleasing to you? You may not like the material it is made of, the color, or the design, but chances are the proportions are awkward as well. Perhaps the back is too high or too low. Perhaps the chair looks squat. Visually pick the chair apart, element by element, then re-see it in better proportions. When you look with the eyes of a designer, you identify the problem and come up with the solution.

All things are noble in proportion to their fullness of life.

JOHN RUSKIN

Proper Proportion Among Different Objects

Understanding proportion requires understanding how different objects relate to each other. Are they basically compatible? Are the proportions linked, one to another? Look at two similar objects together. Examine a lemon and a lime, for example. How are they different? By seeing the likeness of two objects, you can see what gives each its individuality. A lime is fatter, rounder, and smaller than a lemon. You can use such comparisons when you examine the proportions of arms on chairs or of legs on chairs and tables.

Now look at very different objects—a table and a lamp on the table, for example. How can you determine whether the lamp and the table have proportions that work ideally together? First, look at the relationship among the parts of

Maybe it takes genius to see genius.

JAMES HILLMAN

the table. Do the elements work well together? Are the lines pleasing in relationship to each other? Now look at the lamp. Critique it for ideal relationships, parts to the whole, just as you did the table, including the lampshade. If the lamp and shade are proportional, now step back and look at the juxtaposition of the lamp and table.

Your eye must decide whether the dimensions of the lamp are pleasing against the table. Each individual object may have good proportions, but when they are placed side by side, they may look incongruous. Let your eye distinguish how the table and the lamp feel to you when they are juxtaposed. Trust your eye. If they are compatible, chances are you feel peace and comfort when you look at them. You might not have a mathematical rationale for your conclusion, but you know that you are right in your judgment. Be proud that your eye can't be unpleasantly fooled.

Here are some other common pairings in the home where compatible proportions are important:

- *A sofa and upholstered chairs.* They should relate in their basic style, curves, and general proportions, including the height of the back. Look at the arms of a sofa for clues to how the arms of a chair should look. Because the chair is smaller than the sofa, the arms should be scaled down appropriately. If they were as fat as those of the sofa, they would look extremely awkward.

- *A dining table and the surrounding chairs.* The style, the wood, and the scale of the legs of the table and chairs should all be in harmony. If you have a large dining room table and small side chairs, you can correct the disproportion by placing many chairs at the table. This makes sense when you have a large family or when you regularly entertain eight or more people. Two small side chairs at the head and foot of a wide rectangular table look attractive and are proportional.

Generally, dining room chairs should not be too heavy in scale, because they are constantly moved around and

you want your guests to feel that the chairs are not immovable. You can pull up small chairs when you have a bigger group without some people feeling they're in temporary chairs. The height of all the chairs, regardless of their scale and style, should be the same. The height of the back of a dining room chair should be at least eight inches higher than the tabletop.

- *Sofa and end tables.* Relate the sofa arm height to the table. If the arm of the sofa is too low, it will make the end table look and feel too high. If you have low end tables to accommodate the low arms, however, the grouping will look squat, and any traditional table lamps will be so hopelessly low that you'll see the bulb from the top of the shade while you're sitting on the sofa. An ideal end table height for a sofa with low arms is approximately 26 inches—three to four inches below average, but high enough to accommodate lamps. If you have a low grouping, consider lifting it up by hanging swing-arm lamps on the wall on either side of the sofa. The center of the back plates of the lamps should be approximately 48 inches above the sofa back.

- *Flowers and vases.* A tall cylindrical vase looks attractive with one long-stemmed flower. You wouldn't want to see a single stem in a bulbous vase.

- *Mantels and chair rails.* In a room with a fireplace mantel and chair rails, the mantel should be substantially higher than the rails.

When you train your eye to see and understand the nature of one thing juxtaposed to another, in time and with patience you will also understand that the eye needs not only harmony but also dynamics. Flowers such as tulips bending down, for example, capture your interest more than if they stand straight up in a vase. There is a balance between the flowers looking rigid and the tension caused by their curves. Curved stems also make the proportion of the vase less heavy in comparison to the delicacy of the tulip stems. The tension between pliant stems and solid vase enhances your pleasure, and because the stems are in the water, your eye doesn't concern itself with the flowers' well-being.

- Go on a practical treasure hunt around your house, exploring the proportions of your objects and their relationship to one another. Is the saucer of a coffee cup in proportion to the cup, not too big, not too small? Are the legs on a living room table in pleasing dimensions for its design, and for the thickness of the top? Examine the relationship of a mantel to the size of the fireplace. If you have an oversized mantel that is too high, too long, and projects out too far, next to it place a large wicker basket filled with logs. Together they will be in good proportion.

Look at individual objects and focus on the parts that make up the whole. Look at a lamp. We all have so many, and they are the trickiest objects to get in ideal scale because the shade is so often out of proportion to the base. First, examine the lamp to see if the shade is the right proportion for the scale of the lamp base. Is it top heavy or too big? Most lampshades are too large for the lamp. Study the dimensions. An opaque lampshade will look 20 percent smaller than a translucent shade. Now stand back and examine the lamp in relationship to the table. Is the lamp too tall or too short? Too skinny or too fat? Is it too big or too small for the table? If a lamp is too skinny—for example, if it is a candlestick design—consider using a pair of such lamps to correct the scale.

This treasure hunt can be fun. After you've cast a critical eye upon the proportions of some of your own decorative objects and furniture, you'll want to stay in the rhythm of evaluating the proportions of things you see outdoors as well as in your friends' houses. The world is your laboratory. You need continuously to exercise your seeing skills, practicing them wherever you are. You are a student of seeing. What you observe well will train your eye. Open your eyes wide, in the room where you're reading. If you do this regularly you'll be amazed at how much better you see each day. Your innate curiosity will be stimulated wherever you go.

Each according to his own way of seeing things, seek one goal, that is, gratification.

IMMANUEL KANT

Spot a tree with its trunk out of proportion to the branches—for example, a huge old oak that has lost major branches to a storm or disease. Look at a house that is out of proportion to its small yard. Observe the tiny garden that is so overgrown with trees and foliage and flowers,

Learning how to see well is empowering.

you have no room to sit and have a cup of tea. A garden's reason for existence is a person's pleasure. No matter how beautiful something may be, if it gets out of hand and loses its human-scaled proportions, the entire purpose of its existence is defeated.

Scale

We have mentioned scale several times in our discussion of proportion. The size of something is its scale, determined by physical dimensions and presence. Everyone and everything, from a vast mountain range to the tiniest ant, has scale that falls in the range of small to large, short to tall, or refined to bold. Personality, design, material, distance, placement, and color all influence scale. These variables can either heighten or diminish an object's physical size by illusion. To see well, it is essential to visually and mentally comprehend the concept of scale in all its complexities, including its close relation to proportion. When you understand scale, you can assemble more harmoniously scaled possessions for your rooms, creating a comfortable living environment, as well as being able to see how scale operates in the larger picture of life. When we get older, for example, we downscale in order to have more freedom.

Where there is no vision, the people perish.

PROVERBS 29:18

The Elements of Scale

People who are visually inexperienced tend to juxtapose unrelated objects that are widely different in scale and feeling—a small, dainty coffee table with intricate carving placed in front of a large, square-armed, tailored sofa, or a large heavy lamp on a small, delicate end table. The result is a jumbled, jarring feeling.

To distinguish and integrate classes of objects according to scale, you need a sound understanding of measurement. This applies to the full dimensions of an object as well as to the scale of its ornamentation. Take a moment now to notice the ornamentation on a table, sofa, mantel, chair, or bed hangings, window treatments, and tabletop accessories. Designs range from delicate and extremely intricate to large and bold, making a difference in how something appears in proportion or relationship to the other objects in the space.

The eyes indicate the antiquity of the soul.

EMERSON

Objects come in distinct classes or styles. The best way to observe scale is to see a wide variety of things, disciplining yourself to look at all the different types of a given object so you can appreciate the effect of scale on them and their surroundings. You become familiar with French ladderback chairs and understand their tall, narrow scale. You learn that

Louis XVI chairs have oval backs and are relatively small-scaled. Look for the measurements and design that connect each element to the whole, rendering it harmonious and right to the eye. When you see what styles and types go together, you find their link despite differences in the scale and proportion of their parts. A simple French farm table goes well with Windsor chairs because of their straight-forward lines. You may have a side chair, an open-arm chair, and a chaise longue with different scales, but if they are all Louis XVI, they look harmonious together.

Half seeing is half living. We suffer whenever we don't live up to our potential to see.

Plato told us thousands of years ago that measurement is not sufficient to understand proper scale. You need a dash of genius or divine guidance. Our genius is our ability to see all the details and their influence on scale, and to understand how scale can be beneficially manipulated, depending on an object's design.

Juxtaposition and the Illusion of Scale

I once went to a museum exhibition that showed a room empty of all but one object, isolated from everything except walls. Because we are used to juxtaposition, the absence of it was dramatic. This room illustrated how most of us and the objects in our life are not in solitary confinement but are in relationships and groupings. Seeing the scale of something well requires assigning it a place in the whole. We see an object's size, color, and distance in relationship to the elements of its specific environment.

The more you see, the more discerning you become.

The scale of an object has less meaning if there is no basis for comparison. For example, an architect's rendering often includes a human figure and trees to make the size and dimensions of the potential structure more meaningful to the eye. The architect is using juxtaposition to illustrate scale.

Scale is neither good nor bad; it is relative. For example, in relation to or juxtaposed to other American females, I am considered tall because I am taller than the average American female. However, if I were standing among members of a male basketball team, I would be classified as short, even though my height remains constant in both categories.

When you place objects side by side to form a relationship, you juxtapose. When pairing a chair and an ottoman, for example, or a chair and a sofa, you should first consider scale. You scale a bench to fit appropriately at the foot of your bed. You don't want to trip over it in the middle of the night going

Patience is the companion of wisdom.

SAINT AUGUSTINE

to the bathroom, but you don't want it to look dwarfed by the bed, either. Chairs placed opposite each other should be in the same scale even if they are entirely different in style.

I do the very best I know how, the very best I can.

ABRAHAM LINCOLN

You can even observe this juxtaposition in nature: When you look up at the moon and the stars in the blue-black sky, you may feel that the moon is about a mile away and a few feet wide. You see the stars that shine the brightest as being closer and the dimmer ones as being farther away. Another illusion of scale dependent on location can be perceived when the sun sets on the horizon: Because of its relationship to the land, you feel the setting sun has a larger scale than when it is high in a blue, cloudless sky where it looks rather small, like a yellow balloon.

Because scale is relative, juxtaposition is perhaps the most crucial element of scale. If you change an object's location, its scale changes. An average-sized table can look oversized in a small room where it is squeezed into a tight space. When we learn to see and feel certain qualities of scale in objects, we can group them in harmonious ways.

Skill in discrimination goes beyond mere measurement. If more people had this skill, we wouldn't have the vast majority of lampshades hideously out of scale for the lamp, the table, and the room.

Scale and Color Juxtaposition

To achieve harmonious scale in your home, it is important to learn the power of color juxtaposition. Color has a huge influence on scale. White and light colors have the power to enlarge objects or a space visually, while dark colors do the opposite, diminishing scale. This is perhaps one reason why many women wear so much black clothing—and why women like to see men in black tie and tails.

Get two identical clear glasses from the cabinet. Pour milk into one and tomato juice, prune juice, or black coffee into the other. What do you notice about how the two containers relate to each other? Your eye is drawn to the glass with the juice or coffee in it. The milk seems to expand beyond the outline of the glass, appearing light, whereas the lines of the glass with the darker liquid appear more defined, heavier, stronger. The darker the color, the

more visual weight the object acquires, attracting your attention. A black-lacquered coffee table in a yellow room will be eye-catching, and while it won't appear larger than its measurements, it will be noticed immediately because of the high contrast between the yellow and the black.

How can you use this knowledge to enhance the rooms of your home?

- If you want a small room to appear larger, painting the walls white will visually double the space. Whenever you see a need for expansiveness, consider white. If you want to feel cozy and enclosed, bring your walls in toward you by painting them a dark color—bottle green, French blue, Chinese lacquer red, or wine red. Paint the bookcases, the cabinets, and all the trim the same color so you feel cradled in the space.

Just a tender sense of my own inner process, that holds something of my connection with the divine.

PERCY BYSSHE SHELLEY

- In a room with low ceilings, if you have old wooden beams overhead that appear heavy to your eye, consider changing their color. They could be fake, made of Styrofoam, but if they're dark, you feel they might fall on you and hurt you. A heavenly blue color will visually diminish their weight, softening their edges. The lighter the color, the more airy, expansive, even ethereal, the ceiling will appear. If you do not want to paint over the wood, paint the ceiling between the beams sky blue in order to avoid the problem of too high a contrast between a white, light ceiling and brown, heavy beams.

- White bed sheets will look expansive and appear to float. Dark sheets make a strong statement, drawing your eye, visually outlining the proportions of the bed.

- Choose white or light bed hangings to achieve a light, fresh, and airy look.

- A bleached floor looks expansive because it gives the illusion of being a higher floor. By the same token, light on a floor tends to heighten it. A dark-stained floor would look as much as a foot lower. Look around your house to see this for yourself.

Color can appear bright or subdued depending on its juxtaposition. Look at a black coat with black buttons. Visualize how brass buttons of the same size would look on the same coat. How does the color affect how the buttons appear? The brass buttons will appear significantly larger than the black

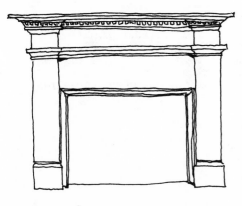

buttons, even if they are the same size, due to their juxtaposition against the black coat. The contrast in color, bright against dark, enhances the presence of the brass buttons, while the black buttons fade into the background. By the same logic, a golden-yellow sofa will have more presence and appear larger against a blue wall. If the sofa and the wall were the same color, the sofa would appear much smaller.

Sight is the most piercing of our bodily senses.

PLATO

Here are a few tips on the use of color and its effect on scale:

- When you want to diminish the scale or dimensions of a large piece of furniture, paint it or cover it in the same color as its background. Recently, I designed for a client a bottle-green study with birchwood bookcases on two opposite walls. The client questioned whether we should paint over the wood. I never intended the bookcases to be anything other than green so they wouldn't stand out in the small room. In their natural honey color, they looked out of scale against the dark green. Once they were painted they looked just right, visually half the bulk as when they were unpainted.

"I have done my best." That is about all the philosophy of living that one needs.

LIN YUTANG

- If you have an ugly side chair or footstool, paint it the same color as the wall so it will fade into the background. If you have an oversized piece of nonquality furniture—an armoire, for example—paint it the same color as the wall so that it will look less prominent.

- A dark coffee table on a dark rug feels anchored. A light-colored table against a dark rug appears to float, feeling unstable.

- A dark object placed on a white shelf has a strong presence. If the same object were made of crystal, it would not be nearly as noticeable. If you place the dark object on a high, white shelf, the eye will be drawn to it even though it is not at eye level.

- If on a large wall you have an object—whether an architectural fragment or a decorative ledge—that contrasts in color with the wall, the outline of the form is prominent and the piece appears to be larger than it is because the strength of its shape gives it character and a sense of weight.

- In a small space, use the same hue in a variety of different shades so that the objects do not stand out and take up too much visual space.

Other Ways to Manipulate the Scale of a Space

Color is not the only way to manipulate scale in your home. Here are a few alternative ideas:

- Rather than clutter a small space with small objects, try a few well-selected, large-scale objects against light walls to enlarge the appearance of the area. Your eye is drawn to the large, bold objects and away from the unobtrusive walls. The furniture will also fool you into thinking the room is of a substantial scale. If you put a lot of things in a small space, it looks fussy.

- You can make a large room feel more cozy by arranging several different seating areas, using an average scale and visually breaking the room into several spaces.

- If large-scale objects are too close to one another, they "fight" for breathing space and dominance. For example, you shouldn't have a king-sized bed close to a large armoire. You want to see both with space surrounding them.

- If you like large-scaled furniture, use fewer and well-proportioned pieces, or your room will look crowded. The woods should be compatible. Repeat the fabric on upholstered pieces to create a sense of unity.

- If there is a view, however humble, leave the windows uncovered and keep them squeaky clean. If you have space, install an indoor windowbox to bring the outdoors inside year-round. Or, if you have a deep ledge or counter space in front of one or more windows, place some flowering plants in front on individual matching dishes.

- A picture frame can increase the presence of a small painting substantially. So that the frame does not look pretentious, select a simple molding in a shiny gold leaf or colored lacquer that complements the painting.

The Influence of Style on Proportion and Scale

Style is a key element of proportion and scale. You can juxtapose a small oak stool to a huge oak dining table; because they're both the same style, they are compatible. If all your furniture is wicker, you can combine large- and small-scaled pieces in a room and they will be compatible. The basic style or likeness of furniture binds them together harmoniously.

There are many examples where style determines how furniture and objects relate to each other:

- If you have a collection of oriental lacquer furniture—perhaps a nest of tables, including a large coffee table and small oriental prayer or tea tables—the curved Eastern design of the leg and the lacquer finish group them together. Even if the pieces are different sizes and have contrasting proportions, they are of the same family and relate well to one another.

- French Provincial furniture shares basic design elements that tie the pieces together regardless of scale. They aren't fussy, and they all have similar "personalities." You recognize this style by the delicacy of the shapes, the curves in the apron, often carved, and the graceful lines of the legs. The tabletops are often shaped. Like nature herself, French Provincial has no straight lines.

- Chairs from the Louis XVI period, from large bergères to open-arm and side chairs, are well suited to one another because they all have oval backs. Repetition of shape can be just as important as scale when grouping furniture.

- You can cover a variety of different-scaled pieces of furniture in one patterned fabric, and they will unite in harmony, much as members of a sports team unite by wearing the same uniform.

- The same kind of wood unites unlike pieces. Recently I saw a nest of three tables, each one a different shape and size, that held together because they were all mahogany. Though the designs were not identical, they were compatible, with each tabletop having openwork.

The true art of memory is the art of attention.

SAMUEL JOHNSON

You have more direct control over your eyes than you do your mind.

I am still learning.

MICHELANGELO

- A collection of porcelain vases in a variety of shapes and sizes creates a harmonious grouping because they are of the same material.

- If you have some painted Swedish furniture, whether huge cupboards or small writing tables, your eye sees that the pieces relate well to each other. Rooms are more interesting when there is a wide range of scale, but the pieces must be orchestrated under strict discipline of similarities or style.

Setting an Appropriate Scale for Your Home

The proportions of a human being directly affect the scale of man-made structures and objects. (*The New Yorker* illustrated this principle with a cartoon of a skinny teenager holding a skateboard in his right hand, with his left hand in the pocket of shorts that hung down to drooping socks at his ankles. On his T-shirt was printed ONE SIZE FITS NONE.) We are all sensitive to human scale, specifically the scale and dimensions of our own body. Our environment should reflect this sensitivity. If you are a tall person, you will not likely be drawn to a small, delicate chair. If you are a tiny person, you will be less likely to bury yourself in a huge chair. A large man is not going to be attracted to a small sports car or a dainty antique twin bed. A large woman rarely carries a small purse. She is large scaled, and so is her handbag; they are proportionate to each other.

The endless variation of the human scale is one of the factors that makes each of us unique. I have tall friends who feel claustrophobic in old houses with small rooms and low ceilings. They feel out of scale, like a bull in a china shop. Scale will always be significant in our lives and need not be complex. Your eye as well as common sense will guide you.

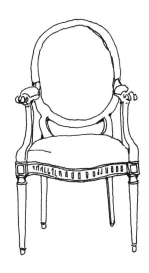

You should feel comfortable in your daily life, finding a scale that fits your size and suits you emotionally. Everyone eventually finds a scale that enhances a sense of self-worth and feels comfortable. Over time, people's sense of scale may change.

Usually furniture and objects are scaled to accommodate average-sized people. Because of this industrywide deference to the average scale, we often find ourselves accommodating to a less-than-ideal scale.

I find that I am especially sensitive to the scale of chairs. Peter and I collect old chairs, odd chairs, one-of-a-kind chairs. We also collect children's chairs, including a few high chairs. Every chair has its own scale. By looking at each one individually, you can envision what size person would fit right into each seat. We have a selection of various-sized chairs around our dining room table to accommodate everyone as comfortably as possible. A friend who is six feet four inches tall doesn't want to be seated in a flimsy Windsor side chair. The seat height of a large, substantial armchair is the same as that of a side chair, but its scale makes all the difference in physical as well as emotional comfort. A chair collection rather than a set of chairs is actually pleasing to the eye, adding charm and interest so long as the seat height is uniform. Providing appropriate scale for your family and friends is an essential ingredient in a comfortable home atmosphere.

Study your own collection of chairs. Envision your family and friends seated in them. Do you have a favorite reading chair? Is it the right scale for your build? Study these chairs one at a time to learn about scale and proportion in your home. Then look at how they are grouped in your rooms. How are they scaled, one to another?

When the eye wakes up to see again, it suddenly stops taking anything for granted.

FREDERICK FRANCK

For wisdom is a most beautiful thing, and Love is of the beautiful; and therefore Love is also a philosopher or lover of wisdom, and being a lover of wisdom is a mean between the wise and the ignorant.

PLATO

Prepare your mind to receive the best that life has to offer.

ERNEST HOLMES

Usually forms relate to the human scale, but human beings have evolved, through better nutrition, into larger people than they were in the seventeenth and eighteenth centuries and earlier. Go to a museum that displays suits of armor, and you'll be amazed at how small the men were. Go to a costume institute, and look at the size of the clothing worn in the eighteenth century. Look at porcelain. Some of the finest eighteenth-century examples of teacups and saucers are too small in scale for us today, because the handle is too small for our index finger to fit into comfortably.

Opening Your Eyes to Needed Change

People become blind to the eyesores in their homes because often they've spent huge amounts of money on things that are obviously so wrong. It is embarrassing to buy a pair of expensive wing chairs and cover them in a pretty chintz only to discover, once they are in place, that wing chairs are too high-backed and the fabric is far too busy. What can you do? Cry, certainly, but many clients pretend that their spouse loves the look and won't let them change it. But if one person in a family detests something, seeing it as all wrong, change it. Life is too short to live with a mistake.

Once the art of seeing is lost, meaning is lost and life itself seems even more meaningless.

FREDERICK FRANCK

Seeing well can create defining moments in a partnership. The one who sees with new eyes should be able to articulate why an object is wrong without his or her companion becoming defensive. Once you see well, you can be exceedingly articulate about why a particular form and its scale, proportions, material, or color are not harmonious.

To create is always to learn, to begin over, to begin at zero.

MATTHEW FOX

When Harmony and Sentimentality Do Not Mix

In 1917, my husband's parents received for a wedding present a huge, German-made, mahogany grandfather clock from Peter's father's older sister. The clock's chimes were robust—Trinity and Westminster. Peter inherited this family treasure in his twenties after his father died and his mother moved into a smaller apartment. Although Peter was extremely sentimental about this clock, he didn't have an ideal place for it, squeezing it between the kitchen and library doors. The clock was extremely large-scaled, awkward, heavy-handed in its design, and dark in color. I loved its deep-throated tick-tock and its melodious chimes. Even the children's friends loved the clock

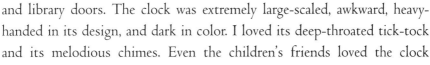

because when they were little they would get in their sleeping bags on the floor and stay up all night talking, listening to the music celebrating each new hour, half hour, and quarter hour. But hearing is entirely different from seeing. This clock was all wrong in proportion and scale to the only space it would fit into in our apartment.

One day, at the right moment, we sat by a crackling fire to discuss the clock. If Peter were willing to part with this nostalgic object—this symbol of his family, that day and night for years had rung through his parents' apartment and then his own, as the sound of home—would we be able to replace it with a clock that had a more ideal scale and proportion for the space, and receive the same joy?

Peter's eye saw that the clock was out of proportion to its space. He agreed to sell it at auction and use the money to establish a clock fund. We would replace this clock. The day the movers took away the

One learns by doing a thing; for though you think you know it, you have no certainty until you try.

SOPHOCLES

The beginnings of all things are weak and tender. We must therefore be clear-sighted in beginnings.

MONTAIGNE

clock, the girls came home from school and were shocked to see it gone. They inquired what had happened and became angry at me when I told them. "How could you do that? We love that clock!"

The wall between the library and kitchen now had space to breathe. It was easy to envision a smaller, more delicate clock in place of the old one. We antiqued endlessly, looking at graceful American-made clocks. We looked in museums and in books, at antique shops and antique fairs, and at auctions. Then, miraculously, when Peter's Aunt Ethel died, she willed to him her most treasured grandfather clock, an English antique that had been purchased in Philadelphia from J. E. Caldwell & Co. The clock had the perfect scale and proportions for the space that had been so cramped for the heavy German-made clock. Peter, feeling buoyed up by the improvement in scale and proportion, became reconciled with the removal and sale of his parents' clock.

Often we are blinded by sentimentality and nostalgia. We all have to see with our eyes and brains and pay attention to the stirrings of our hearts. In many cases, our parents and grandparents may have lived on a grander scale than we do; therefore, many of their possessions will be the wrong scale for our rooms. We can't warehouse objects in our limited space and throw our rooms out of harmony. Beauty and love may rest in the eye of the beholder, but scale and proportion cannot be ignored. Something that looked gracefully proportioned in one space may be awkward and inharmonious in another. See for yourself and decide.

A dwarf standing on the shoulders of a giant may see farther than a giant himself.

ROBERT BURTON

Understanding the Relationship Between
Proportion and Scale

Scale and proportion, properly understood and studied, can help you distinguish if an object's line, form, curves, and shape are pleasing or offensive to the eye, so that you can improve or resolve the problem as necessary.

The interrelationship of scale and proportion can sometimes be difficult to grasp if you have never studied architecture, interior design, or the fine arts. To the architect, designer, and artist, these

abstract ideas become second nature, but not without lots of trial and error, hard work, and practice. Still, these principles are unchanging and available for anyone's use. Learning to see acutely takes the mystery out of scale and proportion. Generally, proportion is a less technical concept than scale, pertaining to the overall form of an object rather than to its actual size. If an object is larger than average, it is considered large or extra large scaled. If it is smaller than average, it is considered small scaled or petite.

Just remain in the center, watching. And then forget that you are there.

LAO-TZU

Scale and proportion, working together, can create a sense of order or one of confusion. Proper scale and proportion should always work synergistically to create harmony and comfort.

Think of scale and proportion as going hand in hand, as salt and pepper or bread and butter. We want a touch of both salt and pepper. They complement each other. You need to know the difference between scale and proportion, but you don't need to separate them, just as it is important to know the difference between a man and a woman, but there is no need to keep them apart.

The science of proportion and scale takes time to learn. Be patient with yourself. You may want to reread this chapter after you spend some time looking about, seeing where ideal scale and proportion

There is no happiness where there is no wisdom.

SOPHOCLES

The first necessity for clear seeing is attraction. You need to be charmed by what you observe.

Sight is located in the highest part of the body.

FICINO

have been achieved. Begin in your home, where you can do something about less-than-ideal scale and proportion. Absorb the difference between the scale or size of an object and the proportions of each object's parts that make up the whole. Examine the juxtaposition of one object to another. Let your eye and brain judge if you are seeing harmonious proportions. Is your kitchen sink and counter high enough in relation to your height and the height of any kitchen stools you may have? What about the bathroom sink height in relation to the height of those using it and the towel bar? Is the tub long enough in relation to your body? Are your end tables big enough in relation to the large sofa and upholstered chairs?

Here are a few examples to help illustrate both the difference and the relationship between proportion and scale:

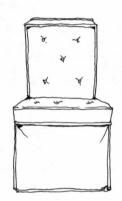

* You can have a variety of different-scaled tables in a room, from a 12-inch-round drinks table to a 78 × 30-inch writing table, so long as their proportions are not too disparate. You can combine a variety of sizes and styles, provided that none of them is too extreme in its proportions or too delicate or too massive in scale.

* If you put a coffee pot in an empty room, you can't evaluate its scale because there is no visual basis for comparison. But you can critique its proportions. You can keenly observe the relationships of each part, evaluating whether the parts render the object graceful or awkward, regardless of scale. How do the shape, form, and curves of the handle relate to the pot? Is the spout graceful and in proper scale to the handle? Is the lid attractive, completing the design? How do the pattern and color add to the overall rhythm and harmony?

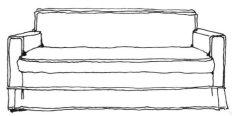

- A room, a rug, a garden, or a dining room table with good proportions is neither too long for its width nor too wide for its length, regardless of its scale.

- Look at a hard roll on a butter plate. Because of its scale you see it as a roll. Now visualize a roll blown up to eight times its size. You now have a round loaf of bread. The scale has changed from small to large, but the proportions have not changed. The scale of the butter dish was ideal for the roll, but a large dinner plate is the appropriate scale for the loaf of bread.

- A table can have beautiful proportions, each part in harmony with the whole, but if its scale is diminutive juxtaposed to other furniture in an arrangement, the table will appear awkward despite the proportions of the other furniture.

- Every man-made object has specific dimensions that can be measured for length, width, height, and other parts that make up the whole. Regardless of the scale of an object, be it a car or a water glass, the relationships between these measurements—the proportions—have to be evaluated separately. Think of a nest of ten oval Shaker baskets, from small to large. Someone designed the ideal proportions for one basket—the relationship of the length to the width to the height and the overall shape—and created baskets in several different sizes using these relationships. Whether the basket is tiny or huge, it has the same pleasing proportions.

- Most flower and plant containers are too big for the flowers and plants they hold. The scale of the container is usually too large. When arranging flowers in a vase, select a smaller container

I will not take the whole of the subject, but will break a piece off in illustration of my meaning.

PLATO

than usual. Cut flowers should have the water changed every day in order to extend their life. Cut some of the stems if necessary. Let your eye judge whether you have improved your flower-arranging skills. Make sure the vase doesn't overpower the delicacy of the flowers. The container, just like a lampshade, is utilitarian and should not be the focal point.

There is a practical reason for flowering plants and trees to be in containers that are a larger scale: to be sure there is enough room for the roots, soil, and water. Yet the eye is bothered when the beauty of flowering plants is obscured by functional containers, just as it is when cut flowers are overshadowed by a large-scaled decorative vase. The solution to this scale and proportion dilemma is to plant trailing ivy around the main plant or add some African violets or primroses.

By assiduously seeing proportion and scale, you can become sensitive to how graceful elements harmonize and relate to each other. Rudolf Arnheim, the author of *Art and Visual Perception: A Psychology of the Creative Eye,* put it well: "We need undiluted vision." Proportion and scale not only involve measurement and juxtaposition but also unite line, tone, color, direction, shape, and movement—all visual forces. In your endeavor to see proportion and scale better, I urge you to muster your full deliberate effort. The result is worth it.

While we teach, we learn.

SENECA

Finding Harmony and Comfort

Symmetry, Order, and Balance

It is the familiar that usually eludes us in life.
What is before our nose is what we see last.
— WILLIAM BARRETT

How can we seek and find harmony and comfort wherever we are, whether at home, inside, out in the yard, on errands, or away on a trip? The more you learn to stop and look at what is in front of you, seeing with greater penetration, the faster you'll see the underlying qualities that will bring you comfort, serenity, and harmony.

Order, symmetry, and balance are three principles essential for you to understand

The universe is an exercise in harmony as much as in shape and color and texture, and none can doubt that there are celestial sounds as well as visions.

PAUL JOHNSON

True simplicity consists . . .
in forgoing over-indulgence,
in maintaining humility of
spirit, . . . even though these
surroundings may properly
be characterized by grace,
symmetry, and beauty.

BOOK OF DISCIPLINE OF
THE RELIGIOUS SOCIETY
OF FRIENDS

in order to see well. Whenever your eye is pleased, you can look for the elements that support what you see. Is there order? Are things arranged in a logical way, providing ease and enjoyment to moment-to-moment living?

Disorder causes anxiety and nervousness, while order is soothing and reassuring. Symmetry is present in all things we find harmonious and comforting. It brings us physical stability and peace of mind. We stand on two legs. We respond to matching pairs of things, each echoing the other. Symmetry simplifies, organizes, unites, and connects visually as well as mentally all the interrelations among objects. When a couple get along well, people say they are a "real pair" or "two peas in a pod." But sym-

Beauty shows off an idea.

metry has to do with placement, not just two objects that are identical. Objects must be placed in a certain way so that the whole image is symmetrical. Identical does not necessarily mean symmetrical, but when matching pairs are placed where one part echoes the other, symmetry results.

Balance is the stability that creates harmony and proportion, keeping everything in equilibrium. We seek evenness, wanting one thing to connect comfortably with another. We weigh ourselves, we balance our checkbook, we seek the truth by listening to both sides. We use a level to be certain our floors are balanced; we balance our nutritional intake to try to maintain our health. Balance is crucial to our health and our sense of contentment.

This chapter will illustrate how vital order, symmetry, and balance are to seeing well. If something is symmetrical, it will be inherently well organized and balanced.

Yet all in order, sweet and lovely.

WILLIAM BLAKE

Whether you are laying out a garden, preparing a meal, setting a table for dinner, planning a vacation or decorating your house, order, symmetry, and balance are the underpinnings of harmony and comfort. When you can see these elements in sights and events that appeal to you, you will become empowered to seek, create, and enjoy more order, symmetry, and balance in your daily life.

And there is no greatness where there is no simplicity, goodness, and truth.

LEO TOLSTOY

Symmetry

Symmetry is the echo of one part in another. Symmetry is exact correspondence of form and configuration on opposite sides of a dividing line or axis. Examples of symmetry exist all around us both in nature and man-made structures. What are some images of symmetry? The moon, a flower blossom, a bridge, an apple, a table, a vase, a glass, a beach ball, a chair.

The Greek temple is the quintessential example of man-made symmetry. You can draw a vertical line down the center of a Greek temple and the left half will be a mirror image of the right half. The beautiful relationship of the parts to the whole makes the structure balanced and harmonious. It is well grounded, delighting our senses with a feeling of stability through symmetry.

There is divine orderliness.

Although many of nature's structures may not be perfectly symmetrical, our eyes perceive them as symmetrical. For example, a tree is never perfectly symmetrical (its symmetry depends on wind, water, light, and the other trees around it), but many trees give the effect of symmetry to the eye and brain. Though we often take it for granted, symmetry plays an essential role in both physical and mental stability. Without it, buildings would collapse and we would have difficulty standing.

Leaves, flowers, a road, a valley, a mountain, and a wave all have basic symmetry. Balls, balloons, eggs, tomatoes, lemons, loaves of bread, and bottles of wine have their own symmetry. Slice open a tomato and see the symmetry of its cross section.

There are two general types of symmetry: symmetry along the horizontal axis and symmetry along the vertical axis. Draw the three basic shapes—the square, the circle, and the equilateral triangle— on a sheet of paper. All squares and circles are both horizontally and vertically symmetrical, because whether they are divided along a center point, top to bottom, or side to side, the result will be two exactly equal parts. An equilateral triangle, however, is only symmetrical vertically. If you draw a straight line from its apex to it base, the result is two identical right triangles. But if you draw a horizontal line from the center point on the right leg of the triangle straight across to the left, you have a smaller triangle on top and a shape on the bottom with two parallel lines called a trapezoid.

What I have, really, is that I see better than anybody else—and I hear better. Maybe that's a blessing.

GEORGE BALANCHINE

Regardless of the form of an object, you usually see symmetry as an interplay of vertical and horizontal lines. Vertical symmetry is much more important to human beings and the natural world than horizontal symmetry. Generally, we are much more concerned with the up-down direction, because of the influence of the laws of gravity and our need for stability. The law of gravity often requires perfect symmetry of the vertical plane. A chair, lamp, table, and vase all rest on horizontal surfaces and must have correct verticality to be sure they rest evenly on a horizontal surface and do not tilt or fall. When a table is not level with the floor, it tilts back and forth and is unsettling.

Bilateral Symmetry

All things that move, whether human beings, animals, insects, fish, airplanes, cars, boats, or vacuum cleaners, are never symmetrical front to back. However, if you hung a plumb line from the center of your forehead directly down to a level floor, the line would divide your body into two halves that are mirror images of each other. This bilateral symmetry along the vertical axis is characteristic of humans and animals. When you have two identical sides on a vertical surface or plane, you have bilateral symmetry.

All animals have evolved to be bilaterally symmetrical. The form of the human being, the most highly developed of all animals, can be considered the most perfect because of how it has evolved perfectly to serve our needs. Symmetry is crucial to the relationship between the human physical form and its functions.

Look at some slides of you and your family taken on a vacation. Look at them the way they were taken, then flip them so you see the mirror image of your family. How does this exercise alter the way you experience

the pictures? Do your family members look noticeably different? Probably not, because they are bilaterally symmetrical.

Natural objects are also bilaterally symmetrical. Consider: an apple, a cypress tree, a daisy, a four-leaf clover, a scallop shell. The next time you take pictures of nature, use slide film. When you get the slides back, put them upside down in the carousel (so that they will project right side up), and turn each one around so you will view it in a mirror image. Look at all of the slides in this way before you look at them the way you took the pictures. Most people think they look just as good reversed, because left side and right side in nature are generally equally balanced, giving the illusion of exact symmetry.

Bilateral symmetry exists throughout nature. Go on a hunt to find an exception.

The Power of Definiteness

Aristotle believed that "the chief forms of beauty are order and symmetry and definiteness." You can't think about or discuss anything of importance without having exact and discernible limits. In architecture it is no different. Harmonious architecture is based on symmetrical groups that are unambiguous. All wholes are made up of parts. A whole should have a definite beginning, a middle, and an end. There should be a scheme in the way the parts are arranged; each room in a house should be related in size to a greater whole. Within rooms, one side of a room generally echoes the other side in architectural elements. Ideally, there should be symmetrical placement of windows, doorways, moldings, and

Vision is a process that produces from images of the external world a description that is useful to the viewer and not cluttered with irrelevant information.

DAVID MARR

pilasters. These details should be clear, not vague.

The human eye is nourished by the definiteness of classic shapes and forms and by the axis line that divides an object in half. Vertical symmetry is basic to our sense of stability. You need two legs arranged symmetrically to walk and run, two hands and arms to lift and hold, and two eyes to see well. Instinctively, we feel secure in the presence of vertical symmetry.

If the maxim "repeat shape for harmony" describes symmetry achieved by placing two similarly shaped objects side by side, consider the symmetry achieved by two vertical parallel lines. Parallel lines never intersect, thus maintaining a constant distance from each other. Parallelism is inherent in symmetry.

Throw some kitchen matches on the floor. Notice that pairs fall at different angles but rarely parallel. Play with some Pick-Up-Sticks. A cupful of pencils will do as well, but be sure to throw them on a rug so the points won't break. Parallel lines rarely occur in nature; they are usually the result of human design. Parallel lines are rarely accidental. Pick-Up-Sticks fall so randomly, we instinctively want to pick them up to bring order. When two sticks are *almost* parallel, our eye is displeased. We tend to like parallel edges. Two columns or pillars are more attractive to the eye than one, and it is no coincidence that two identical, symmetrically placed, parallel columns make a building more structurally sound as well. Something that is symmetrical is balanced, well-proportioned, orderly, and strong.

The Simplicity of Symmetry

The Greeks insisted upon symmetry because it was logical and, as a result, simple to design. The greatest and most lasting architectural styles derive from

Seek, and ye shall find.
Saint Matthew

Beauty addresses itself chiefly to sight.

PLOTINUS

the classical Greek temple design. (Even on a far-away Caribbean island, thousands of miles from Greece, there are symmetrical, temple-style buildings, adapted to the tropical climate with overhanging roofs to provide shade.) The sixteenth-century Italian architect Andrea Palladio continued the Greek tradition, influencing the English style in later centuries, and eventually American architecture.

Many of our municipal buildings echo the classical style, instilling a feeling of discipline and order. When you go to the courthouse, you sense justice will be served; at the bank, you feel your money is safe. The axial balance in the columns of these buildings instills trust and security, a feeling of a greater power protecting us.

Size is another important aspect of symmetry. The eye can't take in vast structures at a glance. When something is too large, we can't see its symmetry. For symmetry to have impact, your eye must be able to see it instantaneously. Greek temples, never too large, allowed the human eye to absorb and experience the nobility of the entire well-integrated composition, and thus to benefit emotionally from the symmetry.

Symmetry in the Home

The charm of symmetry is its permanent power to please because it balances the tensions of the eye. Our eye and hand tend to discover objects from side to side, not from top to bottom. Providing muscular balance in the eye is one of the great values of symmetry. When an arrangement is symmetrical, it will always contain at least one pair of items. Because our houses and apartment buildings often have an awkward lack of symmetry and are not ideal, it is important to see how to create the illusion of symmetry by having pairs of objects in these spaces. If you knock out a wall and discover a support beam that cannot be removed, the eye will not be pleased even if you cover it with a fluted Doric column. Add an identical dummy column, appropriately spaced, and you have classical symmetry.

Pleasure is very seldom found where it is sought; our brightest blazes of gladness are commonly kindled by unexpected sparks.

SAMUEL JOHNSON

Our house is our refuge, a place where we invite our soul to enlarge. We want to be soothed by the peacefulness that results from symmetry. Here are a few examples:

+ *Mantels.* Everyone instinctively wants to arrange the objects on a mantel in a symmetrical way. Begin by placing two matching objects on the left and right of the mantel shelf. A pair of cachepots filled with ivy is appealing year-round. You may add a pair of decorative plates of the same size and pattern. In the space between, select objects that are like-spirited. They don't have to be in pairs as long as they are of the same family. For example, you could have two brass boxes, or two paperweights, or two porcelain fruits or vegetables. Each object can be unique but should be connected to its partner on the opposite side of the mantel.

  The same principle can be applied to create symmetrically appealing arrangements on any long surface—a sideboard, a serving table, or a front-hall table. The candlesticks, lamps, or vases that you place on the far left and right should be a strictly matched pair. These "anchor" the symmetry of the horizontal axis. The center should have a simple object as a focal point. The other objects do not have to be in pairs, but should be of the same spirit and balanced compositionally. The arrangement on the left should be repeated, with flexibility, on the right.

+ *Sofas.* The arrangement of pillows on a sofa should be symmetrical. If you want a center pillow, it should not be identical to the pillows on the right and left.

- *Candles.* Whether you have two candles or four on a table, they should line up in strict symmetry. Votive candles, because they are low and less conspicuous, can be placed where you want to highlight objects.

- *Windows.* Generally, what you display on one window ledge should be repeated on the others. If you have two window ledges on either side of a wall, the object on the far right of one ledge—perhaps a cachepot with flowering plants—should be repeated on the far left of the other. This will make the two windows appear to be one whole unit, creating a sense of spaciousness in your room. Place similar but not matching 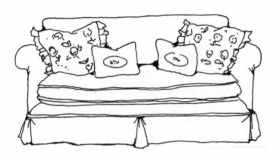 objects on both ledges. I like colored glasses holding one or two flower blossoms, small pots of African violets, glass paperweights, crystals, small paintings on easels, English blue poison bottles, and brass or ceramic canisters of various sizes.

The Danger of Too Much Symmetry

Strict symmetry, when things are too matchy-matchy, can seem cold, even redundant. Think of symmetry in the larger context of balance and harmony, as a series of beautiful associations between the parts. Move away from absolute symmetry toward a more flexible but balanced arrangement. In the earlier example, on your mantel you could have two identical cachepots placed on the ends, and in the center, three porcelain objects that belong together but are not identical. You could have a porcelain cabbage in the center flanked by a bunch of asparagus (lying down) and an artichoke. The center composition is balanced but is not entirely in pairs.

There should always be something whimsical, something unusual or even humorous in your arrangements. When arrangements are too symmetrical, they feel sterile, and the atmosphere is uninviting. Establish symmetry as a framework, then create relief and variety within it. Nature has laws, but within those laws there is almost unimaginable variation. Symmetry, too, should contain surprises.

Seeing what is in front of one's nose requires a constant struggle.

GEORGE ORWELL

To keep the world from chaos, forms must be repeated. But beware of too much repetition in form. Both a picket fence and an iron fence are symmetrical. Though they may be charming and attractive because of their endlessly repetitious forms, they can also become somewhat boring and do not sustain our interest. When forms are repeated over and over, something more visually interesting is needed to engage us and heighten the impact of the whole. Add some rosebushes to the picket fence, using the symmetry of the fence as a frame for their profusion. If your child were seated on the stairs, you would admire the symmetry of the banister and steps, but the whole is energized and your heart is more stirred by your child's presence.

Beauty is a kind of harmony and concord of all the parts to form a whole . . . a certain relation and order, as symmetry, the highest and most perfect law of nature, demands.

ALBERTI

The Illusion of Symmetry Through Asymmetry

Asymmetry, the lack of symmetry, can still achieve visual equilibrium, but of a more complicated nature—asymmetry does not *always* mean visual equilibrium. You can achieve the illusion of symmetry in an asymmetrical arrangement by using objects with similar rhythm, pattern, and shape.

If a form—for example, a fireplace mantel—is generally symmetrical but has some relief carving that is asymmetrical, the composition of the design, when it is well balanced, will have counterpoise and will feel symmetrical to the eye. On the north facade of the

Helmsley Building in New York City is a clock flanked by gilded relief figures of a man and woman. The design is balanced, but it is not strictly symmetrical. One niche in a foyer could contain a bust of a man, and another niche the bust of a woman. Though they are not identical, a feeling of symmetry results. Relief work on the facade of buildings often represents different animals on each side, as well as human figures. Strict symmetry would require mirror-image repetition.

And now forgive the past and accept the present, and be gracious and merciful to me, and do not deprive me of sight, or take from me the art of love.

PLATO

Seeing Symmetry and Asymmetry

Look around you and notice things that lack symmetry. For example, you may see someone wearing only one earring, or several in one earlobe and none in the other. Someone's hairstyle may be a different length on each side. A house that keeps being added onto lacks the harmony induced by symmetry. Careless clutter has a random composition and therefore is never symmetrical.

Symmetry has a delightful sense of completeness because it clarifies, resolving confusion. There is unity in parts brought together in harmony, and simplicity in emphasis on repetition of elements. Humans seek harmony, a state of ease.

As you look for symmetry in your surroundings, be aware of how you feel. Every act of seeing is a magical experience of feeling. Symmetrical objects and arrangements generally open your eye up to feeling pleased by the visual experience. Your eye and brain feel more responsive to shapes that are classical, functional, and simple.

Visual ambiguity is psychologically upsetting. Recall that the three basic shapes are vertically symmetrical—the square, the circle, and the equilateral triangle. The symmetrical shape is the image of perfection and peace. Look for these simple shapes underlying much of what we see.

Simple classic symmetry is beautiful to the universal eye. Studying and appreciating symmetry and the necessary role it plays in providing us with order and stability in our everyday lives allows us to find harmony and comfort at home or wherever we are.

Architectural beauty more than any other object is enhanced by favorable light.

ARTHUR SCHOPENHAUER

Order

Order is a condition of logical, comprehensible arrangements among the separate elements of a group. By stacking towels, bed linens, and blankets on separate shelves of the linen closet, or organizing mail into different categories—bills, personal letters, business correspondence, invitations, bank statements, and third class mail—or arranging groupings of china, crystal, food, and bottles, we create a sense of harmony for ourselves and our life. Order may also be a sequence, the following of one thing after another in a logical, uninterrupted way. Stacking books or boxes so that the largest is on the bottom and the smallest on the top in a pyramid looks and feels best because of the comfort of stability.

Order plays an essential role in bringing disparate elements into a unified aesthetic, harmonious whole. Without order, we would live in chaos, feeling scattered and unfocused. Order, on the other hand, opens the way to further seeing. (You are

Such vision is for those only who see with the Soul's sight—and at the vision, they will rejoice, and awe will fall upon them.

PLOTINUS

more likely to be drawn to a mosaic tile backsplash in a friend's kitchen when the sink is empty and the dishes have been put away than when pots and pans fill the sink and food covers the counters, just as you are more apt to be enticed by a garden path that is neatly trimmed than by one overgrown with weeds.) Order, because it is not random but disciplined, lays the foundation for more profound seeing and living.

How can we become more visually aware of the order that surrounds us every day and its effect on our life? How can we take this knowledge an extra step and create and maintain a greater degree of order in our homes?

The Necessity of Order

It seems we humans have a natural hunger to live with order and avoid turmoil and disarray. While disorder is easily identifiable, immediately causing unease, the positive presence and effect of order is often subtle.

When we see order, we experience a sense of well-being. Before you sit down to write, you want a clear desk, free of distractions. Having all the necessary elements of your domestic and creative life systematically arranged frees you from unnecessary tension as well as from the wasting of precious time. When your house is well organized and the time is right, you are then free to do anything you choose because you are prepared.

For example, a well-ordered clothes closet, with each element of a wardrobe having its own section of the closet, is enormously satisfying. You can find your shoes, shirts, ties, scarves, and

Lovers' happiness depends on their self-control; if the better elements of mind which lead to order and philosophy prevail, then they pass their life here in happiness and harmony—masters of themselves and orderly— . . . and when the end comes, they are light and winged for flight.

PLATO

slacks without having to dig, enhancing the pleasure of dressing and undressing. Because I like to wear colored stockings, I have a blue drawer, a red drawer, a green and yellow drawer, and a pink and purple drawer of stockings. I can easily select stockings that go with what I plan to wear. Next to the stockings are two drawers where I keep neatly folded, colorful scarves, making it fun to choose from them each day. By having colorful blouses, scarves, and stockings easily available for coordination, I can quickly put a twist on whatever I wear.

The Soul must be trained . . . you must search the souls of those that have shaped these beautiful forms.

PLOTINUS

The same holds true for everything in your house and office. To see at a glance that everything is there, in view or categorized and stored in a logical storage space for easy use, is calming and reassuring. The more organized you are, the more effective you become, and your capacity to enjoy a full, stimulating life increases.

The better your ability to see, the greater your capacity to visualize the arrangement of objects in a practical, systematic manner. Organization should always come before any event and should never preclude an experience from fully blossoming. Being well organized, at its best, aids us in undertaking more creative endeavors, enjoying the process and gaining pleasure in seeing everything run smoothly. In my book *Living a Beautiful Life: 500 Ways to Add Elegance, Order, Beauty, and Joy to Every Day of Your Life,* order is discussed before beauty. Without order there is no beauty.

Your dividend of happiness may derive from the simple things unnoticed by most people.

When your possessions are well arranged, you are ready to cook a meal, set a table, write a letter, pay a bill, read a book, change your bed linen, get dressed, go for a hike, do a puzzle, or take pictures, because everything is neatly in its place. When you have an organized life, you are more free to reach for more visual adventures. If you are arranging flowers, not only do you want the flowers at hand but you also need to be able to see your vases and containers and scan them for the form, shape,

Curiosity is a key ingredient in seeing well.

Seeing and hearing are sensations, not senses directly felt as in the case of touching, smelling, and tasting.

color, and size that are compatible with the flowers. The more interests you have, the more need for putting your different categories of things carefully away so they are shipshape and ready for your enjoyment and use.

Restoring and Maintaining Order in the Home

All of us have a lot of stuff around the house that has been acquired over the years and tends to stay around almost unnoticed. When there is too much to absorb visually, the eye tends to blank out. Usually it takes repainting a room or moving, when you have to pack up everything, to enable you to see your familiar things—now disarrayed—in a new, enlightened way. Many of us should pretend we're downsizing and put our rooms on a diet, removing the objects that no longer have meaning to us.

. . . to make of the chaos about them an order which is their own.

HENRY MILLER

Editing is a practical exercise that results in nostalgia as you remember how, when, and where you acquired each object. Everyone tends to be sentimental, but that shouldn't make you blind. There are probably some seriously ugly trinkets scattered around your home that could make a Saturday tag sale more colorful. The resulting clarity in your rooms will give you great pleasure.

Set aside one apron as your puttering apron. This is not the apron you will use to barbecue chicken. This single-purpose apron, when you wear it, will signal your brain to edit your possessions. When things have become overwhelmingly cluttered, you will have to do some major de-thugging. No matter how lean and clean we are at one stage, possessions accumulate gradually, fooling our eyes into not seeing the difference. What about all those books piled on your bedside table? What about the mismatched, half-used candles in the drawer? What about towels and linens that are too worn for use? What about that jacket you bought that never looked "right" with anything? What about the bright blue shoes that are a half size too small? What about the old magazines you know you'll never have time to read? What about those pot holders that are disgustingly burned and stained? You'll need at least forty-five minutes at a time to de-thug. Set a timer, because you'll inevitably get carried away. Put your apron on, get a few trays and some large plastic garbage bags, and focus in on one area at a time.

The contemplation of the beautiful effect of the light upon these masses lifts us, as does all beauty, into a state of pure knowing.

ARTHUR SCHOPENHAUER

Some objects obviously need to be thrown out. Others need to be given away, sold, or removed from view. Do this alone. After you have evaluated what you don't want, don't like, or don't need, then you can consult a spouse or child about what to do with the stuff. Remove your blinders, look and see, attacking one zone at a time. Put the fragile things on the trays. You'll need a clear surface that you can think of as your editing table. Be guided by common sense and intuition. You may look at an object and ask yourself, "Have I ever liked looking at this?" Or, "Is this me?" Or, "This has always bothered me; why don't I do something about it?" No one can do this but you. There is a time for certain objects in your life, and there is also a time to eliminate excess so you have space for the really meaningful objects you have grown to love. The better you train your eye to see refinements, the more decisively you'll be able to discard stuff you've outgrown to make more space for better objects to be seen. Always upgrade what your eye sees.

My photographs are a picture of the chaos in the world and of my relationship to that chaos. . . . But the works of art living on year after year are vital proof before our eyes that the reconstruction of form, of order, is eternally going on in our world.

ALFRED STIEGLITZ

This editing exercise should be done inside drawers, cupboards, and your toolbox as well as on your mantel, window ledges, desktop, end tables, and coffee table. You will smile as you remove

He receives the effluence of beauty through the eyes.

PLATO

the eyesores, one by one, because you will realize that having put up with confusion and jumble means that you haven't been seeing well. Every mediocre item you eliminate is a sign that you are seeing better now. While maintenance is one of the keys to an attractive room, regular editing is as important in your home as it is when a writer writes. Editing refines and polishes, inviting you to open up your senses to what you're experiencing.

If you still like looking at certain objects, but your eye tells you there is too much of a good thing, you can store some of your treasures in a drawer or on a shelf for a future rotation. You will immediately see that many objects of less importance were choking your favorite personal possessions.

Last fall, after my daughter Alexandra returned from her honeymoon, she and her husband came to spend the weekend with us in New York. Several months of travel, lectures, and book deadlines had conspired to keep me from de-thugging the kitchen in our apartment. Alexandra and her husband saw that the kitchen counters were stacked high with mail and other clutter. Our eyes had adjusted to the mess but never found it pleasant. The cupboards were crammed full. If I

emptied the dishwasher, I would run out of shelf space. I turned my back on the difficulty, hoping it would all go away. In reality, the situation was a growing problem. There was no longer order but runaway chaos.

I know Alexandra felt sorry for me because I'd just been too busy to deal with the mess, and when you have too much stuff, things begin to show signs of neglect. Nothing gets polished or dusted, and your treasures become a hodgepodge of clutter. Alexandra came into our bedroom with her cup of coffee and we had a talk. She offered to come up for a weekend to do nothing but help me de-thug the apartment. She sympathized, knowing I couldn't do it alone. I have the hardest time parting with some-

Symmetry is not abstraction.

JOHN RUSKIN

thing even though rationally I know it is bogging me down.

When Alexandra told me her plan of attack, I jumped up. "Let's do it now!" "OK, let's." And we were off. As we began to put the kitchen on a diet, we laughed. It was *really* bad.

We attacked old canned goods in the cabinet and the contents of the freezer and refrigerator. We weeded out baskets and vases. Brooke called us from her apartment, and when we told her what we were doing, she came up to have a look. "I've got to see this. I'll be right there." The laughter continued. Peter and Alexandra's husband, also named Peter, came in from the living room by invitation once we'd made a dent in the project and had progress to brag about.

I scrubbed and cleaned the shelves after emptying them. I Windex'd the glass shelves in the refrigerator. The grime and filth were disgusting, especially in the deep, high, back shelves where no angels had ever cleaned.

Alexandra knew how much I love my butcher-block counters, but now we could hardly see them, they were so laden. I'd spread out the office to the kitchen and the maneuver had gotten out of hand. And how hypocritical of me to let this persist, to refuse to see this mess, when I was writing *Open Your Eyes*.

Nature goes her own way, and all that to us seems an exception is really according to order.

GOETHE

Never does nature say one thing and wisdom another.

JUVENAL

What a joy to put all the candles in flat baskets stored in a kitchen cabinet so I could see at a glance the pretty colors and shapes when making a selection. What a pleasure to have the colorful paper napkins all together and neat inside a cabinet. What a good feeling to be able to sand the countertops and have Zen, empty, clutter-free surfaces. What a liberating feeling to have regained order. I couldn't have done it alone. I needed help and encouragement. We were all so pleased. We laughed and giggled. It was time to face reality and deal with the situation head-on. This event reminded me how draining it is to live with mess everywhere.

The cleaning up didn't end there. My desk had to be attacked as well as the linen closet. The library looked neat, but we'd run out of bookcase space, so we had to weed out books. As someone who has a hard time parting with things that carry lots of accumulated visual memories, I was glad to have a family who loves me to help me through this process.

A fool sees not the same tree that a wise man sees.

WILLIAM BLAKE

There is no doubt that weeding out brings order to your life and heightens the look of every area of your home. I know there are times when you, too, will be in denial, times when your eyes will gloss over what they see. But none of us can be too busy to see for long. Eventually we realize how much we're missing when we don't make the best of what we have.

Creating Order to Enhance Beauty

When we apply the principles we believe in, not only do we see a whole lot more beauty, we become a co-creator of beauty. Everything can be improved upon, and when you focus on creating order through your unique way of seeing, you highlight the objects that hold great meaning for you.

Every surface used in our daily life can be made more beautiful. The bathroom sink, the tub area, the desktop, the dresser top, the kitchen countertop, and the window ledges all can be beautiful as well as practical. When you focus on enhancing what you see, moving things toward beauty, you'll want to make some adjustments. Be grateful you have a home that can echo your spirit. Arrange things so they work for you. Some people need a lot of clutter around them; to feel comfortable they have to see it all before their eyes. Others like having a system where they know where everything is, and can bring it out when needed.

Before you can create something aesthetically pleasing, you have to lay some groundwork. By taking a walking tour to assess what you see, going from room to room, you'll observe certain areas that delight you and other places that look cluttered. See clearly what's going on in all the different areas of your home, including the ones that are not working. If you don't see the problem, you can't see the resolution.

Assess what works best for you in all the different areas of your home. In your kitchen, decide whether you want your pots and pans visible and handy or stowed away in cabinets. Some people like solid cabinet doors to hide what is inside, while others prefer open shelves or glass-fronted cabinet doors. What kind of kitchen do you have, open or closed? Where are your spices stored? How neat are you? How orderly are those you live with? If you have children, do they tend to be meticulous or messy? Are you reasonably happy with what you see as you look around? In a notebook, jot down areas you would like to work on. Remember that order brings style and enhances beauty.

Know that you must cultivate your taste by deliberately looking, and learning by what you see.

Every aspect of your life has an effect on you. While there are things you can do to enhance your workplace and even your hotel room, it is essential that you do what you can to set up your home in an ideal way. Keep in mind that what others see is not necessarily more significant than what your own eyes see. When you consider how often you see the inside of a kitchen drawer or cabinet, how often you go to the linen closet or medicine cabinet, or how often you are in your clothes closet or front-hall closet, you realize how important it is for you to have a working system to arrange and organize your things into categories. The ideal is to have a place for everything and everything in its place. We all fall short of this goal, but we can heighten our pleasure in our domestic life by understanding the value of organization and how visually satisfying it is to put in shape the practical necessities of home life.

See the world through searching eyes.

You will be training your eye by making your

When you experience true beauty, you find yourself being lifted by the wings of harmony.

environment orderly. Focus on one area at a time. Start out being exceedingly strict. If you are a hoarder, be hard on yourself. Make piles of possessions to give to a thrift store, church, or school. I had saved magazines since the sixties, until one day I threw them all out. When friends send me flowers, I save the containers until I see I have more than a flower shop. I tend to save letters, newspaper clippings, and thirty-year-old towels and sheets.

Beauty . . . is the blossom of goodness: as it grows out of goodness, so it leads those who love it to the good.

FICINO

We can try to maintain a balance between too little and too much. Mrs. Brown's warning "Be careful what you throw out" needs to be counterbalanced by a meticulous de-thugging. If something is chipped or cracked, and you know you will never use it again, don't keep it. If something needs to be mended or repaired for future use, put it in a specific place so when the time comes for you to put it in condition, you'll know where it is.

Make a list of all the areas of home that need to be put in order. What do you want to see and what do you want to hide? What is visually pleasing and what looks like a hodgepodge? You will need to designate certain areas where you can leave your tools out for convenient access. The laundry room works best when you have open shelves, because you can't function as efficiently when supplies you use several times a day are behind doors. I prefer open shelves in closets for folded clothes, as well as clear plastic bins for socks and underwear.

Every category—from matches to napkins, candles to flower vases, pitchers to platters, trays to glasses, plates to bowls, cups to saucers, mugs to flatware—needs a logical storage space. Put matching sets together and sort items by size and pattern. Enjoy pleasing your eye by creating an attractive still life. Repetition always is attractive, so put everything together that relates to form a

You shape your taste by what you see. Your life is forever changed.

grouping. Put all your pitchers together, all your bowls in one place, all your flower containers in one area, and your teacups and saucers in their own space.

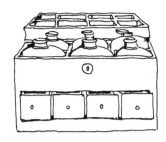

Upgrading Your System of Organization

As you take a critical look around, see if you can upgrade some of your necessities so they are more cheerful and colorful. The stool in the laundry room can be a color other than white, the dustpan and brush set can be a chartreuse plastic, and the wastebasket in a supply closet can be a cobalt-blue plastic.

Set up an attractive sewing box or basket for your ribbons and wrapping supplies, including decorative tissue and shopping bags. Buy some decorative, colorful boxes, available at housewares stores, and use them for storage of photographs, negatives, postcards, and file notes.

Rarely do people have enough storage space. Eventually, you end up exposing in rooms and hallways things that shouldn't be seen. Sometimes this can't be avoided, but generally try to have the things you see regularly as eye-appealing as possible. If the box your envelopes come in is gray cardboard and you keep it on an open shelf, your eye will be disappointed at every glance. Throw the dingy box away and put your envelopes in a brightly colored storage box. In the future, save for storing postcards and notecards the attractive boxes that often come with social stationery.

All are mirrored in every other.

PLOTINUS

You can find brightly colored, striped and patterned boxes in a wide variety of shapes and sizes in catalogs as well as in discount stores and stationery stores. You can store everything in them, from newspaper clippings to unpaid bills, paid bills, bank

Seeing enlarges your capacities to become emotionally and intellectually involved in everything around you.

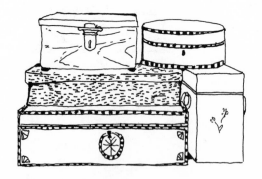

statements, and letters. I have several "idea" boxes where I keep book, decorating, gift, and menu ideas, and I store my slide carousels in some hatboxes. Whether you want a place to store unframed photographs or negatives, or recipes or ribbons, you can find an appropriately sized attractive box to fill your needs.

Boxes are true blessings, because you can keep several empty ones around the house, stacked on top of each other, ready to be filled. They can be moved from room to room and become an attractive addition rather than something dull and strictly utilitarian. I have a box for each client stored in open cubbies in my office, so my client's file folders don't get bulky with rug and tile samples and fabric and trim cuttings. When you slip the lid over the box, you feel secure, knowing that nothing will fall out. The more projects you have, the more clutter you'll accumulate, but there is no need to feel overwhelmed. Everything can find a temporary home in a cheerful, colorful box. Children love these boxes for housing their treasures.

Of all man's works of art, a cathedral is greatest. A vast and majestic tree is greater than that.

H. W. BEECHER

Have a box for small things that need to be mended—a dish, a bud vase, or a porcelain vegetable. Put some Krazy Glue inside the box as well. When you have time, you can repair several things at once. In the meantime, you don't have to look at the chipped, cracked, or broken plate. Put clothing to be mended in another colorful box and place it in the linen closet until you are in the mood to sew on a button.

Look and you will find it— what is unsought will go undetected.

SOPHOCLES

My Zen Room (my office in our cottage) is a riot of Matisse colors. Things are every color of the rainbow except the old floorboards, the old wooden table, and a few natural wicker file boxes. I store documents and manuscripts in boxes covered in bright primary colors. There are also colored pencils, hand-marbleized papers, patchwork and appliqué quilts, ribbons, painted baskets, colorful paperweights, and vibrant paintings. Sitting in this bright, cheerful, sunny room gives me energy and enthusiasm. I wouldn't have it any other way. Why work in a lifeless, colorless space if you can change it?

Be a thinker and *a seer.*

Go to an office supply store and replace your dull manila folders with a colorful selection of red, orange, yellow, green, blue, hot pink, and purple. Buy some colorful paper clips and rubber bands. Buy a colored inexpensive plastic clipboard for notes on projects you want to see checked off your to-do list. Paint the inside of a kitchen cabinet a fun pastel color so you see your drinking glasses in a new light. Line the drawer of an end table in your living room with a colorful paisley or geometric-patterned cotton so you are surprised by the stimulation of color and pattern when you open the drawer to get out a coaster or a napkin.

Arrange your clothes so they are pleasing to look at as you select what you choose to wear. Put a rag rug on your closet or dressing room floor to add color. Keep going until you feel you've added energy and order to all the areas of home. Open up drawers and ask yourself what's wrong. Empty each drawer and sort through the accumulation of things. Rearrange objects until you feel you've streamlined your possessions so they are useful and in good condition. You may want to move your wine to a more convenient storage area. Do you want to see the bottles or do you want them behind doors? Repeatedly ask yourself: "Do I want to see these objects, or not?"

Where do you store your linen napkins, tablecloths, and place mats? Are they in a place where you can use them readily? We have a shallow closet with shelves in our dining room, ideal for stacking them so we can see at a glance our choices. This arrangement is far better than stowing them in a deep drawer of a commode where you have to fumble around to see what's in there.

Only when you are intensely engaged will you elicit pleasure and meaning from visually stimulating encounters.

Where do you keep your candle supply? Are they near your candlestick collection? Where do you store your gift-wrapping supplies? Is it near a large surface convenient for wrapping packages? By having an attractive place where you always go to wrap gifts, you can have more fun being creative and bringing cheer to a loved one. Recently, while wrapping presents for a granddaughter, I created Matisse-esque packages in vibrant colors with intensely saturated

ribbons. To decorate a package wrapped in white paper, I cut out different shapes from four-inch-square sheets of bright origami paper and felt like the master himself with his scissors and cutouts. Origami is the Japanese art of folding paper into decorative shapes, but the paper is also wonderful for cutting into fun shapes. The most modest present can be enriched by an attractive wrapping. Just as writing a letter is a gift to yourself, so you can have fun playing with colorful boxes, tissue, ribbons, and bows. Through your flair, you show how much you care.

When I SEE I am all eye;
ego is momentarily forgotten,
I am nothing but a focus of
awareness.

FREDERICK FRANCK

By visualizing ideal scenarios of how you want to use your space at different times of day, you can see the logic of placement more clearly. Then you can intelligently approach the setting up of the different areas of your home life, achieving both greater fluidity and order. When you see the functional areas of home in a more ideal arrangement, placing loved objects around for the eye to feast on, the creation of beauty becomes an alive, spontaneous, joyful, natural activity. If all your flower vases are in one place, shiny clean and ready to be filled, you have the full range of possibilities to choose from at a glance. You visually take in your entire inventory, searching for the one most appropriate for the flowers, the colors you want to use, and the size and proportion of the table you'll put it on, and you instinctively are drawn to one over all the others.

You begin seeing better right where you are.

The Danger of Too Much Order

A warning: Never let your desire for order and neatness blind you to seeing the wonder and beauty around you. Any imbalance, where you become a perfectionist with unrealistic standards about order and cleanliness, will take you off your seeing path. There is no need to sacrifice the view of the children playing outside or the cardinal flying by the kitchen window, its feathers red against a brilliant blue sky. Some imperfection adds to beauty. In nature, nothing is perfectly ordered. The trees in the forest do not grow in a grid, and the blossoms on an apple tree are not distributed in a perfect pattern, but both are still wondrously beautiful and should be appreciated just as they are.

Reaching Out to Order and Beauty

Always keep in mind that seeing is a *reaching out*. To see, we have to pay close attention. When you pick a bunch of daffodils and need to choose a container, concentrate on the yellow and visualize it against a cobalt blue, and select a blue pitcher or vase. In order to take something ordinary and make it extraordinary, you have to focus on what you want. You have to forget about everything else and make an intimate connection between one object and another, one juxtaposition and another, balance and counterbalance. Seeing is not automatic; you have to make a seeing date with yourself. See through the prism of your true self. When you see with mind, heart, and soul as well as with eyes, you see with integrity, trusting your intuition.

When you are alone, get in the habit of enhancing what you see throughout the day. You'll grow to believe in the value of intimate, immediate contact with everything around you. When you unpack groceries, create an edible centerpiece of fruit in a colorful ceramic bowl for a vision as attractive as a Cézanne painting. Place one little bud or flower in

*Two men look out through
the same bars:
One sees the mud, and one
the stars.*

FREDERICK LANGBRIDGE

a cobalt-blue vase and set it next to the sink so the light from the window illuminates the blue glass. Set a pretty tea tray for your afternoon tea with a favorite blue-and-yellow teacup and saucer, the same color combination that Claude Monet used at Giverny. When you sip tea from this cup, you absorb some of your guru's inspiration. You see his garden and think of his contribution to your life.

Even the inside of the refrigerator can be a pretty sight. Put flowers in the refrigerator as flower shops do. You can go away for a week and come home to fresh flowers. Often I keep a little bud vase with a flower or two in it to make someone smile when they reach inside for juice or milk. I like keeping a bowl of oranges in the refrigerator for their high-energy color and the treat of knowing they can be put in the blender for fresh juice or sliced for a salad. Whenever a brown carton comes into the apartment or cottage, I try to unpack it and cut it up for recycling as soon as I can, because its dull presence dampens the mood of a room.

No evil can touch him who looks on human beauty; he feels himself at one with himself and with the world.

GOETHE

If you look around and feel something isn't right, but you don't know what's wrong, take a picture with a Polaroid. Because a picture isolates the setting from its surroundings, you can see with better vision what looks right or wrong. Photographers do this before they shoot film and will fiddle with a setting until they correct whatever didn't look right.

This practice can be helpful in planning a pretty table for a party or when you want to improve your eye while setting a table for your own lunch. Obviously you won't have the time or interest to take a Polaroid on a regular basis, but when you do, you'll see in minutes what is wrong, saving a lot of time and trial and error. And do take time to photograph what you see when you've created a vision you love. I have a friend, an avid gardener, whose flower bouquets are over the top with lush scale, vibrant colors, and beauty, including the fragrance that perfumes her home. Betty got in the habit of photographing every arrangement she made. By keeping a camera in the pantry, she can easily snap photos of her arrangements before she puts them around her house. Who wouldn't love to have a record of their flower arrangements and pretty table settings created over so many years?

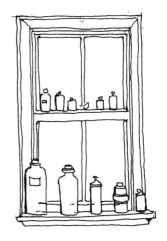

Seeing openly requires a commitment to making an improvement. If you empty a wastebasket and see that it needs cleaning, after you clean it thoroughly, go the extra step and put a white doily or perhaps a colorful cocktail napkin in the bottom, depending on the shape of the base. Looking outside, you may notice that your windowsill needs scrubbing. Do you also need to repaint it to make it look fresh? Perhaps you'll add a wind chime to tinkle in the breeze, creating natural, rhythmic sounds that awaken your heart as the view refreshes your eye. The inside of a drawer is easily over-

Learn to see, and then you'll know that there is no end to the new worlds of our vision.

CARLOS CASTANEDA

looked, resulting in its becoming grimy, dusty, and filled with assorted items that belong somewhere else or should be thrown away. Consider putting a cotton place mat on the bottom to give the drawer a clean, happy look. To add an aesthetic touch of order to doing laundry, use one brightly colored laundry bag for laundry waiting to be folded and another for items to be ironed. Use a third to line a wicker hamper in your closet.

If you enjoy setting a pretty table with a variety of different linens, and your eye becomes accustomed to the added colors and vitality, how can you use this awareness to improve the appearance of other areas in your life? What about your work environment? Are there ways you can bring more beauty to your workplace? I like to bring a few colorful, personally meaningful possessions to my work area so my space reflects my personality, and I would encourage you to do the same. You can have a colored glass, paperweights, a silver letter opener, a pretty in- and out-box, framed pictures of your children, a bouquet of flowers, or a favorite painting or print on the wall. Life is too impersonal. Offices tend to be too impersonal. Although it's important not to take things so far as to be intrusive to our coworkers, we need some toys and small treasures around us.

I don't use a computer, but if I did, I'd drape the screen with a favorite cotton fabric when I wasn't using it. All visible technology, when not in use, is an eyesore as grim as a gravestone. I love my brightly colored memory boards hanging on the wall with art postcards attached to help me remember a special day of seeing at a museum, or displaying photographs of family and friends. I always keep something alive on my desk to remind me how precious time is. Whether African violets, ivy in a pot, or freshly cut flowers, a living plant gives off energy. You will also feel more harmonious in a room where there is something alive and growing that needs tending.

We collect old English cobalt-blue poison bottles and display them on window ledges so the light shines through them. If we arranged them higgledy-piggledy, the eye and the brain would be distressed, but when we order them from the smallest to the largest, they are extremely satisfying.

When we are with other people every day, we don't see small changes in their appearance. But when we or they are away and then return, we see them with a fresh eye. The same thing occurs with our house or apartment. When we're in the midst of all the clutter and confusion, we can't see the forest for the trees. When we go away and return, however, we open our eyes to what is around us. Piles of paper on a desk, stacks of books on the floor, and clutter on the kitchen countertops offend us, because we aren't immediately engaged in the stuff that surrounds us. We've been other places where we've been exposed, influenced, and often inspired by what we've seen.

Use this clarity to seize your own space and organize and rearrange your things so they are more orderly and harmonious. Once you have brought your possessions into order, you will see with new eyes further changes that will improve your spaces. The smallest details can make a big impact. Once you have de-thugged an end table, you might look at the lamp and see with clarity that it is too big for the table. Looking around, you may discover another lamp that is too small for its table. Scale and proportion are closely linked to order. You may feel there are too many things on your tabletops. Use this time of clearer vision to make minor improvements.

Look at your kitchen sink. Look at the counter-top first on the left and then the right. What do you see? Tackle the left-hand counter first. Remove everything. Count how many things you had sitting out. Put the objects away or on another counter temporarily. Scrub the surface clean. (In my case, I have to sand the maple counter.) Do the same with the right-hand counter. Count each separate object. Add the numbers from the two surfaces together. How many items did you have out on the counters? How many objects would you like to keep on them regularly? You will be amazed at how much you accumulate, robbing yourself of Zen workspace. This exercise should be repeated every three or four months.

One of my rules is that I never put something back on the counter without cleaning, polishing, or repairing it. Most often, I end up with lean spaces after I've removed everything, because I feel such expansiveness after seeing all the space.

Look at your counter with the eye of a photographer's stylist. If you have a Polaroid camera, take a picture of the counter. If you don't, take a picture with your regular camera. By the time you get your film developed, the counter will probably look quite different.

When you have eliminated the clutter and the space is now spare, is there anything you want to add? You may want to fill a small bowl with lemons. Or you may want to put some juice oranges in a clear glass bowl next to the shiny chrome juice squeezer, ready for tomorrow morning's fresh-squeezed juice.

The eye and the brain seek order in all things, both natural and man-made. Look around the train station. What eyesores do you see this week that you didn't see last week? Look around the diner where you go for a cup of coffee. By opening your eyes to see the places where you go regularly, you'll be able to translate to your home this heightened sensitivity to your environment. As you see clutter and things that are run-down, try to visualize how they could be improved. You can't put the world in order, but you can rearrange things at home attractively in order for them to be inviting.

Pretend that a magazine photographer is coming to photograph your house, inside and out. Who knows, he or she may want to photograph your closets for fresh storage ideas. What's going on in your closets? Do you have anything to hide? Every house has a few messy corners, but it's enormously satisfying to put your house in order. Attack one zone at a time.

Do nothing without purpose.
SAINT AUGUSTINE

Where do you begin? What catches your eye? Look around at the bathroom sink. Remove everything. Scrub the surface clean. Look at the tub area. Remove everything. Clean the surfaces. Do this routinely area by area. The top of the chest of drawers needs a look. The front-hall table becomes a catchall. Even your briefcase, tote bag, or pocketbook needs a look and a clearing out.

You can buy colored storage boxes with label windows to tidy the mess on top of your desk. Everything will be safe in these cheerful boxes. Even if they serve as temporary storage until you have time to deal with the work or file things away more permanently, it is worthwhile to tidy up. Keep pretending that the photographer is coming soon. Open your eyes to what you wouldn't want in the pictures. You'll feel so good about your house after you've tidied up room by room, closet by closet, that perhaps you'll want to have friends over for dinner. There is nothing to entertaining if you're "party-ready," but few of us are ever party-ready without the adrenaline-inducing deadline of an upcoming celebration.

Goodness is said to be the outstanding characteristic of God.

FICINO

We all close our eyes to certain things—the dusty row of vitamin pill bottles on the kitchen window ledge could be placed inside a cabinet with the juice glasses. You'll see them when you reach for a glass and remember to take them. Mystery is important in your private spaces. We all may take vitamins, but we don't necessarily want them bared, in clear view of everyone.

To any vision must be brought an eye adapted to what is to be seen, and have some likeness to it.

PLOTINUS

Open your eyes to personal items in the bathroom. When we open our eyes, we intuitively cast our eye around a space to be sure everything is in order to avoid potential embarrassment and offensiveness. Before leaving a bathroom, look around to see that it's ready for the next person. Feng shui experts believe you should keep the toilet cover down when not in use so your fortune won't get flushed away.

Young mothers are usually so tired and overworked that they don't see as well as they could. However, it is a good exercise for parents to see the pacifier on the living room end table and be aware that it is no more attractive to others than plastic bottles are when not in use. Seeing well helps you be more objective, with fewer blind spots because of emotional attachments. Seeing well is thoughtful, because you avoid sending out negative energy inadvertently.

The truth of the matter is that you always know the right thing to do. The hard part is doing it.

NORMAN SCHWARZKOPF

Enhancing beauty through order has nothing to do with money. You can't hire someone to set up your systems and keep them up. No one knows better than you how to arrange your possessions in a logical, harmonious manner. When you see the increase in efficiency, you will value the worth of a highly personal sense of order that helps you to be more effective. Even if you have outside help, you have to have a system in place for others to follow. There is no easy delegation.

Order paves the way to serenity and grace. Putting your house in order, for your enjoyment and convenience, has a powerful effect on your sense of inner peace. Last January, I made a New Year's resolution to be more organized. As a visual person, I'm usually quite organized because it

is second nature to me to want to see harmony. But when I become busy and travel a lot, things pile up, and I turn my back on them. One day I brought a load of freshly laundered towels and cotton throw rugs from the laundry room to the linen closet, and much to my frustration, discovered that there wasn't a free shelf for the clean laundry. The time had come. I couldn't turn my back on this. I stood there, towels and area rugs in my arms, and opened my eyes to the scene in front of me. My resolution to get more organized rang in my ears as my eyes opened wide.

There is no such thing as being half-organized. I removed everything on one of the shelves, one item at a time. I placed the sheets and towels on a bed and rearranged everything into sets of sheets, stacking favorites in one pile and rarely used older ones in another. I refolded some sheets and pillowcases, creating more uniformity. It became clear that it was time to cut up some old, worn-out towels to make into rags for cleaning. I made piles of others to give to a thrift store. I put all my sewing supplies and button jars in a colored box the size of a shoe box. I found some inexpensive, brightly colored, nylon laundry bags at the hardware store in sky blue, pale pink, chartreuse, dark green, and hot pink. They were ideal for stowing our down comforters.

Great knowledge brings great responsibility.

EMMIT FOX

After several satisfying hours, I had styled the linen closet so it looked attractive. In the best of all possible results, I was able to leave one whole shelf empty. Now when I bring laundry to the linen closet, I can rest it on this shelf as I sort things out and put everything away neatly.

I was so pleased with myself that the linen closet became my high altar. I turned on the

I am starting very much from down at the earth, . . . taking a giant-sized stride not from sun to sun but, at most, from mountain to mountain.

GOETHE

76

light, opened the door wide, put a yellow throw rug on the floor, and showed everyone who came to the apartment my accomplishment. The empty shelf was so Zen, I felt proud. "Come see my closet."

Order is a gift we give ourselves. We know where we want to put things once we commit the time and focus needed to become more organized.

When you open your eyes to putting your possessions in order, you will not be bored. These are your personal things. You either like them and find them meaningful or you can discard them. But only your unique eye can make these decisions. Your possessions should be a source of great companionship and entertainment because your personal memorabilia and treasured objects are all pieces of your autobiography. Discriminate between what is necessary, what is meaningful, and what you can let go. We all hold on indefinitely, but eventually we're able to let go of stuff because we've opened our eyes to the reality that it served a purpose at a former time and it is no longer relevant. Think of order as a river. There are tides, times when everything is cleared away and other times when you have too much going on.

We need to be courageous enough to embark on the hero's journey.

LARRY DOSSEY

Set aside one day a month—don't make any appointments for that day—and weed out your things, at the office and at home. If your job doesn't allow you this time, do it at night or on a Saturday. This regular clutter control is important, because it prevents you from developing an indifferent eye. In the end, the organization will save you time. This commitment to order is ongoing. You'll grow to see how stimulating it is to be alone, perhaps listening to some powerful classical music, and feeling your emotional attachment to some of the things around you. Let your instinct guide you. If you're not ready to throw something away, put it in a "slush" box to be revisited. This discipline is a soulful form of meditation, increasing your personal awareness and daily satisfaction.

Knowledge comes but wisdom lingers.

ALFRED, LORD TENNYSON

Every time you figure out the best place for something and set it up ideally, think of it as a grace note. Each time, ask yourself, What am I trying to accomplish? What is my goal?

When you see disorder or irregularity, look to see what is in front of your eyes. Now, envision what would be ideal. How can you create regularity from what you have to work with?

Learning is but an adjunct to oneself.

SHAKESPEARE

Always ask yourself, What will be the most useful way to solve a problem? What will bring the best results? What will make the process more enjoyable? What will make ironing more pleasant? Being by a sunny window with some primroses on the ledge? Where would be the most attractive place to pay bills? If it is the living room, set up your papers on a desk in the path of sunlight coming in from a window.

Self-organization removes the drudgery from day-to-day tasks. When we see for ourselves how fulfilling it is to be in control of our personal life, we feel uplifted and sustained by this feeling of self-control, eager to meet the day. Be strict with your eye and brain to care as much about the areas of your life that you live unnoticed by others—the vast majority of your time—as you do those areas that others see. When you achieve order, then you're free to live with more beauty moment by moment, day by day, wherever you are, whatever you are doing, because you can see the grace and beauty of a harmonious life.

Balance

To know oneself, one should assert oneself.

ALBERT CAMUS

We have a need to organize all stimuli into rational wholes, but the parts don't need to be exactly alike for there to be balance. While strict symmetry demands exact correspondence on opposite sides of a line or axis, balance only requires an equality of distribution, a harmonious arrangement or proportion of the parts on opposite sides of the dividing point. Balance is achieved by using the contrasts between elements—such as light and dark, or weight variations—along with placement to create counterpoise. Therefore, while a symmetrical object is always balanced, a balanced object is not always symmetrical. A balanced object needs to appear evenly weighted on each side, but the sides need not mirror each other. Consider a sugar bowl and a teapot. A sugar bowl is balanced and symmetrical because it has handles on both sides. A teapot is not symmetrical, as it has a handle on one side and a spout on the other, but the two elements are counterpoised, making the object balanced. The eye desires this feeling of equilibrium or composure.

We are all on a constant search for balance, the key to solving all problems. We never achieve a lasting balance. We may eat too much or too little. We may drink too much or too little. We may work too hard or not hard enough. There are competing forces from one side of the pendulum's swing to the other, and somewhere in the middle—the mean—is equilibrium.

When you lose yourself in some positive behavior, you forget your fears and worries; temporarily they cease to exist.

DAVID K. REYNOLDS

Look at the world around you and see all the balance that exists, both natural and man-made. This will make you become more aware of balance and how you can achieve more of it in your life and in your home, leading to harmony and comfort.

Counterpoise

To achieve balance between opposed forces, action is required. A ballerina can support her body on one toe. Her other leg may be at an oblique angle, producing a counterpoise, also called counterbalance, a force or influence that balances or counteracts another. Watch a performer practice counterpoise on a tightrope by tilting a long horizontal balance bar; watch a gymnast place her arms and legs in counterpoise to maintain her position on a balance beam. People riding bicycles will unconsciously and naturally shift their weight to achieve balance, a skill we learn and never have to relearn.

On a 4 × 6-inch index card draw a dot one inch in from the center of the left edge. Stare at the dot. Because it is not centered, it is unstable. What is needed to relieve the visual tension is a counterbalancing dot or weight. When there is balance or counterpoise, intuitively you're aware of equilibrium.

Now draw a dot one inch in from the center of the right edge of the card. Both this dot and the dot on the left should be on the same horizontal plane. Stare at them. Do you feel a sense of balance? The single dot has the same effect as a face with only a left eye. The second dot restores order to the image.

Architects hire builders to use careful measurements to assure balance. The carpenter uses a level, a tool that ascertains whether a surface is horizontal. When a surface is level, the liquid inside the level's rectangle of glass forms a bubble exactly in the middle. I collect antique levels and use them as desk accessories to remind me of the importance and beauty of balance.

The key to balance is the vertical line, the most powerful element in visual satisfaction. It does not matter what objects are placed on the left or on the right, so long as the eye senses a central dividing line and each side complements the other. A common mistake is attempting to achieve balance by using identical objects. Identical objects work well in achieving symmetry, but too much symmetry is boring. Within symmetry, you can play with balance.

Look around your house for examples of counterbalance. If you have a framed picture on the right side of an end table, a lamp on the left side

offsets the weight of the frame and picture. If you have an arrangement of flowers on the right side of a coffee table, a stack of books on the left will compensate for the flowers not being in the center. When you place an object off center, you need another to offset it for a balanced feeling.

Counterpoise is created by many different elements besides scale. Texture, color, pattern, and the nature of an object influence the way something appears. A flowering plant to the right of a sofa can be counterbalanced by several throw pillows on the left side of the sofa where one pillow is strongly patterned in bright blue and red stripes. When you examine still life or landscape paintings, you see that objects are balanced with one another not through symmetry but by offsetting one object against another. A dark tree on the left side of a landscape painting could be offset by a sunny path that leads from the painting's right side. A good picture with a balanced composition should look no less balanced in reverse than it does when viewed normally.

This is the only eye that sees the mighty Beauty.

PLOTINUS

Study paintings to see the artists' use of balance. If you have some slides of master painters' works, deliberately reverse them and see if they look just as well composed to your eye. Most artists achieve balance in their paintings by counterbalancing the elements of the composition in regard to color and weight.

The reason this works is that our need for an invisible plumb line or felt axis has been satisfied. Keep in mind why horizontal and vertical lines are the most harmonious and restful: They represent balance, counterbalance, and equipoise. We human beings have an intuitive sense of visual balance because of our basic relationship with the vertical and horizontal axes in our environment. When you learn to see and feel the power of counterpoise, you can become more comfortable creating your own still life arrangements in your rooms.

Visually, you feel uneasy when you observe imbalance. When something is not balanced, your sense of equilibrium is disturbed by the lack of equality in weight distribution. For this reason, all oblique angles create tension. If you put a glass down on a stack of papers, causing the glass to tilt, you fear it will fall. A lampshade that is crooked is unsettling for the same reason; because the bottom rim of the lampshade is not parallel to the horizontal surface of the table and lamp base, you sense that could topple.

Draw a circle. Draw a line at twelve o'clock from the center of the circle. Now draw another circle. From the center draw a line to the circumference at two o'clock. Notice how the tipped radius of two o'clock attracts more attention than the twelve o'clock radius. It creates an imbalanced image, disturbing the eye. Deliberately tilt a painting on the wall, creating an oblique angle. Walk away, turn, and look at it. You immediately want to straighten it out. Area rugs that lie at an angle to the walls of a room also create unpleasant tension. However, if you place a favorite

Not life is to be valued, but the good life.

ARISTOTLE

object on a table at an angle, it will attract more attention than if it were lined up perfectly with the side of the table. In this case the tension is desirable. I find that placing books slightly over the edge of a tabletop at an angle creates intrigue.

Broken window panes or cracked windows create unsettling oblique angles, as do cracked tiles. Have you ever noticed the oblique angles created by the stairs of a fire escape seen through a window? Examples of disturbing oblique angles that are common in the home and should be corrected are blinds that are askew, shutters that have uneven slats due to missing pins, a duplex outlet that is not parallel to the floor, and a tower of collared shirts that is about to slide right off the shelf because the shirts have not been stacked appropriately—you should reverse the direction of the shirt every other layer for stability.

Study balance in nature. Trees usually grow up vertically with branches spreading out in all directions. If you see a tree trunk growing at an oblique angle, you detect tension, almost as though the tree were in danger of being uprooted. After a hurricane, often trees are leaning over with roots aloft, giving you an unnerving sensation arising, I suspect, in the recesses of our primitive brain, where we have a primordial understanding of the proper relationship of objects to earth and sky.

Pure seeing is always active, never passive.

Balance is steady, consistent, and sensible. Without it, we fall.

THREE

Seeing the Spaces Between Us

Space and Depth

I become a transparent eyeball; I am nothing;
I see all . . .

— EMERSON

We live in all kinds of spaces. We experience wide-open spaces, crowded city spaces, our personal spaces, and the spaces of our family, friends, and community. We travel to exotic spaces in faraway places, always influenced by what we see and feel in these areas between boundaries. Too few people understand the dynamics and atmosphere of space. The spaces between us are where life—words, energy, a glance—happens. Spaces may or

Two things incline the heart to wonder, the starry sky above and the moral law within.

IMMANUEL KANT

may not contain objects. Some rooms are empty, some are full of things; the space is the same but the feeling is different. You can be at the beach alone or with hundreds of people but, while the area is the same, the energy and the atmosphere vary.

Space is where good and bad things happen. For example, when we were younger, couples in New York City would make dates to meet under the clock at the Biltmore Hotel on Manhattan's Vanderbilt Avenue. A special meeting place always becomes charged with positive electricity. On the other hand, the street space where Peter and I were brutally mugged one summer night causes me to feel profoundly sad. I intend to help you to see and feel the energy of the space between us. Even though you may think space is virtually invisible, it is the stage setting of life. All space has personality. In this chapter, you will begin to see what some say can only be felt.

All space has energy, pleasant and awful. We need to learn to read space. Wherever you are, how you feel has a great deal to do with the vibrations of energy in the space. You can go to other people's spaces and feel their vitality and spirit as well as negative energy.

When you understand and feel more comfortable with some of the mysteries of space, you'll know intuitively what spaces are sweet, harmonious, and open up your heart, and how to make the spaces you occupy uplifting to your soul.

The foolish reject what they see, not what they think; the wise reject what they think, not what they see.

HUANG-PO

The spaces we occupy have boundary lines, marking their limits. Your house is on a lot. There is a property line. Your fence or wall separates you from your neighbors. Your house and garden should be one integrated space. If you have bad feelings about any of the spaces in your environment, you will not feel harmony.

Space is not only the area between borders or limits; it is also the aura or ambience among objects and among us. Contentment comes from creating and living in harmonious personal spaces. You learn to look at and really see space with your gut, not your intellect. The abil-ity to identify sacred spaces—places that speak to your heart and soul, that open you up, expand your vision, your imagina-tion, and your dignity—should be cultivated. I intend to show you how essential it is to your well-being for you to create spaces that have this personal spirit of place for you, that you feel a reverence for, that become sacrosanct. You

Stare without moving an eyelash.

SHIVA

love yourself and others when you occupy hallowed spaces. Once you recognize the energy you can't physically see, you will know to flee when a particular space makes you feel discontented. Spaces have as powerful a hold on us as people.

Look! This world is vast and wide.

ZEN SAYING

Think of all the spaces, the places, you are instinctively drawn to, where you feel you belong, where you long to go, where you never feel lonely, where you want to linger—the spaces you remember in your imagination and dreams. Envision space as an invisible expanse that accumulates energy from nature and people, as a three-dimensional canvas you can fill with select objects that add charm and grace, as a place where things and people come together harmoniously, ennobling and enriching your life's path.

My eyes and brain are awake.
The stars stand around me
Like gold eyes. I can no longer
Tell where I begin and leave off.
The faint breeze in the dark pines,
And the invisible grass,
The tipping earth, swarming stars
Have an eye that sees itself.

KENNETH REXROTH

The most blessed, divine spaces can be all the spaces in your own home and your garden.

To truly understand space, you must embrace perspective, our way of gauging distances. When you begin to see and appreciate depth in your surroundings, you will be seeing and living more profoundly. The depth you train your eye and brain to see is echoed in a greater understanding of the mysteries of life. Ultimately, visual perception in space results in more profound insights about one's life.

Space

In order to understand wholly an object, arrangement, or scene, we must learn to accept and to see space as its own element in any visual experience. Doing this involves defining the space around objects, studying the space between objects, identifying negative space, understanding the importance of objects having adequate space to breathe, and becoming more aware of how space makes you feel.

Becoming Sensitive to Space

Because of the human inability to fathom infinite space, many people are most comfortable within confined spaces. Space is the area between or separating objects. Yet space itself has density, otherwise birds and airplanes could not fly. The space between two objects can be just as important as the objects themselves. A house needs a lawn to allow breathing space between you and your neighbor. The Japanese expression for emptiness is "space to breathe." Lovers know to stand on their own and not lean too heavily on each other. Similarly, in all designs, there is negative and positive energy where the breathing space surrounding an object enhances it.

Vision may not work all the time, but we should marvel that it works at all.
STEVEN PINKER

When you see—when your retina registers light and dark shapes, colors and patterns—you see the whole object, not its parts as separate entities. Nor can objects be seen as separate from their surroundings; when you see an object, you always see the space surrounding it. The outline of a beautifully designed house against the sky is as important as the facade of the house itself. The space outlines the object and provides a context for it.

The space between objects helps to define each better. When observing the moon, for example, because of the limitless space around it, we have no proximity clues, so we always see it as a small round object. Only when it is low on the horizon do we see its vastness. Our vision depends on such relative measurements. To help us make sense of space, we need to use all of our senses to test and confirm what we see.

All are clear, I alone am clouded.

LAO-TZU

Whenever possible, touch the objects that draw your attention. Walk around and away from them and notice how their size appears to change. Notice the distance of space between objects. Guess measurements, then check for accuracy. This is a great way to train your eye so you have a greater grasp of spatial relations. When you move through a new space, try not to talk as much as usual as you try to absorb its vibrations. Just look around. Listen only to nearby natural sounds. Hearing tends to open you up to the sense of the atmosphere. Freely touch things in your midst.

The difference between landscape and landscape is small, but there's a great difference in the beholders.

EMERSON

Whenever possible, walk rather than drive. Pace yourself; don't hurry. Walking is ideal, because it allows you to stop and examine objects often. A bicycle is fine, too, because you see best when you use your own momentum to travel. Driving is often passive to the point of being numbing because you have to keep your eyes on the road. Even as a passenger, you're not free to concentrate on what you see, because by the time something attracts your eye, you've passed it. When you move mindfully in space, everything around you is also in motion.

Any opening is space, allowing access. When you examine any kind of open work, whether in metal, leather, lace, or wood, look at the pattern created by the intervening spaces. These are called negative spaces. Notice how the negative space is just as integral to the piece as its solid parts. The shadow also is a critical part of the space surrounding an object, and it is connected to the object. Study shadows. You can learn so much about an object by examining its shadow. Look at the shadow of a wrought-iron fence, a chair, a tree, a flower bouquet, or a pitcher.

Feng Shui: The Importance of What You Don't See in Space

Feng shui, the ancient Chinese system for determining favorable and unfavorable influences in our lives, ensures an optimum flow of vital energy, or ch'i, throughout your space. Feng shui takes into account all the mysterious elements of space to calculate how people may live healthy, prosperous, happy lives. Feng shui involves alignment and balance of the energies of spaces.

I said to the almond tree,
Sister, speak to me of God.
And the almond tree
blossomed.

UNKNOWN POET

Our feelings, our moods, and our attitude affect our spaces positively or negatively. The state of our spaces in turn affects our emotions.

Here are some simple ways to implement feng shui in your home:

+ To draw energy from the outdoors, make sure you are not blocking its entrance with heavy window treatments. Always maintain clean windows.

+ To ensure a continuous flow of energy within your rooms, clear away clutter. Use mirrors, glass, and light-catching objects to reflect energy.

+ Make sure positive energy doesn't escape up an open flue when there is no fire in the fireplace. Place a decorative screen in front of the fireplace.

- Have live plants to add energy. Change the water of cut flowers and plants every day.

- Keep the toilet seat down. You don't want your fortune to be flushed away.

- The front door of a home reveals the energy of the life inside the house. Your front door should open and close easily. The paint should be fresh and the brass polished.

- The best place for the dining room table is in the center of the room.

- The ideal location for the bed is where you feel most secure and private. Never place a bed directly in line with the door.

- Heavy, dark-brown beams on a ceiling may suppress positive energy. Consider painting them white or pastel blue so they will float in a heavenly direction.

- The best location for a desk is diagonally across from the door with the desk chair facing the entrance of the room.

Making the Most of Space

No matter how large or small a room is, the scale of the human form often determines the appropriate spacing between objects. To create a room ideal for moving about with ease, for intimate conversation, for comfortable walking between furniture, you need ample space between each chair, sofa, table, and stool. If a chair is on a swivel, you need to take that into consideration—otherwise it could bang into a nearby table with one turn. Always sit in a chair yourself to decide whether its

Wonder is the basis of worship.

THOMAS CARLYLE

placement is comfortable. For conversation, you should be no more than eight feet away from another person—three to five feet is intimate. You shouldn't have to raise your voice to be heard. One reason to have a chair at either end of a long sofa is for balance; another is for good conversation.

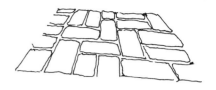

- When placing your coffee table in front of your sofa, make sure to allow enough room for people to walk around without bumping into the table. There is no absolute measurement for how near or far the table should be to the sofa, but human dimensions will help you determine these distances. If you are sitting on the sofa and want to reach for a cup of tea, can you do this without lurching forward? Seated on a sofa with your arm stretched forward, can you reach the coffee table? If you have a coffee table that is lightweight and can be easily moved, once seated you can adjust the table, moving it forward or back to the ideal location.

Nature and books belong to the eyes that see them.

EMERSON

- The furniture in a space should invite you to come into the room, sit down, and feel comfortable. Enter your rooms and glance down at the seating areas to sense whether or not they lure you into the space. Can you visualize being seated in a grouping? Is there plenty of space surrounding the furniture so you won't feel claustrophobic? If you have a chair near the middle of a room, it should be small in scale and easy to move around. Heavier furniture should be positioned around the edges of a room. Be sure high pieces are placed against a wall. Low pieces can float in the middle of a space. The exception to this concept is a flowering plant or floral bouquet on a table in the middle of the room, because it is alive and animate, drawing your eye upward, visually lightening the atmosphere.

Give me the splendid silent sun with all his beams full-dazzling!

WALT WHITMAN

- Always make sure your furniture has plenty of breathing space. Whenever a space becomes too crowded, it becomes unsettling, feeling more like a storeroom than a welcoming place.

- If you have a collection of small objects, consider putting a decorative tray underneath them to unify them in one space. If an object has a great deal of presence—a sculpture, a statue, or an intricately decorated large vase, for example—you need to give it breathing room. I learned years ago that an elephant needs a square mile of space all for himself. Like some animals, some objects need more space than others.

- If you have an important painting, free up the wall space on either side of it so the eye can feast on the beautiful work of art.

- Never fill a space. If you have a long, narrow hall, try not to hang any art on the side walls to prevent further crowding, but instead hang one mirror or painting at the far end, visually opening up the space.

- In a living room, no matter what its size, arrange at least three different places to sit. Create small conversation groupings rather than one large group of furniture. Have a place to sit at a desk as well as a spot to read near a window.

- Put a swivel on upholstered chairs (hidden under a flounce) in order to have one chair work for two different groupings, depending on the dynamics.

- Give every space a strong point of view. Use each space as an opportunity to express something personal.

- Always define breaks in space. If you have an architectural molding, whether a cornice, a chair rail, or molding on a door, contrast its color with the wall or door color to add energy to a room.

- Bring as much natural light as possible into your rooms. Always have clean windows. Avoid heavy window treatments that block light from entering the space. Paint woodwork a shiny white to reflect more light. Use lots of shiny materials to bring in additional light, including polished wood tables and floors, and gleaming brass and silver.

To me every hour of the light and dark is a miracle,
Every cubic inch of space is a miracle.
WALT WHITMAN

- If you have a small space, paint it white. Hang white sheer curtains at the window.

- Be neat. A messy space is not welcoming. When a room is not occupied, it should be well ordered. When you are using the space, it is likely to become cluttered with books, newspapers, water glasses, dishes, and projects. Try to put things back where they belong in order to have the room ready for another fulfilling experience. Whenever we fail to tidy up, we are depriving ourselves of future enjoyment. For the hours of pleasure we receive, a few minutes of picking up, emptying the wastebasket, or dusting a surface is well worth the time. Once you see the value of neatness, make it a habit.

Eyes open. I listen to spring in the four directions.
TAN TAIGI

- Stack and nest objects. By arranging your books, boxes, and other things attractively, you can make your space house more objects without looking crowded.

- Place a flowering plant or a bud in a vase in every space, including the bathroom. Whenever we don't have living flowers, plants, or trees in our rooms, our spaces become stale. The quickest way to pep up a space is to add something growing or blossoming. An indoor tree attractively

The absence of light is a color beyond darkness.
QUENTIN HARDY

lit will produce graceful shadows on a wall. Are flower blossoms finite? Yes, but they also link us to the perennial seasons of our lives.

- See that your spaces have as few negative visual tensions as possible. Whenever feasible, correct lines that are askew and create many positive patterns.

What you do to any part of you that you call your "surroundings" you are doing to yourself. . . . The more you notice and learn about your "surroundings," the more you are learning about yourself.

DAVID K. REYNOLDS

- A client recently asked me what was wrong with the placement of her rectangular kitchen table and four chairs. The chairs were too large to be placed side by side without feeling too tightly arranged. When I went in to take a look, I saw the table crowded in the corner of the kitchen near the sink, sticking out at an oblique angle into the room. There was no symmetry, no balance; it felt helter-skelter. I immediately placed the table in the center of the room, lining up both ends with the sink and stove, freeing up floor space in front of all four counters on the four walls, giving ample space to breathe and move about the table. Remember, you will have exactly the same amount of floor space in a room no matter where you place your furniture. Keep balance in mind and you will place objects logically for a harmonious arrangement.

- The center of a space is visually important. If you have one focal point, as Mrs. Brown did with her large round table in the middle of her living room, all the areas surrounding this eye-attracting object will be balanced and well ordered.

Unity of Space

One of the biggest mistakes most people make in their homes is to compartmentalize their spaces, dividing them into categories where more emphasis is placed on the public spaces than on the private areas where they live each day. Your clothes closet, kitchen, pantry, linen closet, laundry room, bedroom, private study, and child's room are the spaces where you and your family spend most of your time at home. The same attention to detail and the same effort at fine-tuning should be spent on these spaces as on the areas for public view. To do otherwise is extremely counterproductive, because it is based on making a good impression on others. Whenever decisions are made to impress the Joneses, the sense of competition, the obsession with keeping up with what others have, goes against the essence of home as a private sanctuary for you and your loved ones.

I love all waste
And solitary places;
where we taste
The pleasure of believing
what we see
Is boundless, as we wish
our souls to be.

PERCY BYSSHE SHELLEY

To value seeing is to live appreciating light.

No one knows what goes on behind closed doors except the people who occupy the space. If the large majority of our time is spent at home alone or with our family, it is senseless to set up our lives for the 5 percent of our time that we have guests, rather than for the 95 percent of our time when we don't. I feel a need to help people to see how short-sighted and limiting this mind-set is. It actually causes people to be envious and jealous of what others have, and blinds them to seeing all the texture and beauty right in front of their own noses.

The seeing have the world in common.

HERAKLEITOS

The worst part of this tendency to compartmentalize for show is that so many daily sensual pleasures are lost, and life is lived from the perspective of what we don't have rather than from what we have. We look out through a prism of lack rather than one of abundance, gratitude, and blessings.

Whenever we deprive our eyes and the eyes of our family of the delights of variety, the beauty of fresh flowers and blossoming plants, the comfort and visual stimulation of crackling fires, we

Night, when words fade and things come alive.

ANTOINE DE
SAINT-EXUPÉRY

are not infusing our spaces with vital energy. When we don't set a pretty table for even the simplest meal, or prepare an attractive tea tray, we are dulling our eyes because there isn't enough to see in our spaces that is refreshing, stimulating, and uplifting—not enough to see that feeds the soul.

We all care deeply about others and want not only to love people but to be loved, respected, and admired in return. But when we don't see the importance of feasting our eyes on a regular basis, creating little details that make a huge difference, we grow restless and anxious, believing that life is largely a burden. In reality, life is a blessing we should celebrate minute by minute, hour by hour, especially in the intimacy and the privacy of our homes.

Think of the amazing care and attention to detail you demonstrate when you plan a party. This same energy will always be there for you when you are a co-creator, adding your finishing touches to your spaces, making what you see more beautiful. This energy will also be there for you when you see ways to add flair and color to what's at hand.

The evening star,
Love's harbinger.

JOHN MILTON

Every space in your home is of vital importance to you whether it is seen by others or not—the inside of a cabinet, your closet. When you see your home is just that—*your* home—you can arrange and rearrange things so you will be able to stimulate your eye by seeing harmonious proportions, surround yourself with objects that delight you, select materials, patterns, and compositions in your favorite colors, and so make your home a poem you have composed for yourself.

There is really no such thing as bad weather, only different kinds of good weather.

JOHN RUSKIN

If we could see our home as a journal, reflecting our innermost thoughts and feelings, rather than as a published autobiography, where we expose ourselves to the public, we could free ourselves of all the superficiality that narrows our vision, keeping us from seeing well.

If you never had a friend or relative see your house or apartment, how would it look? Would it feel any different? Pretend you could create the space of your dreams where no one else was allowed and therefore couldn't judge your taste. What kind of space would this be? What kind of home would you really live in?

Nature never did betray the heart that loved her.

WILLIAM WORDSWORTH

Your home is so much more meaningful to you than the opinions of others; its spaces need your unique eye to shape them and mold them into places that breathe your life and the life of your immediate family who live under your roof.

How often do you use your living room for your own pleasure? Do you see it through your own eyes, or do you tend to envision what others see? Do you get nervous when people come to your home because you know they will be snooping around? If someone comes for dinner, they can look about in certain areas for three to five hours, but you see these spaces every day. You are also influenced by them at night, in the dark, even in your sleep.

Night hath a thousand eyes.

JOHN LYLY

Spaces that are outer-directed—created to please others—will never feel cozy when you are alone in them. Subconsciously, you look around and don't see or feel yourself there because you are only partially represented in the decorations, colors, and objects. When are we going to achieve a wider, wiser way of seeing, seeing what *we* want to see every day and letting others in on that personal vision and joy?

Space is limitless, but your private spaces are not. You have limited space in which to express yourself. When you see the light, you will live each day seeing the very things around you that tell a personal story and are symbols of a larger message. The favorite objects you surround yourself with will keep you company, will give you back the love you feel for them, because you have formed a bond, a genuine closeness. You are never lonely when accompanied by your personal essence in your home. Whenever you are true to yourself, you feel content. If your private spaces aren't lived in fully, richly, and lovingly when you are alone, even the 5 percent of your life spent at home with guests will be more of a production than a genuine celebration among friends.

What else is nature but god?

SENECA

The Secret Space

Everyone should have a sacred space, a sanctuary where no one is allowed to go without first being invited. When the children were little we created a loft reached by a ladder in a large closet off limits to adults. We called it *The Secret Space*.

Space is an opportunity for something personal to take shape. We must have spaces waiting for us where we have no fear of being invaded. In the cottage, where Peter and I escape from the world, we are even more private than in New York. Both Peter's and my writing rooms, located upstairs in the back of the house, are off limits to others. Brooke's room has a tiny alcove where she likes to paint; she prefers that people not enter freely. Like most artists, she doesn't like visitors in her studio. Peter and I consider our bedroom a sacred space. The sitting room I use as my dressing room is another private space.

For you can look at things while talking or with a radio going full blast, but you can see only when the clatter stops.

FREDERICK FRANCK

We decided several years ago to call the entire upstairs of the cottage "family quarters," off limits to guests. The upstairs is rich with seeing stimulus. The fact that it is for our eyes only does not diminish its beauty, nor does it look less wonderful than it would if we were to expose it to visitors. Maintaining some mystery is not mean-spirited; it is respectful to yourself and your need for a sacred, private space. You don't have to apologize or explain anything. Having friends over doesn't mean you have to give a complete house tour.

It is solved by walking.

SAINT AUGUSTINE

Many people like their bedroom, dressing room, and bathroom to be private spaces. No one is entitled to see everything of yours. It's an unwritten rule that Peter never goes in my Zen Room, for example, without being invited. When we are there together, he is enchanted, because he sees me in every inch of the space. In turn, when I am invited into his writing room, I see Peter, pure and simple, everywhere. He has complete autonomy over what he puts in his space, what he hangs on the walls, what he stacks on the floor or on his desk. Our two writing rooms are connected by a wide, open entryway, but you can't imagine two more different spaces. I enjoy seeing his memorabilia, his treasures, and his organized clutter, and he loves to see my colorful boxes, paperweights, quilts, ribbons, and colored pens and pencils.

Because these two rooms are sacred spaces, they are extremely meaningful to us. We can go to them with a guarantee that nothing will be touched by anyone else. I can go to my Zen Room any time of day and night and it is there for me, safe, private, and a feast for my eyes. I open up to the true spirit of the space, caressed by many nostalgic, colorful objects. I feel safe somehow and see better than ever when I'm there.

Experiencing Beauty Without Ownership

America traditionally is interested in possession—land is important and more is better. Some people don't see well until they own the land or the house or the car or the boat. But artists and poets don't want to possess the sunset or the waves or the birds in flight. Native Americans traditionally experienced the land without a fixed sense of ownership. They felt its beauty and revered it. They felt the land was theirs without a deed and that others could also enjoy it. In a genuine seeing experience, your satisfaction is simply in the moment of engagement without regard to possession.

We would be happy if we studied nature more in natural things, and acted according to nature, whose rules are few, plain and most reasonable.

WILLIAM PENN

Where are some of the places you go in order to see well and experience powerful transformation without any desire for ownership? The mountains in Colorado? An island in the West Indies? The islands of Greece? New England in the fall? Niagara Falls? A nearby beach? A park? When we learn how to see wherever we are, we will be better equipped to look at an empty room and envision the space filled with our energy and spirit, our colors and favorite objects. Far too many people want to be told what to see. Rather than train their own brain, they let others brainwash them. Every genuine seeing experience will enrich your own perceptions, uninfluenced by those of others. Here are some ways to build independent perception:

What I know of the divine science and Holy Scripture I learnt in woods and fields.

SAINT BERNARD

• When you take a walk, explore a new route. Vary your routine as often as you can. You will be amazed how much more you will see because of the novelty. When you take a familiar road or path, notice what has changed almost imperceptibly. You see green buds one day, and yellowing the next, until at last you see daffodils in bloom.

• The next time you take the train home, sit opposite where you usually sit. Notice ten sights that are worth seeing. If you hadn't sat there, you never would have seen the bathers at the beach, the elevated osprey nest over the salt marshes, a church steeple in the sunlight, a sailboat regatta close to shore, schoolboys playing soccer, white birch trees, an old stone wall, a beautifully proportioned colonial brick house.

• Sit in your living room in the morning as you sip your coffee and read the newspaper. Return to the same chair in the late afternoon, as the sun is setting, and sip tea as you look around. This is exactly the same space

The works of nature must all be accounted good.

CICERO

but it feels different, depending on the light. Our living room faces west and south, so the glow of the setting sun turns our white walls and curtains a rosy pink. I can swivel my chair to see our neighbor's cornflower-blue house turn pale lilac as the red in the sunset mixes with the blue.

In his several serial paintings of haystacks, Reims cathedral, and poplar trees, Claude Monet showed us that space is always alive simply because of the rotation of the earth around the sun. He was fascinated by the ever-changing atmosphere and the surrounding air and space as he painted the fog and its density against the sky. Like Monet, pay attention to the times of day. Driving at night is an entirely different experience from driving in the identical space during a sunny cloudless day.

The light will change in your spaces seasonally as well as hourly. In the winter, when the trees are skeletons and the light is low, you see brilliant light that could be twice as intense as in the summer when the trees shade your spaces.

The moon is a different thing to each one of us.

FRANK BORMAN

- The next time you are outside looking at a starry sky, pick some of your favorite configurations of stars, perhaps one including the Little Dipper. Try to count the stars around it. Then stop counting and just look. Count again. The more you stare, the more stars you see. Seeing takes time.

- If you think of a friend, can you visualize his or her image? My mother has been dead since 1980. I can't literally see her. However, when I think of her, I can vividly envision her. She had a favorite gray wool dress that flattered her figure. I can see her, wearing that dress, walking down the stairs of our house in Westport, Connecticut, when I was six or seven, her nails painted fire-engine red and her hair jet black, pulled back in a bun.

The heavens call to you, and circle around you, displaying to you their eternal splendors, and your eye gazes only to earth.

DANTE

Translating Seeing Experiences into Your Spaces

I once was asked if I were to hire an interior designer, who would it be? Whose taste do I most admire? What do you think my answer was? I couldn't think of one designer whose taste is similar to mine. When we see well we see for ourselves; we have pure vision. The spaces I occupy are deeply personal. They are put together over a lifetime. It is my seeing

The sun shines not on us, but in us. The rivers flow not past, but through us, thrilling, tingling, vibrating every fiber and cell of the substance of our bodies, making them glide and sing.

JOHN MUIR

experiences that are the building blocks. What's right for my space is wrong for someone else's. When you train your brain to make the connections from powerful seeing experiences anywhere in the world, your personal spaces will reflect all your seeing. It is not our task to see through the eyes of others. Our goal is to learn to see something that is not literally in front of our eyes but is in our soul.

Before you increase your powers of visualization, think about your space as it looks now. How well do you know the space where you live? Can you close your eyes and vividly picture your rooms? Can you make a list of all the elements in your living room, including the artwork on the walls and the objects on all the tabletops? How many windows does each of your rooms have? How many panes of glass per window? It is important that you know your space well before you change it to make the atmosphere of your home more reflective of who you are.

Visualization Begins with Seeing an Empty Space

We all live in physical spaces. Our house is our ultimate space. When you have real seeing experiences—where you have taught yourself how to be dazzled by an object, a form, a shape, the sunlight on the grass, the shadow on the wall, the sun after a rain that turns raindrops into shimmering diamonds—you will be able to incorporate the essence of these experiences into your spaces. If you can dissect a chair, a table, a lamp, and see it with new eyes, studying the curves, the straight lines, the proportions and scale, grasping the nuances and knowing it well, only then will you be able to look at an empty room and visualize a table here, a chair there, a lamp here, a footstool there. Your eyes see into an empty space. Your brain connects the objects to a new environment. You know a

The sky is the daily bread of the eyes.

EMERSON

chair's dimensions, character, and personality. You trust the mystery whereby a chair is literally in one place but can be seen in another in your mind's eye.

It's far easier to envision your belongings being moved from one house to another if you are intimately familiar with your possessions and the next house is empty. But if you go into a house full of things, color, patterns, and individual style, it is difficult enough to visualize the space as empty, much less filled with familiar objects, colors, and patterns. Practice mentally rearranging objects on a table without moving anything. Walk over to a cluttered tabletop. Without using your hands to physically rearrange things, use your brain. First, mentally remove everything from the table. Now envision placing things in better order, editing out things you don't want to see. Can you do that well? Do you see like objects with like? Is there symmetry and balance? Does your eye now see objects that don't seem to belong together? Is it their scale, color, pattern, or material that is causing dissonance?

You can observe a lot just by watching.

YOGI BERRA

We are peculiarly sensitive to the vibration of light.

You can do this exercise anywhere. You can look at someone wearing silly clothes and you can mentally dress that person in a more flattering wardrobe. You can look at a shop window and see it arranged in a new way. If the shopkeeper could really see, the window wouldn't look so random, junky, and like a hodgepodge. The disgusting sooty beige carpeting in the shop window could be a great blue-and-white checkerboard tile. You have an "*ah ha*" moment of pure seeing, because you were attracted to the blue-and-white tiles years ago when you saw them in the breakfast room of a country inn, and now you have mentally transported them to an entirely different space. You can do this at a restaurant or at a friend's house, too.

Something will turn up.

BENJAMIN DISRAELI

I was sitting with a friend at a favorite French restaurant in New York City when he noticed the arch of a recessed niche and asked me why it was ugly. I knew he longed to know, being the frustrated architect he is. When

I looked at the troubling shape I began to laugh. I love this restaurant so much—the atmosphere, the food, and the memories of such great times there—that I'm inclined when having lunch there to admire the French atmosphere rather than critique it architecturally. However, picking the arch apart, element by element, awakened me to its awkward execution. Though I am sure the heart of the architect or builder was in the right place, the result was really quite appalling. The proportions were off—the arch was too skinny; the workmanship was sloppy, resulting in rough edges; the two sides were not symmetrical left to right, and to make matters worse, there was a column on one side of the arch that was not repeated on the opposite side. This niche, in short, was a visual wreck.

Light is so much a part of sight.

Every time I return to this endearing French restaurant, I smile at this pathetic niche and visualize a more graceful, symmetrical, well-crafted arch. It was fun for me to know just how many architectural and aesthetic sins had been committed in the construction of this one small niche. But seeing the problem isn't enough. Visual literacy involves knowing how to solve the problem. You want to be able to see what is wrong with this niche and how it could be corrected. Let your eye identify what is awkward, then you can determine what would be satisfying and visually pleasing. By studying the harmonious proportions, curves, and graceful shapes of classical architecture, our eye sees why something is wrong and therefore unsatisfying.

If you are seeking creative ideas, go out walking. Angels whisper to a man when he goes for a walk.

RAYMOND INMON

It is the child that sees the primordial secret in nature and it is the child of ourselves we return to. The child within us is simple and daring enough to live the Secret.

LAO-TZU

Real estate brokers often advise their clients to paint the inside of their house off-white so there won't be any chance of its being painted in colors objectionable to potential buyers. I disagree. Off-white is blah and has no energy. Apparently most people can't see beyond what is literally in front of their eyes. But the truth is that you can always improve something once you know how to see it. The knowing how involves tapping into the brain's warehouse. You have visual references you can draw on.

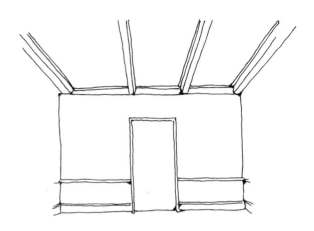

- Peek in the windows of a house that is for sale. What do you see? Is it furnished or empty? Can you envision fresh bright colors with your furniture and taste? Spaces always have character and energy, good or bad. See how you feel when you experience bland neutral empty spaces versus rooms that breathe the life and vitality of the owners.

    One of the greatest selling points of a house may be the happiness of the current owners. If the house is on the market empty—the owners have already moved on— try to get a sense of the former occupants by walking around the rooms. What colors did they use on the walls? What condition are the floors in? How do you feel when you walk around the bedrooms? Do you feel it is a loved house?

When neighbors sell their house, watch with interest what the new owners do to change the appearance. On your regular walks, jot down the changes. See for yourself whether they are improvements or merely alterations. This is fun to do, because sometimes money is wasted on showy, even tacky, additions. Everyone has taste, good or bad, but your private eye can judge when the original character that lends charm is obscured by awkward modern additions.

Your brain can store every real seeing experience without ever becoming overloaded. The more you see well, the greater your seeing vocabulary, and the greater your freedom of expression.

A Decorator Show House Experience

Walking wisdom is natural and lets you learn complex things easily.

W. A. MATHIEU

In the spring of 1997, the Kips Bay Decorator Show/House (benefiting the Kips Bay Boys and Girls Club, a New York settlement house) celebrated its twenty-fifth anniversary. All of the decorators who had participated in the inaugural event, myself included, were invited to return for this quarter-of-a-century celebration decorating rooms in the show house. *The New York Times* characterized us as "the gang of ten."

The morning I went to the mansion on Park Avenue and Sixty-fourth Street where the design show was to take place, I was enthusiastic to find a room that spoke to me. I wanted to bond with the space I'd be putting so much work into for this public event. I took notes as I explored all the magnificent rooms on the several floors—the grand hall, the living and dining rooms on the second floor, the master bedroom and several architecturally fine spaces on the higher floors. I looked at a huge kitchen space and several other rooms as well.

The real voyage of discovery consists not in seeking new landscapes, but in having new eyes.

MARCEL PROUST

But it was not until I reached the attic, on the fifth floor, that something spoke to me. There before my eyes, the last space I saw, was *my* room. As I looked south down Park Avenue through the two quarter-circle fan windows installed on their ears that also overlooked a church, I fell in love with this quirky space, originally two separate maids' rooms opened up to create one. The eaves reminded me of being in Paris in 1979–80 in Gertrude Stein's old apartment, where I stayed while working on a client's eighteenth-century house. The family lived in the apartment and I was happily put up in the attic, the most charming space of all. I remember how much I loved sitting at the desk in front of the window looking out at Paris. I'd stay up late and write, hoping some of the karma would rub off onto my writing paper.

Instantly I knew I'd transform the room into a writer's atelier. During the three months of preparation and the three weeks that this room would be open to the public, I'd put my heart into enhancing this charming space so it would take on even more character. I'd create an ideal room where I'd be inspired to write. The fact that the room was on the top floor, tucked away from everything, gave it a cool aura of calm and a distinctive quality of privacy. You *felt* the atmosphere.

You must learn to be still in the midst of activity and to be vibrantly alive in repose.

GANDHI

The first thing I did was remove the shallow fake mantel installed the previous year to give the illusion of a working fireplace. If there really had been a working fireplace, I would have replaced the mantel and kept it as the room's focal point, but I found it pointless to have something artificial disturbing the integrity of a room, particularly a writing room. There was a tiny broom closet on the wall opposite the windows. By removing the door, I turned it into an alcove where I hung botanical watercolors on the three walls, and on the floor I stacked several colorful hand-marbleized manuscript boxes with fresh grosgrain ribbons.

Openness, patience, receptivity, solitude is everything.

RAINER MARIA RILKE

Over the walls was stretched spring-green Thai silk donated by Jack Lenor Larsen that turned out to be an ideal background for a selection of my favorite Roger Mühl paintings.

In the course of those months, the room took on a distinct personality. The windows needed to have layers of paint stripped, and I sent the hardware out to be refinished. My friend the ceramist Lady Anne Gordon created a new collection of her porcelain fruits and vegetables to be placed on hanging shelves above the windows and on the surfaces to the left and right of the windows. An American glassblower agreed to execute some colored glasses I designed to place on the window ledges to hold flowers. I wanted a swirl of chromatically intense colors—red, orange, yellow, green, blue, and violet, the whole spectrum of primary and secondary colors—holding lilies, peonies, and roses, with light streaming through the

*He only can enrich me who
can recommend to me the
space between sun and sun.*

EMERSON

colorful glass. Between the handblown glasses were colored glass paperweights, all bought on vacations in Italy.

I envisioned all the colors as clean, fresh, and happy, and selected a silvery blue Thai silk for the chair cushions, and a purple-and-green plaid for a huge ottoman and two antique fruitwood footstools. Under both windows were bookcases, which we painted white with periwinkle blue on the back walls to match the ceiling. A wonderful electrician installed some subtle yet dramatically effective lighting, including strip lights along the bookcase shelves and two projector spotlights hidden in the ceiling, one to frame a painting placed over a French Regency carved commode between the bookcases and windows, and the other to spotlight the eighteenth-century French Provincial writing desk placed in the center of the room.

Because the room was to be my fantasy, all the antiques came from Pierre Deux Antiques, a favorite shop on Bleecker Street. In addition to the writing desk and commode, I placed an antique three-drawer dessert server under the eaves on the west wall, complemented by an antique wine-tasting table on an adjacent wall that I used as a dictionary stand. A seating area against the east wall was furnished with modern wicker furniture stained a tobacco tone.

*We can, at any time, double
the true beauty of an actual
landscape by half closing our
eyes as we look at it.*

EDGAR ALLAN POE

I filled the bookcases with colorful memorabilia including my books, diaries, and notebooks. *The New York Times* noted that this room was the most personal, even including a painting by my eleven-year-old granddaughter, Julia Hoyt. I'd taken four small paintings to Anthony Fair, a superior framer who made simple white-lacquer frames that I hung on a narrow wall above a French Provincial child's chair.

A few days before opening to the public, I had the door to my room removed so I could hang an attractive painting in the space to the left as you

*Retinal art appeals mainly or
exclusively to the eye rather
than to the mind.*

CALVIN TOMKINS

entered that would otherwise have been blocked by the open door. I loved walking into my room after climbing the five flights of stairs, anticipating spending time there, arranging flowers and writing.

Everything I love was represented in this room; it became a symbol of my life. Whenever you have an affinity for every detail in a space, you heighten the value and usefulness of the room because you are innately drawn to it, wanting to spend time there. Here, in this writer's atelier, I had perfect freedom to create a dream room. It was a fantasy of a well-ordered, sunny, cheerful, colorful room, complete in every detail, in all its elements. I could go there and sit, read, and write in an atmosphere of timelessness and peace.

You can't depend on your eyes when your imagination is out of focus.

MARK TWAIN

I became so attached to this intimate room in those months of preparation that I wanted it all to myself. I wanted to be able to go there alone and write. But what I created for my own private pleasure was, in reality, a room for public display, where thousands of people from all over would come and take a peek. They'd walk in and their eyes would move from right to left, ceiling to floor; gradually, they'd take in the sight. When I was there, I invited them to come in, sit down, and relax. Standing up in a writer's atelier is not the same as sitting down. Everything in the room was designed to be appreciated by someone who is seated at the desk or in a reading chair.

I found myself getting up early to go to my show house room—in theory, to do the flowers. But I knew I needed to be there, to be alone, to be silent, and to let the room speak to me. Whenever I was in town and free, I'd stay in the room to talk with the visitors. Peter loved the space as much as I did. He'd come down to the show house to be in the room and read, and when the public came through he would answer their questions and point out some of the most interesting features. He pointed out the amazing lighting that both framed a painting and spotlighted the center of the desktop.

The three weeks after the opening flew by. There were lots of parties to celebrate the silver anniversary, and it was a wonderful reunion for the once-young designers who are now more seasoned, many of them the most successful in the interior design field, all of them enjoying one another and the stimulation of the people who came to take a look around.

The last night of the show house there was a black tie party. After an elegant dinner with toasts and laughter, I looked at Peter and told him I needed to say good-bye to the room. The next morning we were flying to Ottawa and Toronto to give a lecture and do a television show, so I would never see the room again in three dimensions unless we dropped by on our way home up Park Avenue. Smiling, Peter said, "You really need to say good-bye, don't you, Alexandra? Let's go." That afternoon when I had left the room to go back and change into my evening clothes, I had felt choked up, but it was nothing as powerful as how I felt climbing that spiral staircase, turning to the left, and seeing my writing room for the last time.

When it is dark enough, you can see the stars.

CHARLES A. BEARD

My eyes are stuck to the point I look upon. I feel they would bleed if I tore them away.

PAUL CÉZANNE

Peter and I lit candles, sat on the comfortable wicker chairs, removed the silver tea tray on the ottoman so we could put our feet up, and held hands. "I've never loved any space more than this. What's wrong with me? Why do I feel this way?"

It is unusual for anyone to put so much enthusiasm and passion into a room that lives, completed, for only three weeks. As much thought went into planning every detail as in planning a wedding. There, with a drizzle outside reminiscent of London or Paris, I felt a profound sense of loss. I got up to sit at my desk for the last time. I stretched my arms out wide and stared at a silver pitcher holding dozens of lavender sweet-pea blossoms. My belief that you can transform a room into a private sanctuary had been proven to be true. Even though my writer's atelier was open to the public, it was intensely personal.

The visual memories associated with this show house will never fade. The early morning visits to arrange the freshest spring flowers and flowering branches, the private moments seated at the desk in the hours before the house opened to the public, the friends and acquaintances I'd see, the many strangers coming in who left as friends, and the feeling of collectively raising a great deal of money for a charity that gives children a head start in life made me feel good indeed. Was it a lot of work? Yes. Was it worth it? Yes.

I had given my heart, soul, and vision to this brief Kips Bay chapter where a humble space transcended its awkward structure to become an epiphany. I've come to realize that I don't need this room to exist in my real life. I'm glad it was a dream come true. I'm grateful I was able to take an inanimate space and bring it to life where the invisible energy was so heightened, where I enjoyed spending quality time both creating the atmosphere and experiencing the results. There is nothing you can't transform into a personal gem if you put your whole spirit into it.

The sense of sight is the keenest of all our senses.

CICERO

Making a Punch List

Put a pad of paper on a clipboard. On the top right-hand side of the pad, write the date. On the top left-hand side, write "Punch List." Items on a punch list should be numbered and should contain key words to identify areas that need to be remedied. Select any room in your house to write up all the areas that need improving. After the workmen leave a decorating job, invariably they have to return to touch up the paint, put on a switch plate, paint a screw white, or remove paint from a brass hinge. I've had punch lists with more than a thousand items that needed attention. The idea of this exercise is to notice, to see everything. Pretend you are a rich perfectionist who won't pay the bill until every detail is corrected.

Beautiful sorrow! It can do nothing wrong.

J. W. WATSON

You don't need to renovate or decorate to have a long punch list. Your eye becomes complacent when you settle into a space. Clipboard in hand, look at your room as an inspector or a doctor. You want to make a report, an evaluation. What room did you select? What doesn't look right? What bothers your eye? This is the time to be critical. Are your windows clean? Is there a missing pin that should be holding your shutters together? Is there a full wastebasket? Is the chair where you like to read worn out and dingy? Is the lampshade on your desk crooked, dirty, and much too big? If so, it's wrong. Take it off the lamp and throw it away. Look at the lamp with fresh eyes. A bad lampshade can completely alter the way you see the lamp—and the room!

My heart leaps up when
I behold
A rainbow in the sky.
WILLIAM WORDSWORTH

Look up at the lovely chandelier. Turn it on. Does it need to be cleaned? No matter how delicate a crystal chandelier is, if it's dirty you can't see the color spectrum in all its facets. What wattage are the bulbs? Are all the bulbs lit? Notice the crystal ball in the center and the triangular piece of crystal that hangs down at the bottom. See the iron chains with star designs. Simply by cleaning this fixture you discover a gem. The walls are all aglow in the aura of the prisms of crystal.

Dancers need music, but
walkers are their own music.
W. A. MATHIEU

As you write down each item you intend to fix, number them. One item might be to clean the marble hearth. Another might be to tidy up the books in the bookcases. Perhaps your wooden baseboard needs to be touched up, or you are missing a drawer pull. Try to find at least thirty-five to forty details that can be improved. I've never walked into a room that couldn't be made more harmonious, more charming. Sometimes a room is too rigid, needing to be loosened up. Don't consult anyone; let your eye negotiate the truth.

We do not learn by
experience, but by our
capacity for experience.
THE BUDDHA

Glance down at your pad of paper. What color is it? Is it lined, plain, or does it have a grid? What color are the lines? What color is your clipboard? Are you using a pen or pencil? What color ink or lead are you using? Is the clipboard attractive or is it office-supply brown? You probably grabbed it without seeing. I use clipboards all day long, for writing and for my decorating notes. I see the objects in front of me intimately and they become part of the appearance of my desk. Make a note on your punch list to go to an office-supply store and get a fun-colored plastic clipboard if yours is ugly. You will see that this inexpensive item can make a difference in the pleasure of your project.

If you don't care about the utilitarian items you see in front of your nose every day, the things you touch and hold in your lap, how will you be able to see well the things located at the far end of your living room? Every object in a space can be attractive. Even a pencil has better energy if it is freshly sharpened.

You will be amazed how much better you see when you have a clipboard in hand and are making a punch list. You'll see spots of dirt, a ripped piece of fabric, a seriously ugly end table, a rug lining that shows, a spot on the wooden floor under your desk worn out by the chair going back and forth. The switch plate could be dirty or crooked. There could be a missing piece of plaster or a broken mirror. You might look at the dried hydrangea bouquet and feel sad because you see them as dead brown flowers. Remove them.

Eventually you should have a punch list for every room. Your sight improves with every item you have on your list. When you are at a friend's house, your eye will notice things it didn't the last time. You will see the harmony of good workmanship and feel disappointment when you see something sloppy where someone didn't take pride in their work.

Decorators, architects, and contractors keep running punch lists, trying to notice everything that needs to be corrected before our clients complain. You can see for yourself what needs to be fixed. One day I stood at my kitchen sink and was appalled at the dirty white sponge and the gunk under the broken cake of soap. I threw the sponge away, polished the white porcelain and the brass faucet, and put a fresh blue sponge down as well as a new bar of almond soap. Why shouldn't I have the treat of my favorite soap when I wash my hands at the kitchen sink?

If you want to see a mess, open the cabinets under your kitchen sink. Look in your broom closet. Look at the grime around your dustpan. Look at the inside of your washing machine. Do you see caked soap and dirt? Look at your dryer. Is the dial panel dusty? Look at your ironing board cover. What color is it? You see this fabric so often. Why not look at something pleasant? Look at your iron. If you use it regularly, you should notice what color it is. Can you remember the color of your broom handle? What about the mop? Utilitarian spaces, private spaces, and public spaces are all seen by your eye regularly. You don't have to love your mop, but it is a good discipline to see it well. The reason some spaces lure you into them, inviting you to open up all your senses and feast your eyes, while other spaces make you feel uneasy, is the energy of the seen objects and how they affect you. The more you "love up" your spaces, the more you will love being in them.

There shouldn't be any depressing space in your immediate surroundings. Remember, how you feel has to do with what you see. If you have positive seeing experiences in a space, the space will have good karma, good feelings.

We dignify ourselves when we see well how we can improve each space where we live. There is never a dark, disinherited space that can't be transformed into a useful place filled with positive energy. See how you can alter your spaces into more fertile spots. If you want to create a library where you feel cocooned, you should be surrounded by books, if possible, on three walls. When you are surrounded by books you feel balanced. Whether used as a refuge for reading or as an uplifting place to iron, all sizes and shapes of spaces can be turned into oases. Look and you will see.

Rethinking Hidden Spaces

Conventional wisdom tells us to put doors on closets and cupboards to hide what's inside. While most people have doors on storage areas for this reason, rethink what you can do with these spaces to bring them into view. All space is precious and should be looked at with fresh eyes. Many of the possessions you are storing are full of color and pattern and will add life to your spaces.

We hunger for what we somehow intuitively know brings us happiness.

- Rather than stashing your linens or china away in a dark space behind a closed door, consider displaying them as decorative elements. When we bought our eighteenth-century cottage ten years ago, the buttery on the north side of the kitchen was a frightening sight. It wasn't just the dung-colored peeling paint that disturbed us; the whole space was depressing because of the buildup of dirt and the obvious neglect, to say nothing of the tar paper on the floor. But this tiny rectangular space had a window at its far end with a view of the red house where the nineteenth-century American artist James Abbott McNeill Whistler lived with his mother. I saw that I could put a window box outside this window. With some scraping, sanding, and painting, I knew I could transform the buttery into an interesting space to display our plates, pitchers, and flower containers. We now keep the door open and the light on in the buttery because the space is too charming to hide. It adds character to the kitchen, making it a decorative resource rather than a mere storage space.

Truth should be highly valued.

PLATO

- Our coat closet in the cottage also has a window with a window box, filled with geraniums in the spring, summer, and fall. I have wrapped a blue-and-white polka-dot ribbon around the coat rod and placed cobalt-blue bottles on the ledge. When we're home alone, I often keep the door open and the light on in order to appreciate this cozy nook.

Sight is the prelude to perception.

- At the end of a bedroom hall you can place a high cabinet with open shelves to store your towels. Why stash this feast of color behind a closed door when you can show it off? It is charming to see a display of terry cloth as you approach the bedroom and bath in your home. I store linens in an old blue-painted high cupboard with open shelves in our upstairs sitting area. It feels intimate and sensuous. I always enjoy seeing the colorful stacks of sheets and pillowcases.

- Look around your spaces. Are there areas where you can remove a door or cabinet door to expose some of your loved possessions, or can you use the space in another way to add intrigue to a room? Whenever there is a storage area behind a closed door, the tendency is to disregard the possibility of an aesthetic arrangement because the eye has no aesthetic expectations.

What can we do to expand and refine our ability to see? Do you see, express what you see? Do you keep a seeing journal?

- Clients moved into an apartment with solid doors on one wall in the dining room for china storage. Because they had a large collection of lovely china, we wanted to create an attractive pattern by displaying it on the shelves. We installed glass upper cabinet doors to allow the glory of the colors and forms to be a central part of the room decoration.

- When I created a tiny alcove from a closet by removing its door in my Kips Bay atelier, I was able to look at a beautiful vista from my desk, complete with compelling art and an attractive arrangement of marbleized boxes, rather than a white door and frame. This tiny space added depth and character to an otherwise ordinary space because it offered an element of surprise.

- Always question each space. Flip the space over in your mind, asking reverse questions. If there is a door, do you need it? What if this closed cabinet were open? You could use it to display books and decorative objects. Turn things upside down, asking "What if?" Space is so valuable; rather than having hidden storage areas, think of them as spaces for surprise displays of china or for a favorite collection of vases. Many bookcases have closed cabinets below. One client removed the doors and used the space to display a collection of colorful Chinese vases. What you see is not necessarily what you want in your space. Personalize every detail.

- When you go into a housewares store, you see all the objects for sale on display. Nothing for sale is hidden from view. When you see all these functional items attractively arranged, you can get ideas to help you see how to open up your once-hidden spaces. The key is to have objects you like to look at frequently. I have a large collection of antique quilts collected over thirty-five years. I love to look at them every day because they feel like old friends. I have a stack of them in our bedroom, making it easy to put a different one on the bed each time we change the linens. I'd hate to think of them crammed in a dark closet behind a closed door. In this case, rather than putting my storage space on display, I brought favorite objects out of storage to decorate the space. When you have pretty things you love, often you can place them out in the open.

To what higher object . . . can any mortal aspire . . . than to be possessed of all this knowledge, well adjusted and ready at command.

JOHN ADAMS

Look around and soak it all in.

I know of no more encouraging fact than the unquestionable ability of man to elevate his life by a conscious endeavor.

HENRY DAVID THOREAU

- A client had a storage cabinet on the wall separating her kitchen from the breakfast room. It was a clever design with cabinet doors opening on either side. Even though there was counter space below with a pass-through, the arrangement seemed boxy and separated the spaces in a jarring way.

When the doors were open, the cabinets revealed pretty china crowded together. Because there was a pantry next to the breakfast area, I suggested removing all the cabinet doors. Immediately this integrated the space. Opening it up allowed us to put the prettiest forms and patterns on display and the rest went into the pantry on open shelves. If a space was designed in an era when storage and serving areas were closed off from living areas, and you now want the spaces to be more accessible and open, you often will be able to accomplish this without major construction.

Living with the Unavoidable

Without light we would be unable to see, we would die. Light is life. Light is energy.

We all have pots and pans we can't store away because we've run out of space. One solution is to hang them up on racks. Gleaming copper pots displayed this way add charm to our kitchens.

There's always a way to have fun with the unavoidable, including the eyesores you can't remove or rip out despite your strong desire to do so. If you're renting an apartment, either you aren't allowed to make structural changes, or you don't want to invest money renovating someone else's property.

- A client moved into an apartment with a red thermostat in the center of one wall in the octagonal foyer. This rectangular box jutted out two inches into the space. What could we do to hide this unsightly object smack in the center of a wall, as though it were an intended focal point? It couldn't be completely concealed because of its functional purpose of adjusting the heat. We couldn't hang a painting or a plate over it because the decoration would protrude too much. We needed a shape similar to a colander or a basket that we could display with its bottom facing out. One solution was to hang a two-and-a-half-inch-deep ledge underneath the thermostat to rest some pictures on. What we ended up doing was tossing a fun straw hat over it. Often an awkward feature is an opportunity to add a surprising touch of whimsy.

Whenever possible, eliminate distractions and completely focus.

◆ The apartment of another client had cornice molding that protruded six inches into the room. It looked strange, dangling out into thin air, as cornice molding should always hug the wall. Studying the problem, I discovered that the windows extended to the ceiling and opened into the room. If the cornice molding were in the right place, the client wouldn't be able to open the windows. Left alone, however, it looked awful. We decided to hang white sheer curtains with a leaf design to allow light to filter through and provide privacy from office buildings nearby. The cornice molding now is in front of the soft folds of the fabric and feels integrated with the wall. It may not be perfect, but it is no longer an eyesore, and replacing all the windows, or keeping them closed, was not an option.

My river has never seemed so beautiful.

ABRAHAM MASLOW

Bringing Energy into Our Spaces with Mirrors and Crystal

Space contains wavelengths of energy that can be augmented by the wavelengths of the light in your spaces. The next time you see a beveled mirror

A presence that disturbs
me with the joy
Of elevated thoughts;
a sense sublime
Of something far more
deeply interfused,
Whose dwelling is the light
of setting suns,
And the round ocean
and the living air,
And the blue sky . . .

WILLIAM WORDSWORTH

in bright light, look for the spectrum in the bevel. Do you see fuchsia, reddish orange, yellow, and blue? Look all around you. The spectrum of light may be shimmering on a wall. A beveled medicine-cabinet mirror is ideal for this exercise because you can move it around, seeing the chromatically intense rainbow fall on a variety of objects. Even a white trellis garden wall with mirror behind it can bestow this electricity of color and energy.

A beveled crystal paperweight will have the same effect as the mirror because the color is in the glass. Carry it to a window in bright sunlight and move it around in your hand until you see the spectrum. Choose a room with white or pastel-colored walls in order to get the highest contrast between the rainbow and the wall color. At first you may see only white light. Move it around a few more seconds and you will see the spectrum.

A prism from a crystal chandelier will also work. Often you can find odd pieces at an antique shop. They probably won't be displayed, so ask the dealer. You may want to keep some cut crystal on your desk to play with when you're on the telephone. If you ever find a crystal prism at a nature store, buy it to take with you on walks. Hold a piece of cut crystal up to a flower and see the unparalleled spectrum inside the blossom.

Be careful where you place a piece of cut crystal, because you can start a fire. I had a sunny office in New York City where the sunlight reflected off the East River. One day I walked into my office and smelled smoke. The stack of papers under the crystal paperweight were burned with a brownish-black hole over an inch deep.

Mirror and crystal bring energy to your spaces. Sometimes you see the light and colors

I wanted to be quiet with my own heart and open to my own spirit. I sought especially the answer to the question of the relationship of the beauty of nature to the Infinite, to what some people call the Absolute and others call God.

ROLLO MAY

and sometimes you just feel them and know they are there. Mirror opens up space, reflects light, and brightens our spaces (if you have awkward proportions in a space, reread the section on mirror in chapter 1). Crystal shines and creates color and light on surfaces. Both mirror and crystal bring life and harmony to spaces.

Light comes first, and everything else—line, color, shape, direction, texture, scale, dimension, and rhythm—is secondary.

A Touch of the Orient: Experiencing Your Space from a Different Vantage Point

Every room can be improved with a touch of the Orient. For example, a Japanese tea table makes an ideal coffee table for a sitting area. Traditionally, westerners didn't have low coffee tables; they used high English tea tables appropriate for serving formal tea. The Japanese tea table is a convenient height and is well designed for providing ample surface space for decorative objects as well as room for a tray. If you have an oriental table in your living room, pull it into the center of your space. Put some pillows on the floor and enjoy an exotic

The moon like a flower In heaven's high bower, With silent delight, Sits and smiles on the night.
WILLIAM BLAKE

evening eating Chinese, Thai, Vietnamese, or Japanese food. Do you enjoy using chopsticks? You can buy them inexpensively, lacquered in a variety of colors and patterns. You are in your living room, but the fact that you are sitting on the floor creates an entirely different mood; and you are transported into other worlds. Look around you. See how high your ceilings appear. You will see your space from an entirely different perspective when you are sitting on the floor rather than at a chair-seat height of approximately eighteen inches. To awaken your seeing skills, create these special rituals where you see your spaces differently.

The spirit down here in man and the spirit up there in the sun, in reality are only one spirit, and there is no other one.

UPANISHADS

Depth

Every time I sit in an airplane taking off outside Manhattan, I look out the window and see the transformation of a city to a model drawing of a metropolis. This may be an apt description of the powerful impact of space and depth perception on how we see. Depth perception is a vital element to seeing well. Some researchers conclude we are born with an innate appreciation of depth. Babies prefer simple dimensional objects to flat representations of the same shape.

Snowdrops bloom in the snow, but when the daffodils open you know spring is here.

ANNE RAVER

To understand the complexities and subtleties of depth perception and to sharpen our seeing skills, it is necessary to study our three-dimensional surroundings as well as the deliberate illusion of depth in two-dimensional drawings, paintings, and photographs.

Come forth into the light of things,
Let Nature be your teacher.

WILLIAM WORDSWORTH

Why will knowledge and training about depth perception help you to see better? Depth, or distance intelligence, is essential to understanding the world around you. Where is something located in space? Is it near or far away? Without perspective you have no depth perception and are in effect living in limited dimensions. When you study depth perception, you have the potential to bring the world to you. Dimensional visualization is extremely complex, but with practice and study you can learn to see and record it well.

The Illusion of Depth

Two-dimensional objects such as drawings can only imply a third dimension. The lines and shading are intended to produce a feeling of reality. Study Rembrandt's great use of chiaroscuro, the dramatic emphasis on light and shade, to create perspective in his paintings and etchings.

Almost half of what you experience is two-dimensional. Books, magazines, newspapers, television, film, photographs, drawings, paintings, and graphic designs are all flat surfaces, lacking depth. Yet, because of scale, tones, shading, lighting, and shadows you imagine three dimensions; you achieve a sense of depth perception through illusion, imagination, and the use of geometric perspective.

Nature has always been the inspiration.

Consider the artful peculiarity of photographs. They are merely flat projections on a surface. Intellectually, you know you can't compress a three-dimensional object into a two-dimensional surface. Yet a photograph artificially flattens a subject, in perspective.

Perspective is all about depth and the illusion of distance; what you see goes far beyond the information your eye perceives.

The Evolution of Perspective in Art and Architecture

Although everyone sees in three-dimensional perspective, artists have not always portrayed three-dimensional reality in their art. In fact, geometric perspective—the realistic portrayal of depth in art and architecture drawings—is a fairly recent development in recorded history. Most paintings executed before the Renaissance had no perspective. Cro-Magnon cave drawings from 24,000 to 30,000 years ago were the exception. These paintings had rudimentary perspective. On the walls of a cave discovered several years ago near Avignon, France, were brilliant animal paintings drawn in perspective with some depth.

Remember that the most beautiful things in the world are the most useless; peacocks and lilies for instance.

JOHN RUSKIN

As inventive and advanced as the Egyptians were, they never used geometric perspective but only drew flat images with no visual depth. Did they understand perspective but deliberately choose not to depict some people or objects as being smaller than others? (Even a tall mountain should look like a molehill in perspective, if it is meant to be seen as being far away.) Because they made no representation of surfaces, but only profiles and edges, the Egyptians' drawings lack vital depth information. Children's drawings are quite similar to the flat-surfaced Egyptian art, where the whole picture is free of depth.

Ancient Greek Architecture and the Use of Optical Illusion

The Greeks showed slanting, sloping planes in their art but probably never used strict geometric perspective, though they obviously understood it because they used it to erect their temples and similar buildings. According to one theory, the Greeks were able to create such graceful temples because the temples were originally wood structures, making it easier to modify the dimensions. Through trial and error they were able to look at the buildings from every viewpoint until they accomplished the sublime, adhering to the proportions dictated by the golden mean.

The Greeks provided us with sterling examples of their understanding of depth, accommodating our eye's distortion of reality in their architecture. Perhaps the most outstanding example is the Parthenon, built between 447 and 432 B.C. under the direction of Pericles and considered one of the seven wonders of the world.

There is so much beauty to see and appreciate out-of-doors in the natural world.

When building the Parthenon, architects actually manipulated the structure's measurements so it would look perfect to the eye. At first glance it appears to be a simple rectangular building, perfectly symmetrical, but in truth it is quite complex. The corner columns, set closer together than the columns placed in the center, are separated by six feet, whereas those in the center are separated by eight feet. The more than 200-foot-long horizontal base connecting all the columns is not perfectly horizontal; it curves upward along the ends. The corner columns as well as the columns lining the long walls lean in slightly toward the center of the interior space. The columns are slightly thicker in the center. Understanding that the eye bends a straight line into a concave (bending inward) curve, the architects designed the columns of the temple facade with a slight, almost imperceptible bowing outward to achieve the illusory "perfect straight line," making them convex to compensate for the warping phenomenon of the eye. The columns also taper upward so that they don't look wider at the top than at the bottom. The diameter at the bottom is 6 feet 2 inches and only 4 feet 10 inches at the top to compensate for our perceptual distortions. The Parthenon is a brilliant experiment, creating beauty for the eye to appreciate with maximum fulfillment and awe.

> *The eye should not be led where there is nothing to see.*
> ROBERT HENRI

Italy in the Early Renaissance: Florence Cathedral

Contrary to the optical illusions created by the Greek architects of the Parthenon who tapered their columns at the top, the painter Giotto actually did the opposite when he designed the bell tower, also called the campanile, of Florence Cathedral (Duomo) during the early Renaissance in Italy. Begun in 1296 by Arnolfo di Cambio (Giotto was appointed master of the cathedral works in 1334 after Cambio's death), the cathedral was considered so spiritually uplifting that its architect was exempt from paying taxes. The decree read: "The Commune of the People of Florence, from the magnificent and visible beginning of the said work of the said Church, commenced by the same Master Arnolphus, hope to have a more beautiful and more honorable temple than any other which is in the region of Tuscany."

> *Nature's beauty as well as art's beauty expresses our spiritual longings.*

Giotto's tall campanile had to look right from many viewpoints. He used negative perspective in his design, making the top of the tower considerably wider than the bottom. He did this to counteract the usual way tall buildings appear when viewed from the ground: They look as though they were leaning backward. You can experience this distortion yourself: Aim a camera upward toward a tall city building. Do you see the building as though it were falling backward?

I look out at the sun and the wonderful colors in the sky and I'm totally complete.

SYBIL CONNOLLY

The relationship of scale between the bell tower and the cathedral was terribly important; one had to enhance the other. Architects needed spatially accurate technical drawings so they could envision and execute the result in three-dimensional space. The architect Brunelleschi, who built the cathedral dome, was the first Renaissance architect successfully to develop geometric perspective, though the principles of geometric perspective were not to be set down formally until the innovations of Leonardo da Vinci in the fifteenth century. Geometric perspective allowed architects to render realistic designs of three-dimensional space to show to wealthy patrons—government and church officials—for approval.

A few years ago, Peter and I went on a seeing vacation in Italy and France. We spent three and a half weeks opening ourselves up to all our senses, especially our eyesight. On our final day in Italy, before flying to Paris, we were picked up at our hotel in Fiesole, a town in the hills above Florence, by a taxi driver named Luigi.

There are unknown forces within nature; when we give ourselves wholly to her, . . . she leads them to us; she shows us those forms which our watching eyes do not see.

AUGUSTE RODIN

Turning a corner and seeing the green-and-white marble Florence Cathedral bathed in sunlight hit me in my solar plexus. The perfection, the harmony, stunned my perception. I asked Luigi to stop so I could pay my respects to a favorite sacred space. When he observed my joy, he said, "We don't see how beautiful our city is. We drive around and don't see." Not all taxi rides to an airport are that confessional—or charming—but Luigi's wise remark conveyed a message for all of us who hurry through life.

The Revolutionary Use of Depth
by Italian Renaissance Painters

We see the world from one vantage point: If we move, our vantage point moves with us. However, the mind's eye is rich with knowledge about the object or scene that is not in direct view, providing us with a more complete vision. The early perspective paintings of the Renaissance depicted scenes viewed from different vantage points, creating several paintings within a single painting.

These multiple perspectives were later used by the cubist and surrealist painters who broke the convention of geometric perspective by jumbling many different vantage points, showing their subjects from all angles simultaneously.

Everything you've learned . . . as "obvious" becomes less and less obvious as you begin to study the universe.

BUCKMINSTER FULLER

Depth Cues in Our Three-Dimensional
Surroundings

You need information to ascertain depth. If you are looking across a desert or at an ocean with no islands, it is impossible to gauge the distance between you and a faraway point. The scale appears vast, endless. Your eye doesn't have anything interesting to focus on to indicate depth. If your eye can look at an island, at land, or a boat, you can see with more accurate perspective and are better able to judge distances. As a result, the overall

The eye is often described as a camera.

R. L. GREGORY

impression is more intimate and therefore more stimulating, in much the same way as looking at a cloudless blue sky and suddenly seeing a balloon or a kite brings depth and meaning to the sky.

When you are by the ocean on a calm day and you look at the horizon, it seems to be a certain distance from you. On a rough day, when the surf is up and there are waves and whitecaps, the horizon seems farther away because you have so much more to see between the land and the horizon line. Your brain uses the waves as depth cues. A placid ocean is deceptive.

Compare looking out across an ocean to staring down a city avenue. It is two and a half miles from 100 Park Avenue in New York City where we once had an office to our current Park Avenue address. The same two-and-a-half-mile distance seems shorter when you stand on a beach and look out over the water at an island. Why? Because there are no obstacles. When you see something in clear view, it seems nearer.

Charm, lightness, crispness—all these are passing sensations.

MATISSE

Be on the lookout for a house being built in your neighborhood. You see the shell before you see the wall partitions. The large hole is divided into a series of smaller spaces. Breaking up the space provides depth cues, giving you a clearer perception of actual size. This is an excellent way to train your eye. I remember seeing the frame of a friend's new house before any walls were installed. I loved walking through the open space, absorbing the views from all sides, envisioning the different rooms and placement of the windows with the vista from each, and where the furniture would be placed. When you see a house being built, fantasize that it is yours and set your imagination loose.

How can we apply our understanding of depth cues to decorating our spaces?

◆ A space appears vaster or smaller than its actual dimensions when there are no depth cues to indicate distance. A large empty space will seem vaster than a large space containing a lot of objects, because your eye absorbs the depth. Furniture groupings create intimacy, giving large spaces a cozy human scale. When you have large plants, columns, or furniture, your eye focuses on objects in the foreground, not on the actual depth of the room.

When Mrs. Brown bought an amateur theater on Long Island to use as a weekend house, she turned the forty-foot-square space with twenty-two-foot-high ceilings into a living space, sitting area, and dining area by placing a six-foot-round table in the center of the room, and kept it brimming with fresh flowers. The eye was drawn to the focal point of the table and the living flowers, not the vast space of the other half of the room. Each arrangement of furniture and objects spoke of comfort and intimacy, creating a human scale within a large space. There was a secretary against one wall in the far corner of the space where she loved to write letters and do desk work. She created a large seating group surrounding the fireplace. There was a study space with bookcases, and there was a dining space. She was years ahead of her time in her decision not to add walls to separate these areas, allowing this open plan to maintain its ideal proportions, including the high ceiling.

As we shift our attention away from the external world and into the internal one, we learn symbolic sight.

CAROLINE MYSS

- In a small, well-proportioned space, logically arranged furniture can give the room a feeling of depth, actually making the space appear larger when furnished than when empty. Select fewer, larger pieces of furniture, well spaced in order to open up the room rather than fill it up.

- The rule of "the nearer the island is to you, the bigger it appears" can be applied to decorating your spaces. If you have a large piece of furniture, place it on a far wall to make it look smaller, less dominant. If you put a weighty piece near the entrance, the room will look crowded, the large piece dwarfing the average-sized pieces at the opposite end of the room. Remember where Mrs. Brown put her large mahogany secretary—the far end of her huge open living space.

  As you take seeing walks, try to gauge distances. Stand at the end of your driveway and guess the distance to your house. Now measure it. Look out at your front lawn. Try to guess how many yards there are between the house and your street. As you walk toward a church or a library or a friend's house, guess the distance. Pace out these distances. Every day deliberately guess a distance and pace it out. How long is a city block? How long is the lobby of your office building? If you don't know the size of the rooms in your apartment or house, guess, then pace them out or measure them. This is a fun exercise with lots of surprises. Learning how to refine your depth perception is useful in everyday living and helps you experience your surroundings with fresh eyes and insights.

Opening Our Eyes to Everyday Optical Illusions

Our eyes basically deceive us every day. The clouds we see in the distance appear to be approaching the earth, though they are at the same altitude as the clouds directly above our head. Parallel lines, such as two sides of a highway or railroad tracks, seem to converge in the distance, though we know they never meet.

Things are not always what they seem.

PHAEDRUS

The whole discussion of distortion in visual perception is fascinating, full of surprises and proof that our eyes are not always accurate detectors of what they are seeing. If you're so inclined, try some of these exercises. You'll see how profoundly your vision shapes your world. Have some fun with them, as I have.

- Draw a series of horizontal zigzag lines on a piece of paper, pretending you are drawing a chevron-patterned floor. Shade in every other stripe with a dark color. Notice how the dark color in concert with the white of the paper causes the lines to look as though they were literally popping out at you. If you bleach and stain a chevron floor, the same optical illusion will occur. Look at other floor patterns that fool your eye with depth cues. Some inlaid marble floors fool the eye into believing you can't walk on the surface because it is spiked with pieces of marble coming up at you.

- On the left-hand side of a piece of paper, draw a vertical line. Put arrowheads on each end. On the right-hand side of the paper, draw a vertical line slightly shorter than the one you just drew. Put a V on the top and an upside-down V on the bottom. What do you see? Does the line with the in-facing arrows appear shorter even though you know it is slightly longer?

- When you look at a photograph of yourself, you see what everyone else sees. You see the right side of your face on the left side of the image. However, when you look in a mirror, the right side of your face is in the right side of the mirror, the opposite of a photograph.

  Throw a shirt on a chair. Look at the buttons on the left of the shirt and the buttonholes on the right. Look at the shirt in the mirror. The buttons are now on the right, the buttonholes on the left. If the shirt has a monogram on the left as you look at it, it will appear on the right when you look at the shirt in the mirror.

  One evening an ambassador came to an awards dinner at the Waldorf in full regalia. As he entered a ballroom, a dignitary leaned forward and whispered to a colleague, "The ambassador has his decorations on the wrong side of his white-tie jacket." The friend replied, "I often make that mistake myself. He probably put his jacket on the bed and attached his decorations on the left side. When he dressed and put his jacket on, the jacket decorations were now on the right-hand side. Protocol requires decorations to be over the heart, or on the person's left."

The sky will be a dull thing to the dull appreciator, it will be marvelous to the eye of a Constable.

ROBERT HENRI

- Compare how the objects of your affection appear to you in regard to scale and distance with less meaningful objects. Human emotions can influence depth perception, making loved objects or people appear closer than they really are. When you look at a framed picture of a child on a table, the photograph appears bigger to you than it actually is because of your strong feelings of love. One study finds that a woman just back from a honeymoon doesn't see her husband as being smaller when he is at a distance. Her being in love makes her perceive him as larger and she senses his nearness emotionally.

Perspective Tips for the Home

Here are a few more ways to use space and depth perception to enhance the rooms of your home:

- To increase the appearance of depth in a room, hang paintings that have perspective. Even a small picture can have great depth, taking your eye into infinite space.

- When hanging paintings that have depth, hang them at eye level when standing so the impact of their perspective won't be lost.

- If you are framing a painting that has perspective, select a frame that splays out from the wall to intensify the feeling of depth.

- If you are hanging a painting high on a wall, the frame should be graceful, curving back toward the wall. Remember, you will be looking up at the bottom of the frame.

- If you want to enjoy framed prints while taking a bath, hang them under the sink so as to view them at eye level without distortions.

- If you have a pair of hanging lamps, hang them slightly lower than eye level when standing, otherwise you will see too much of their bottom, and they will look awkward and heavy.

- If you have a beautiful bowl attractively colored or decorated on the inside, place it on a low surface—a table or server—in order for the eye to appreciate its interior in addition to its outside form. Many objects are misrepresented in shape when they are placed too high up on a shelf, losing the refinement of their proportions.

Understanding space and depth perception is invaluable when planning any kind of designing and decorating. As we move about in our spaces, we are constantly seeing our possessions from different perspectives. Our eye will continue to fool us, but the more aware we are of the mysteries of space and depth perception, the more we will be able to please the eye.

FOUR

Recognizing the Objects of Our Affection

Form, Material, and Composition

Everything we see passes through the eye, to be filed in

a little room and then amplified by the imagination.

— MATISSE

Spaces contain objects of a variety of forms in a wide range of materials, usually seen in juxtaposition. When we stop and look, we can explore associations between objects. Some forms go together, others don't. Why? What are the guidelines that help us to find and use the associations between objects to make a harmonious composition? Where do we look for clues for compatible connections between objects and materials?

In this chapter I will tell you how to see the objects of your affection in a new way. The fundamental change in your outlook will be to see all objects—just as space—as alive, with distinct personalities. You will look at forms and materials organically, seeing the forms' inspiration from the marble or the wood. You will see the Vermont verde marble and visualize it in the earth. You will see the connection, the intimacy, of a form detailed in silver or brass or glass. You will see the interconnections that link the forms to their substance and composition.

The forms and materials we are drawn to in nature can be re-created symbolically in our daily lives at home. If you love trees, you may want hardwood floors in your house. The objects you gather over your lifetime should all be rich with associations, alive with spirit and energy, tangible representations of the intangible mysteries that give our lives meaning and significance. We don't see these forms and materials in isolation but put them together as artistically as our eyes and brains are capable of doing. This chapter will give you the tools, through seeing exercises, tips, and secrets, to compose the life you dream of for yourself, your family, and loved ones, using your treasured objects.

Form

The physical structure of a single object in its entirety—its outline, shape, and volume—is its form. The essence of form, however, transcends its tangible reality because the true power of a form lies in the emotional effect it has on the observer. To see well, it is necessary to interpret the forms that surround us. How do they influence our state of mind? Every object, no matter how minute or grand, has a form. A statue, a person, a palace, a vase, a table, an apple, all have form, whether they are real or part of a two-dimensional illusion, such as a painting or photograph. But form is not the first element perceived in an object. Most people see color first, then ornamentation. When you see a friend on the street, you notice first what he or she is wearing. You don't immediately envision the person's physical core, or naked form. This is why, when you go to a custom upholstery shop, all the furniture is covered in white muslin—so the customer can discern, without distraction, the form, the proportions and lines, of the chair, sofa, love seat, or ottoman. Once you really see the bare shape of something, you can better visualize how it will look covered in a color and pattern.

Man-made forms tend to be colored to fit our human needs. The red traffic light represents stop. The green light means go. Because red and green are vibrant colors in the color spectrum, they become more intense when contrasted with each other. There is no potential for ambiguity or confusion. When you watch a football game, each team has a brightly colored uniform so you can follow the color as the players move in different directions.

The Power of Form

Seeing pure form, when it is graceful and sensuous, is a transforming experience. You can be transported beyond the function of an object to recognize and appreciate its essence. Look around your home. What objects have become spiritually uplifting to you? An antique high chair, a porcelain teapot, a Ming vase, a brass carriage clock, an antique carved table, a ladderback chair, a candlestick, a book, a ceramic pitcher, a mantel? The form can have such integrity that you see it as a beautiful object for its own sake.

To the attentive eye each moment of the year has its own beauty.

EMERSON

Fernand Léger, an artist whom critics praise as the single greatest figure in early twentieth-century French modernism, had a stunning "seeing experience" as a young soldier in the awful trenches of World War I. Léger recalled the transcendent moment: "I was dazzled by the breech of a seventy-five-millimeter gun that was standing in the sunlight: the magic of white on metal. Once I got my teeth into that sort of reality, I never let go of objects again."

Professor Sheila Danko of Cornell University has a student whose life changed as a result of taking her class Making a Difference: By Design. This student is raising her daughter differently. Rather than watching television, they play a new game called "What can you see?" and go on seeing adventures together. The game is designed to open you up to the joy of seeing. What forms can we see at the zoo? What can we see at a park? What can we see on the street? What can we see at the market? When my daughters were children, we called these seeing adventures "grooves." We still groove to see better.

Recognizing Forms

The right hemisphere of the brain perceives whole shapes, while the left hemisphere recognizes shapes of the parts that make up the whole. We recognize approximately ten thousand things by their shape. Children at the age of six recognize a few thousand, adding dozens to their visual vocabulary each day.

Certain forms or arrangements of forms recall specific associations in our mind. For untold generations, the shape of a Ming vase has always been associated with beauty, dignity, and grace. Every time I see a Ming vase, I recall drawing a rare one kept in a display case at the Metropolitan Museum of Art in 1959, when I was a student at the New York School of Interior Design.

If one shape is used for something that makes you feel uneasy, your eye and brain will recall that association even if you use something of a similar shape for an entirely different purpose. Certain shapes disgust us. A urine-collection bottle in the shape of a wine carafe makes you not want to drink white wine out of a carafe even though you know it does not contain urine. In this case, ugliness is the other side of beauty. I also often see bud vases shaped like test tubes that remind me of chemistry class. I don't hate the vases, but I can't help feeling that lab equipment somehow got loose in someone's home.

Bird-watchers recognize birds in flight by seeing the small differences that are not detected by most people. As you learn to see the details of things, you, too, can look for the most unusual features in an object. Study its geometry, the relationship of points, lines, surfaces, and solids. Look at a pelican's beak, an elephant's ears. Each time you see what is noteworthy about an object, you are stocking your brain with conceptual memory-images of form you'll be able to retrieve in the future.

Recognizing faces is different from recognizing objects, because you have probably seen people from different angles at different times. Objects don't move about, but human beings do. Facial expressions, movement, and mannerisms all increase the recognition factor. But with an object, you have to establish an intimate relationship in order to know its "expression"—its personality, character, and mood.

The mind houses images. Recently a group of psychologists urged their subjects to close their eyes and asked them to imagine and identify images from descriptions read to them. They were asked to rotate the letter D to the right 90 degrees and put the figure 4 above it. Most people reported seeing a sailboat.

There is material enough in a single flower for the ornament of a score of cathedrals.

JOHN RUSKIN

When a shape is upright, we recognize it quickly. When it is tilted or upside down, often we don't recognize it. Turn a handwritten letter upside down. The words look as though they were written in a foreign language. Your brain needs significant time to rotate the letters 180 degrees.

Form gives an object the essence of its character. When we focus our eyes on an object, we are affected by its form on both a conscious and subconscious level. Every detail of the form evokes a different emotional response.

The Power of Lines

The abstract expressionist artist Irving Kriesberg wrote about pure seeing: "Our eye responds to assemblages of lines, colors, shapes, masses. Real objects may be seen abstractly; abstract elements may be seen as reality." As you look around you, study whether the forms you see are angular or undulating. Are their lines vertical, horizontal, or diagonal? When Peter's youngest daughter, Andrée, was a student at the Rhode Island School of Design, a professor asked the students to find a hundred straight lines outdoors. She saw how few there were in nature, but realized that they were there when you really looked. The experience led her to see architecture with fresh eyes. By examining the lines of objects, you grow more knowledgeable about what elements constitute a form, and how central lines are to everything we see.

Draw a diagonal line on a piece of paper. Your reaction can range from feeling it is unstable and upsetting to finding it stimulating. There is more tension in the diagonal or oblique direction than in any other direction. Now draw a vertical line in the center of a piece of paper. On a third piece of paper, draw a horizontal line. Try to see these lines in the forms around you. Take a few minutes to see oblique, vertical, and horizontal lines.

Straight Versus Curved Lines

Look for straight lines in nature. Can you find any? Even the horizon has irregularities because of the movement of the ocean and the curve of the earth. The straight line suggests strength more than the curve and is the simplest of forms. Consider the foundations of a house, flagpole, or window frame. Straight lines are rare in nature. Humankind makes straight lines. Straight lines are rigid and stiff compared to curved ones. Because straight lines are necessary for the vertical and horizontal axis humans relate to, we find ways to curve the edges and soften the angularity.

All Forms Comprise Three Basic Shapes

The most elementary forms are the three basic shapes—the square, the circle, and the equilateral triangle. The dimensional versions of these shapes are the cube, the sphere, and the pyramid. More complicated forms are composed of an arrangement of these shapes.

What do you want from an object? Satisfaction? Awe? Stimulation? Usefulness? Charm?

Look around you and see the circles, squares, and equilateral triangles. The human figure is made up of these three shapes; so is a tree. The trunk of a tree is a cylinder or column. If you cut through a tree trunk, you will have a disk and will see concentric circles similar to a spider web. A child's simple drawing of a tree is a triangle on a rectangle.

The three basic shapes are unique in character. The circle is different from the square, and they are both different from the equilateral triangle.

In the twinkling of an eye.
I CORINTHIANS 15:52

The Circle

The circle is the simplest visual pattern, a perfect shape. It is infinite because it is one continuous curved line. What comes to mind when you think of a circle? The moon, sun, earth, and other planets all have circular shapes. The rings we put on our fingers are circles. Draw a circle. A circle represents endlessness, as well as warmth and protection. The circle is all curves. There isn't a hint of a straight line. You can't feel steady with this circle, however, because it has no axis, but if you draw a vertical line through it you immediately feel it is stable as well as symmetrical. It is stable because it is self-contained and has a vertical axis. Add a horizontal floor or base and feel even more stability. The form is now grounded.

Like any hunter he hits and misses. He is looking for what he loves, he tries to capture it. It's found anywhere, everywhere.

ROBERT HENRI

The circle is satisfying in its closure, beautiful in its purity and simplicity, having an emotional quality. The circle is symbolic of life and continuity, and lacks any stimulating quality. A circle is peaceful, balanced, round, fat, cozy. There are no hard angles, no sharpness.

Circles are always seen as elliptical except when they are flat on a vertical surface and at eye level. Draw a circle on a sheet of paper. You never see a circle just that flat; visually, you see circles in perspective. Look straight on at a child's hoop. You see a circle. Give the hoop to a child, and it becomes an ellipse. Because the eye is accustomed to this distortion, perfect flat circles are rarely seen in art. Study the fruit in still life paintings, and notice how the round pieces of fruit are actually elliptical. Ellipses are never dull, because the variation between their width and height is stimulating.

Small circles, such as buttons, have a different effect on the viewer. We see them the way we see dots or stars, as points, and instinctively want to make forms out of them by connecting the dots, as we form star constellations in the night sky.

The Square

Draw a square. You have four 90-degree, or right, angles and sides of equal length. What associations do you have with the square? It is extremely stable, having both a vertical and horizontal axis. Draw a vertical line through the center of the square and you have two symmetrical rectangles. Similarly, you can demonstrate horizontal symmetry with a square by drawing a horizontal line through the center of the square. Because the square is grounded, vertically and horizontally symmetrical, it is inherently satisfying. Now, with a red pencil, draw a square. Tilt the square so that it is a diamond shape. Label the four points north, south, east, and west. What do you see? If you draw a vertical line north to south through the center, you have two symmetrical triangles. The same happens when you draw a horizontal line east to west through this diamond-shaped square. Look back at your other square. Feel its solidity. Now look at the red square. All four sides are at oblique angles, causing tension. Our innate sense of gravity makes us feel that it is balanced on one sharp point. In front of a large office building on Wall Street in New York City, there was a fifteen-foot-square sculpture positioned just like your red square. People were fascinated by its tension but would not walk near it for fear it would fall on them.

The difference between Einstein and a high school dropout is trivial compared to the difference between the high school dropout and the best robot in existence.

STEVEN PINKER

The square, when grounded on a horizontal axis, is a positive visual statement. Draw a square. Stare at it. Draw another square. Now put a dot at one o'clock inside the square. How does the dot make you feel? Do you feel more tension, more active stress from the square with the dot? The eye prefers the simple square.

The western culture is rectilinear, bounded by straight lines. We depend on the right angles they form—boxes, tables, rooms, buildings.

Visualize how two lines define the edge of a square. Look at the corner of the page on your book. With your right index finger gently curl back the corner of the page approximately one inch. Do not fold the paper. See how you can soften the edges of a sharp square corner. Think of a curved kitchen counter or a dining room table or a bathtub to see how their corners can be softened while still maintaining the strength of the square.

The Equilateral Triangle

An equilateral triangle is simpler than a square because it has the least possible number of sides necessary to create a form. Triangles are usually classified according to the size of their angles. Draw an equilateral triangle. You have three 60-degree angles. How would you describe a triangle? What do you see? You have a horizontal base that gives it stability. Now, rather than two parallel vertical lines, you have two diagonal lines converging to a point, the apex. Turn the triangle on any side and you feel the same solidity. Yet because it has diagonal lines, a triangle is more tense, more acute, more dramatic than a square. The ancient Egyptian pyramids have square bases, with triangular sides that slope at an acute angle to the ground and meet at an apex. See the triangle in mountains and trees. An obelisk with its tapering sides is a similar shape. These different shapes are regarded as having certain meaning. Some obelisks celebrate a significant event in a community or nation. Napoleon brought back numerous obelisks from Egypt that he used throughout his empire to communicate his own victory and power. Triangles sweep upward toward an apex; they have the look of aspiration or triumph.

Zen is like looking for spectacles that are sitting on your nose.

ZEN SAYING

Shape Preferences

Of the three basic shapes—the circle, the square, and the equilateral triangle—what is your favorite? Number them one, two, and three. If the circle is your number one form, think about transposing this preference to your dining room table, an end table, or a patio and a garden table. Even the stepping-stones on a garden path can be round.

Most people have definite shape preferences even if they aren't aware of them. Strict geometry could be too rigid for your romantic personality. Every shape and pattern represents something and has the power to express a mood. If you like circles, your doorknobs can be spherical, like balls. If you prefer the egg shape to the circle, you can have oval doorknobs instead of round. If, however, you picked the square as your favorite, you will have to compromise. Square doorknobs do exist, but they are rare because they don't feel comfortable to the hand. An alternative is to have round, saucer-shaped doorknobs (think of a round brass cylinder cut up into doorknobs one inch thick, like a stack of coins).

Look at the shape of your kitchen pulls or knobs. Do they please your eye? Look at the hinges on your doors. You can soften them by adding ball tips on the top and bottom if you like round shapes. Look at your lampshades. Do they have straight sides? Or are they rounded, fluted, or pleated like an accordion? Do you prefer a drum shape, or do you like the bottom to flare out? Examine your silverware. Would you describe it as rectilinear or curvilinear? Study the backs and arms of your sofas and armchairs. Are most curved or straight?

We exercise our shape preferences often without knowing why we prefer one object to another. When I ask clients to name their favorite shape, most often they say that they like them all, but upon careful inspection of their house you see certain shapes repeated.

Someone who likes circles usually has rounded pitchers, cylindrical flower containers, and even round place mats, napkin rings, and serving trays. What shape are your coasters? I have some that are round and neutral in color. I also have some that are square with stripes of blue, white, green, and red. Because I am drawn to the color and pattern, I prefer the square ones. Would square coasters be as appealing as round ones? You decide. Would the round neutral coasters be more appealing if they were square? It's up to you. Most of my candles are cylindrical; some are tapered and some are not. For a candlelit dinner, most people prefer a tapered candle, even selecting the shape over the color. Tapered candles are more delicate than those with the same diameter at both ends. They add elegance to a table. If you prefer an object to be round or square rather than triangular, you will probably choose a cylindrical candle that is not tapered, even if it looks less graceful. A brightly colored candle that is not tapered tends to look wider at the top than the bottom.

The simple perception of natural forms is a delight.

Would you select color over form when setting the table for a festive dinner celebration? Pretend to reach into a candle drawer containing a variety of candles. Generally, you like tapered ones, but you see some blue beeswax candles that are not tapered. You love the color, and they'll add to the table setting with its primarily blue theme. Would you sacrifice the color to have the elegance of the tapered shape? I wouldn't. To me, color speaks louder than form.

Do you have any fat square candles? I like four-inch-square candles that not only come in great colors speckled with stars but are also scented. Because most candles are cylindrical, it is satisfying to have a different-shaped candle to light. Look around at candles in a store. You'll probably see some that are circles, some egg-shaped, some tulip-shaped, some heart-shaped, and even some in the shape of a teapot. You decide what forms you prefer as well as what colors appeal to your eye.

Regular Versus Irregular Shapes

Regular shapes don't attract the eye as much as irregular shapes. What is balanced, rational, and harmonious, what is regular, symmetrical, and simple, is the most pleasing to our emotions. Forms with bilateral symmetry (where two sides are identical) are less complicated and provoking. Exaggerated, distorted forms are the most emotionally disturbing to the eye. Generally, you want the overall form to be symmetrical. Irregular forms

Seeing is a collaboration of yourself and the object observed.

can be used as accent pieces that will attract the eye, not disturb it, but these should be the exception, not the rule. You could have an Empire sofa whose back curves down on one side, but you wouldn't want a pair in a room. Whenever you use an odd-shaped piece of furniture or object in a room, it should be surrounded or framed by regular forms to ease the eye. You can create excitement and energy in a space without oddness. Usually it is wise to err on the safe side and furnish your home with pieces whose sides echo one another.

Seeing Form: Black and White Images and Color

Looking at black images on a white background and white images on a black background can help you to see the pure form of an object. Once you grasp pure form in a black-on-white or white-on-black image, then your brain can fill in the details of texture, color, and pattern. For example, if you see a black image depicting the form of a teddy bear, your brain fills in the furry texture, the blue glass eyes, the color. To help train your eye, look at black-and-white photography. A useful exercise is to take two cameras with you on a seeing adventure. Take one picture in color and one in black and white. Put them side by side. Study them. Now, remove the colored ones. Looking at the black-and-white images, can you remember the color of a friend's necktie or your daughter's dress, or the color of the roses rambling along the picket fence? Look at the colored pictures to check the accuracy of your recollections. Because we are so affected by color, we often don't see form. When you see form, sometimes you forget color. A Ming vase can be so beautifully proportioned that you see its outline and are in awe. Whether the color is neutral or the pattern nondescript, you remember the form. Flipping back and forth between the two, black and white and

When a man loves the beautiful, what does he desire? That the beautiful may be his.

PLATO

color, will strengthen your skills at perceiving form as well as color, texture, and luminosity.

The Emotional Power of Form

Beautiful forms can convince the mind to seek harmony. Whether you look into a crackling fire or a lit candle, or at a pretty tea tray, birds in flight, seashells on a beach, the sun rising, or a field of daffodils, you experience the joy viscerally, feeling rather than reasoning, experiencing a sense of comfort and peacefulness.

Certain forms make you see empathetically. The architectural caryatids are carved, draped female figures that replace columns as support for the entablatures of Greek temples and other structures. The most famous temple is near the Parthenon. You feel the weight of the caryatid's burden because you relate to her human form.

There are times when we become one with an object or objects. We're able to forget ourselves and fuse with natural or man-made beauty. These are the moments of our greatest joy. Concentrate on one object at a time. Become one with the

We are shaped and fashioned by what we love.

GOETHE

form. If you are looking at a teapot, observe it from every angle. Turn it upside down. Look inside it. Become the "little teapot, short and stout," as the child's song goes. By temporarily living the life of an object, you forget your self and enter a state of contemplation. This is a good exercise to practice every day. Get into the life and spirit of something tangible. Don't look at something. Look out from within its essence. Feel its form as a living, breathing entity.

There are forms I particularly love, objects that stand on their own, that are so satisfying in their entirety, you don't need others around them for complete enjoyment. I have a pair of small antique French Provincial fruitwood footstools (one is slightly bigger than the other) covered in a blue, green, and purple plaid Thai silk. I brought these stools back from Avignon, France, in a flowered tote bag ten years ago, and my fondness grows each day. I love to look at them, rest books on them, and put my feet up on them. I move them around often in order to admire the graceful curves of the frame.

Often I select a colorful glass paperweight, remove it from the collection on a table, and bring it to a window to play with it in the light. I love to move it around to see the design from different angles, admiring the round shape and the delicacy of the colored cones of swirled glass.

So much of human life and happiness is subjective that we should be fools not to take advantage of this subjectivity unashamedly and learn to cultivate the seeing eye.

LIN YUTANG

There is beauty in form. You are drawn to objects, the nuances of surfaces—lusciousness, transparency, shine, and patina. If we take one object of our affection to bond with each day, over time we will know our possessions well and they will become more meaningful to us, more beautiful.

Understanding Complex Forms

We are drawn to what is unusual, what is rare, what is novel. We look for shapes with an interesting arrangement of their parts. We like the simple rectangular tray, but we also like the one with curved handles. We appreciate the subtle proportions of a Ming-style lamp base and its delicately painted decoration with depth perspective. We enjoy a set of dishes with an open border, similar to a picket fence, an unexpected form in a dessert dish.

It takes certain knowledge to appreciate complicated forms. You begin by learning how to dissect complex forms to understand their components. When you were young, you were probably asked by a teacher to describe a spiral staircase. Most children point with their index finger and swirl it up and down in a motion similar to tossing dough for a pizza crust. We all know a spiral staircase goes around and around like a corkscrew, but most of us have only the vaguest notion of how it joins the axis and how the axis is related to the perimeter. A beautifully constructed spiral staircase is a work of great achievement. A good architect has the

intelligence and concentration to engineer the graceful treads and risers around the central axis so the staircase is more than a piece of sculpture; it is useful as well. In order to see form, you have to know the function of an object in relation to how it is made, just as in appreciating nature's forms fully, you need to understand how a plant grows or a mountain develops.

A graceful silver coffeepot that has a swanlike spout and a graceful high handle is in perfect balance. The top curves upward to a finial. You can look at this coffeepot from every angle and find it a work of genius. Your eye is always delighted when you examine it, touch it, and pour from it.

When I look at a pitcher brimming with daffodils in bright sunlight, I see the complex form of the blossom with its lacy trumpet and pinwheel leaves. I can look at shutters at the window and see the light and shadow of the slats. I can look at a desk drawer and admire the brass decoration surrounding a keyhole. One of my favorite tables, bought at auction from Mrs. Brown's estate, has the most lovely marquetry work. Study the subtle forms of an antique secretary desk. You will be awed by the complexity and grace of the series of different shapes.

The more penetrating your examination of an object, the more elements you see and appreciate in a form.

Using Our Hands to See

To understand a three-dimensional form, it is useful to touch its shapes and caress the various lines. Nature-lovers are great touchers, learning about forms and shapes by feeling them. Blind people use their hands to "see" three-dimensional forms as well. (Recently I learned of a blind gardener who grows dahlias. I could see how a blind gardener could know a flower by scent, but dahlias don't have an aroma. I later discovered that he touches his exotic blossoms to differentiate this variety from other types of flowers.)

Paintings, drawings, graphic design, photographs, and films are only two-dimensional suggestions of three-dimensional objects or scenes. By highly refined use of perspective with sophisticated use of light and shade, the two-dimensional surface of length and width, size and shapes, gives the illusion of having three dimensions. We are tempted to touch a painting because our eye and brain have accepted the illusion of form rising from the two-dimensional surface into the representation of three-dimensional space. We are conditioned to see the scene in a painting, photograph, television show, or movie as existing in space.

In sculpture, however, form *is* the reality. The primary essence of sculpture is that it is constructed of solid materials and is three dimensional. Whenever touching is permitted, it should be touched, read, and understood by people with eyesight as well as by blind people. Lorenzo Ghiberti, the Florentine sculptor and painter, observed, " . . . the perfection of such works escapes the idea and can only be understood if we pass over the planes and curves of the marble with our hands." The bronze sculptures in Central Park in New York City are polished until they gleam, attracting children who instinctually touch them.

The virtue of man also will be the state of character which makes a man good and which makes him do his own work well.

ARISTOTLE

One of the best ways to learn about something is to touch it, hold it, and caress it. Hold any object in your hands. Now shut your eyes. Play with it. Feel each curve, each sharp edge. If you are holding a box, open the lid. Is it attached to the box by a hinge? If it is wood, can you feel its grain? If it is stone, can you feel its coolness and texture? If it is cardboard, can you sense the thickness of the sides, or feel the seams where the material is glued together?

By feeling objects with your hands, you become familiar with their shape, size, weight, and essence. A form is solid or hollow, cold or warm, rough or smooth. Think of your objects as your toys and be more playful with them. First study them with your eyes open and then shut your eyes to fondle them. This exercise will help you to see each object uniquely.

Do this with some of your different-shaped stemmed glasses. Do you prefer the feel of certain ones over others? Why? Is it the height of the stem? How wide do you like the rim to be? I prefer drinking wine from a wide-rimmed glass, often referred to as a balloon glass, regardless of whether I'm drinking red or white wine, because the shape appeals to my eyes and hands. Balloon glasses are all-purpose. They are elegant for orange juice, iced tea, mineral water, wine, and ginger ale. They are attractive containers for gazpacho and cold cucumber soup and are equally appropriate for serving strawberries, ice cream, or sorbet for dessert.

Translating Nature's Forms into the Home

Because everything in nature is changing, observing nature makes us more spontaneous as well as more imaginative, because we see our house as a place that is also constantly changing from day to day and seasonally. Objects are alive, interesting, and understandable. When you observe something you like, some natural shape—a favorite tree, certain flowers, seashells—imagine how you can translate these forms into designs in your home. If you love ferns and jack-in-the-pulpits you may find a linen print for the sunroom with ferns and this mysterious flower that you discovered along a path in a wooded area. Or you may find a green, purple, and yellow color scheme that recalls your favorite forms.

I don't have creative pangs. If it doesn't work one time, it will the next.

GEORGE BALANCHINE

If you are fond of the scallop shell, you may choose a flatware pattern with this symmetrical fanlike shell design on the handle, or you can have it embossed in white on Nile-blue paper for your house stationery. Consider displaying scallop shells in a dish on your dresser or in your bathroom. You can find favorite motifs from nature reproduced in tiles for the walls and floors, the carving in wood furniture and marble mantels, porcelain lamps, cachepots, dinner and dessert plates, fabrics, sheets, and rugs.

You might want some tiles in your kitchen to be painted with vegetables, fruits, and herbs. Perhaps complement them with a bowl of some of the same vegetables and fruits on a nearby counter. If you are renovating a bathroom at a beach house, you may want to have some tiles painted with seashells and fish.

When you see something in nature that makes you feel really wonderful, make a deliberate effort to find a way to translate it into your daily life. If you walk into the woods and become conscious of how much you enjoy seeing the bark of a birch tree, you can have a plant container or a fat candle covered in birch bark. Because it is a loose bark, you often find it on the ground in usable pieces. Gather them on your seeing walks when the spirit moves you and toss the curled pieces into your woodbasket for a white accent.

If you enjoy Provence, you can bring elements into your home that make you think of the South of France—rough plaster on walls, ladderback chairs with caned seats, even the scent of lavender, can conjure up visions of Provence.

Everything should be made as simple as possible, but not simpler.

ALBERT EINSTEIN

If you enjoy seeing the fluffy forms of white clouds against a blue sky, chances are you find the blue-and-white color combination soothing. You can buy sheets of blue and white, and line your drawers with cloud wrapping paper. Or you can try painting some soft clouds on a blue ceiling. Keep a glass jar filled with fluffy cotton balls on your bathroom counter or window ledge, a stack of plush white terry-cloth towels on a stool, or a white terry-cloth robe on a bathroom door hook. Even a soft white cotton throw rug on a wood or tile floor will evoke soft white clouds as well as provide comfort for feet.

Animal Forms

Human beings are fascinated by animals for many reasons. The most obvious is their variety and beauty. Animals don't try to be themselves, they are who they are. A lion, tiger, dog, cat, and elephant are all distinctly different from one another. But there are other more emotional reasons that we seek the presence and companionship of animals such as dogs, cats, birds, or horses. Animals are not human, but they have many characteristics and behavioral patterns that intrigue, soothe, and delight us.

If you are fond of horses or drawn to lions and tigers, you will find a variety of ways to bring these forms into your home. You could have brass bookends or an animal-printed fabric for the upholstery in the study. You can have statues and paintings. Maybe you adore elephants. You are fascinated by everything that represents elephants, from jewelry to photographs to a silk scarf you frame as art.

With a keen eye to spot clues, when you are visiting friends, try to determine what forms from nature they are attracted to by looking at the objects in their rooms. Most people have a favorite animal, seashell, flower, or tree. People who love birds may have a passion for hand-carved duck decoys. We have several wooden hand-carved birds "in flight" over the door to the study in our cottage. Perhaps you have a collection of small iron, china, and jade objects depicting your favorite animal.

In art, economy is always beauty.

HENRY JAMES

When I work with clients, I ask them a wide range of seemingly random questions, but each answer is an indication of favorite forms from nature that can and should be incorporated into their homes. By identifying a wide variety of objects of your affection, you can then look around your house and garden and see how you can translate forms you like into different materials. Women can even show their love of flowers—and fish, bees, butterflies, and gemstones—in the jewelry they wear as well as in silk scarves and the patterns of their clothes. I like to garden in a red sundress with colorful butterflies all over it as I watch butterflies flutter around me.

Seeing Forms with New Eyes

There are many objects in your house you have never seen as they really are. For example, you may have an in-out basket on your desk that is basically rectangular. Have you noticed that rather than having four sides, it has eight sides because of the pinched-in four corners? You may have a hatbox that is actually hexagonal, though in your memory it is round. Only when you examine an object in all its detail do you know it well. You think your dining room table is rectangular, but the corners are rounded.

Seeing the subtle details that make you like particular objects will add enormously to your appreciation. If you have a patchwork quilt, study the optical illusions of the design. Count how many different patterns were used in the textiles as well as the design. How many different colors are there? Turn the quilt over to study the stitch work.

Take a moment now to examine one object in detail. Where are the seams, the stitches? Examine the hinges and screws. Look at an inkwell or an inlaid wooden box or a leatherbound, hand-tooled book. Study how the object was made. Feel the silver, gold, crystal, wood, marble, or leather. Make it a habit to take one small favorite object each day and put it on your desk so you can fondle it, study it, hold it up to the light, and see it with new eyes.

Having nice objects is one thing. But by seeing them well you establish a rapport with them. They become alive for you. Whenever you see anything well, it is never a waste of time. All seeing is accumulative. You are always instructed by what you see.

We tend to regard objects according to our emotional reaction to them, whether they stimulate us or soothe us. However, when we open our eyes, we can appreciate the quality and logic behind the forms that create a particular style. We are open to see new forms with greater appreciation. A form can arrest the eye as well as stimulate the imagination to follow new directions and see new connections, enabling the viewer to be awed by new beauty and therefore enriched visually. One day, as I was preparing tea, I gazed at the teapot and was struck with the idea of arranging fresh flowers in teapots. I love the way the spout and the handle connect with the shape of the flowers.

Echoes in Form

When you look at objects purely in terms of shape, you discover surprising similarities and relationships, endlessly repeated shapes creating echoes in the forms. Look at the carving on the back of a French Regency open-arm chair. Now look at the apron of a table of the same style. The carving is similar to that of the chair. Look at the legs, see how they, too, are alike. Look at a bench. In all period styles of furniture you see basic elements, shapes echoed in all forms. Wherever you go, look for these repetitions.

All beauty is founded on the laws of natural forms.

JOHN RUSKIN

Draw a puddle of water on an index card. Look at your sketch. The puddle lies flat on the ground but it appears like a cloud. A puddle and a cloud are the same shape but are located in different places in space. Go into your larder and get some elbow macaroni, a familiar popular shape you will see repeated in your household objects. Before looking around, determine how many objects you think you'll be able to identify that have the same shape as part of their design. Three? Six? Look around. You see this shape in a coffee mug handle, a suitcase handle, the handle on a child's pail, and perhaps the cabinet pulls in your kitchen. Years ago, you could have found the shape in the telephone receiver. Continue this exercise outside your home. Look for an elbow-macaroni shape in an arched window or in the wooden gate to a house.

Look at a clear cylindrical flower vase. That same shape and material can be a lamp base. Add a megaphone to the top and you have a lampshade. The cylinder is an umbrella stand, a drinking glass, or a candle hurricane globe, depending on its size.

Repetition of Form

When you go to the supermarket and see a display of blue-bottled mineral water that pleases your eye, visualize a row of six of the bottles on your kitchen window ledge with the east light shining through them. Even after you drink the water, they'll look great empty or with one flower in each—a daisy, tulip, or daffodil. Buy one or several and enjoy them on a sunny sill. Look at the area around the bottles. See the aura of blue light spilling out of them. Look out the window and see how the blue glow puts a purple cast on the grass or ivy. Repetition calms the eye with continuity, order, symmetry, and balance. You stack matching plates on a shelf as well as put matching glasses together. When you display pitchers on a shelf, the handles all face in one direction. Most of the collections you have contain repetition of form. Use daffodils in a series of bud vases to brighten some dreary corners on a rainy day.

The Skeleton of Form

Look for the skeleton of a form. For example, when you look at a fish, visualize its bones. When you look at a tree in springtime, imagine it in December without any leaves, the bare branches exposed. When you look at a house, envision the framing before the walls were put up. What other shapes can be reduced to a skeletal form? Animals and humans are flesh around bones. See the nuance of the skeleton in a sea horse. Look for the core or bones of forms to understand their true nature. When you look at an object, try to imagine its interior. Mentally dissect it.

All art consists in bringing something into existence.
ARISTOTLE

Several essential forms may be combined in a larger form. When you look at an apple tree, the apples are round, distinctively different and separate from the green leaves. The apples and leaves are different and separate from the pattern of the branches. The apples and other elements of the tree may be separate visual units, but together they make up the apple tree. The apples are bright red, not camouflaged on the tree. The next time you buy some red apples at the vegetable stand, visualize how they look when ripe on an apple tree, and visualize the shape of the leaves. Can you recall picking apples, gathering them in a basket, and going home to make applesauce and apple pie? The more visual memories you conjure up from a past experience, the more you will enjoy the present moment.

Now, slice open an apple, and think of the cornice molding in your living room. To visualize the cross section of the molding, look at the sliced apple. You cut through the molding to see its structural form. When you go to a lumberyard and look at architectural moldings, look at the end of a piece to examine the cross section. Study the projection to envision how it will look in relief in your room. If you can learn to visualize the way a form will appear in a specific space, you'll have a talent that surpasses mere measurement.

When you have limited space, select forms that line up snugly with the wall. A round hamper in your closet will take up more literal and visual space than a rectangular one that can sit tightly against a wall. Chairs that stack snugly, one to another, may be better forms for you than chairs that take up twice the space.

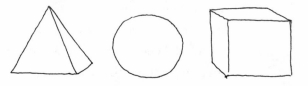

Exercises for Seeing Form

A form is the cumulative effect of the combination of selected elements. The way the elements are combined constitutes an object's character and style. Design puts content into form. Look at an object. Count how many different elements make up the whole form. Look again; you'll see more subtle variances. For example, contemplate a stemmed glass. Remember to look at the transitions between forms, as well as the forms themselves— the place where the glass base curves into the stem; the small knob, perhaps, where the stem joins the bowl.

- Draw the base of a glass. Draw the top. Look at the difference in size between the base and the bowl. Even a water glass that looks cylindrical might not be absolutely straight. To really see the shape of an object well, measure its different elements.

- ◆ When you rinse out your glass jars for recycling after you've used up the jelly, jam, salsa, olives, pickles, and mustard, examine the pure shape of the glass. The shape of the container is never as fully appreciated when it is full of mustard and sits in the refrigerator. I love a brand of marmalade that comes in thick white glass jars. I soak off the labels and keep colored pencils in them. The thick, solid form is stable and soothing, and the white is so pure. You may want to use a hexagonal see-through jar to store colored paper clips, buttons, or thumbtacks. You may find several you want to line up on a ledge in your workroom for nails and screws. They are excellent for saving some paint for touchups. Paint the lid the color of the paint for color matching.

  All things are artificial, for nature is the art of God.

  THOMAS BROWN

  See how many different uses you can come up with for these see-through jars with screw-on lids. They can be used to make and shake salad dressing or to hold a small flower bouquet with raffia or a colorful ribbon around the neck to hide the ridges. Some mustard jars are so attractive they add charm to the table when placed on a butter dish with a small wooden spoon. When they are empty, tie ribbons around their necks and put one filled with lilies of the valley or pansies at each place setting at a dinner party. Give them to your guests at the end of the evening to take home as a memento. I have a friend who makes pesto and puts in it small glass jars as Christmas gifts. A red bow around the top is vivid against the deep-green pesto—holiday colors!

- ◆ Perfume bottles are much too pretty to throw out. They make excellent bud vases for tiny flowers or for one rose blossom. They can also be set in front of place cards at dinner parties to enhance the celebration. Look around your house for other forms you like, finding uses for them beyond the obvious.

- Line up brightly colored favorite coffee cans on a workbench to hold screws, small tools, and other practical odds and ends.

- Go to auctions regularly to train your eye in the different forms of furniture and decorative arts. Go to the exhibitions beforehand so you can touch the pieces. Bring a small flashlight to see unlit places and niches as well as point up the details of the objects. All the professionals touch the objects to learn more. Look at the back of a chest of drawers. Is it finished or rough? Run your fingers along the underside of a tabletop to be sure it is finished smooth. Learn more about oriental designs, porcelain, and textiles as well as furniture. Read and study the catalogs. They are descriptive and detailed.

Our tastes greatly alter.
SAMUEL JOHNSON

- Poke around in thrift stores for the forms that are reminiscent of your childhood. Perhaps you'll find a thick oval gray metal Dutch oven just like the one your grandmother always used for Sunday pot roast. Keep it on a shelf where you can feel its comfort and use it at a moment's notice.

- The next time you go to a concert, as you listen to the music look at the instruments. Examine their size and form, and what materials were used to make them. Shut your eyes and try to visualize the features that differ from one to another. Attempt to see why an instrument is formed the way it is to create the music. When you are at home listening to classical music, try to visualize the instruments that create the sounds.

- Whenever possible, seek direct access to the creator of objects you are drawn to. If you visit Venice, go to the island of Murano to watch the glassblowers create different designs and colors for pitchers, glasses, and paperweights as well as chandeliers, sconces, and lamp bases. Watch lace being made in the nearby island of Burano. In Madeira, watch embroiderers. At craft fairs, watch marbleized paper being made, weavers at the loom, quilters at work, wood carvers carving.

- You have a greater eye for the intricacies of a form when you watch it being created and understand the process. Search out the craftsmanship and artistry of things you're attracted to. If you're interested in jewelry, observe a jeweler at work. Exploring the creative process of ceramics, woodcarving, weaving, and painting can provide you with many hours of pleasure and knowledge.

- There are studios in cities and towns where you can decorate unglazed pottery—plates, vases, bowls, tiles, and other ceramic objects. When you're finished, the shop will fire it for you in their kiln. A few days later, you can pick up your masterpiece. This is a fun activity to do with a spouse, friend, or child.

- When your suitcase doesn't arrive at your destination, you are asked to look at the diagram of different-shaped suitcases and try to identify yours. How good are you at remembering size and color?

- Become a bird-watcher and develop a high level of seeing skills. Birds are usually camouflaged in the foliage of trees, so it is difficult to locate them and discern their color, size, shape, and pattern without keen observation. From knowledge, experience, and a bird guidebook, you can become a skilled bird-watcher. This exercise hones your eye for seeing better in general.

- In a notebook, jot down one or two things you really see well each day. You never have to show it to anyone. This is a discipline just for your eyes. You will see that as you go about your life, you are drawn to the objects you describe, which adds sweetness to your days. Reading over your seeing journal is a way for you to see your interests unfold before your eyes.

When I was in design school, my teachers urged their students to keep a seeing journal. Describing what you are looking at forces you to see more deeply. The same is also true of sketching. You may think a table is a straight rectangle until you draw it, then you see that the top has rounded edges and the edge is a bullnose rather than a straight edge.

- Slice open a beet horizontally. Study the concentric circles. Doesn't it look like a tree that has been cut open? When you serve a cold beet salad, rather than dicing the beets into cubes, slice them horizontally so the inner design enhances the form.

- The next time you slice open a Red Delicious apple, first cut it in half vertically. Look at the inside half. Examine the shape. Does it look like elephant ears? Look at the chartreuse color next to the seeds. Turn it over and look at the sprinkling of stars on the red skin.

> *Art is not handicraft, it is the transmission of feeling the artist has experienced.*
>
> LEO TOLSTOY

When you look at a thick-skinned orange, can you visualize how the skin looks on the inside? Examine the texture of the skin. Slice the orange in half horizontally. Study the internal pattern of the fruit. Slice a section one quarter inch thick. Hold it up to the light. What do you see that is different? How does the color change? Do this with a lemon and lime.

Take another orange and peel it with your fingers. This time, rather than slicing it open, pull apart the wedges. How many are there? Now, take a sharp paring knife and peel the fine skin off an orange section. Hold it up to the light. How different does it look? How does the color change?

- Slice a tomato in half horizontally. Look at both halves' interiors. Turn one upside down. Examine the shape. When you make a salad with tomatoes, do you prefer wedges, slices, or diced pieces? When you slice open a lemon for tea, do you slice a wedge or a round?

Peel one half of the tomato. What is the difference in texture and color? Slice the peeled tomato half in one-quarter-inch-round slices. Now, make wedges out of the other half. Put them together on a white plate. What shapes appeal to you? Hold up one slice to the light and examine the design, the seeds, and the color. Look at a whole tomato. You're now better able to envision the inside when you see the outside. People can cut up tomatoes mindlessly or they can anticipate and then see the beauty of the pattern long before they enjoy the richness of the flavor. Seeing a tomato well adds to your appreciation of the taste. Visualize the tomato turning ripe and red on the vine in the sunlight.

We are less convinced by what we hear than by what we see.

HERODOTUS

- Look at an avocado. Feel it for ripeness. If it appears to be ripe, slice it in half vertically around the pit. Look at the one half with the pit and the other with the hole. Put the two pieces back together. Can you now visualize how the inside looks? Describe the yellow and chartreuse colors. Peel one half and slice it into thin sections. What letter shape do they resemble? Examine the texture of the skin. Look at the inside as well as the outside of the skin. Take the pit out of the other half. Hold it in the palm of your hand. Look at the hole in the half avocado. Examine the shape and colors. Do you prefer to eat the half avocado with a spoon or the slices with a fork? Does it matter to you?

Imaginative Seeing

In order to see, you have to act and imagine. It is half seeing to see only the outside of an avocado when you buy it at the market. You have to become the avocado. You have to see the inside as well as the outside, and to really see well you must visualize how you will choose to serve and eat it. Do you want to put some golden olive oil in the cavity, or a spritz of lemon? Ruby-red balsamic vinegar? A sprinkle of freshly ground pepper? Do you want to add pink grapefruit wedges to the slices? You have to envision the detail in order to see the big picture. All great events begin with envisioning. Even something as simple as slicing, serving, and eating an avocado can be wonderfully rich when you do it with vision.

A thing of beauty is a joy forever.

JOHN KEATS

Perhaps you envision chopping the avocado up into a Cobb salad or maybe you want to make guacamole to enjoy with some chips. If you enjoy the combined flavors of avocado and pink grapefruit, can you see the idea of making avocado and pink grapefruit sorbet? The taste is delicious, the color is soft green, and the texture is buttery smooth.

This way of seeing beyond the obvious is great fun. You can play with shapes, colors, and flavors. Try to visualize five ways to serve each food, based not on recipes but on how you see them visually, how you want them to look as well as taste. How you see a cantaloupe, for example, enhances your enjoyment of the sweet flavor and the orange-colored flesh. You may want to peel the whole melon and slice horizontal rounds with a hole in the middle like a doughnut. Or you may want to make melon balls. Or perhaps

All the arts have a certain common bond of union, and are connected by blood relationship with one another.

CICERO

you see the cantaloupe sliced horizontally in half with the cavity filled with cottage cheese and freshly cracked pepper or chicken, celery, walnuts, and cantaloupe cubes or balls.

If you slice the cantaloupe in half vertically, what do you see? How different does it look from being sliced in half horizontally?

In order to see, you have to be interested. If you don't like to eat cantaloupe, you probably won't see this melon well. If you prefer the flavor of honeydew melon, you will see it better than a cantaloupe. The color also enriches your seeing pleasure.

More Fun with Forms

Are you ready for the advanced course? Here are three more enlightening exercises using form:

- Cut a 4 × 6-inch index card into a four-inch square. Cut out the inside of the square with a single-edged razor or X-Acto knife, leaving a one-quarter-inch-square frame. Line it up so it looks like a window with four points. Label the top left corner of the window A. Label the top right corner B. Label the bottom left corner C, and the bottom right corner D. I suggest you do this before reading on. Look at your square window. Hold it up in front of you. Notice the complete harmony between the vertical and the horizontal planes.

  Simplicity is that element of beauty in a scene that leads gradually from one object to another, in easy harmony, avoiding abrupt contrasts and unexpected features.

  Edmund Burke

  Put your left thumb and index finger over the bottom left corner, C. Put your right thumb and index finger over the upper right corner, B. Tilt A so it points vertically, and D is directly underneath A. A is now at twelve o'clock, D is at six o'clock, C is at nine o'clock, and B is at three o'clock. You have a square placed on an angle, creating a square on the diagonal.

  Next, squeeze C and B together, elongating A and D. You now have a diamond with points north, south, east, and west. A and D are now acute angles, sharp and intense, and C and B are obtuse angles, softer and greater than their original right angles. The measurements of the sides remain the same, but visual perspective changes greatly.

  If you are laying a tile floor, you can set square tiles on the diagonal to create a more active, dynamic look than if they were set perpendicular to the wall.

- Cut two white 4 × 6-inch index cards into four-inch squares. Cut two colored index cards the same size. Play with them. First, create a checkerboard pattern with the white square to the left of the colored square, A and B. Now place the colored square under A in the C position and the remaining white to the right, directly under the colored square. Now tilt the assembled squares on the diagonal, and your eye sees something quite different: a dynamic diamond pattern.

- Cut two white 4 × 6-inch index cards into two four-inch squares and do the same with one colored one. Cut the squares into triangles. Put one side of a white triangle flush with the side of a colored triangle. You now have a square made up of two different-colored triangles. Repeat the same process directly under the square using the remaining halves, but alternating the colors. If you continue to do this with additional squares, always alternating the two colors in the same pattern, you will see a pinwheel design. Your eye will first see the pinwheel in the lighter color or the darker and will switch back and forth between the two.

It is looking at things for a long time that ripens you and gives you a deeper understanding.

VINCENT VAN GOGH

If you're willing to take the time and effort to use a black, broadpointed felt-tip pen to shade in one side of the colored square, you will immediately see how much more dramatic these visual illusions become with high contrasts. Flip the marked sections back and forth to experiment with the changes in contrast.

Understanding how the effects of a form vary depending on the form's angle, size, and color is a helpful tool whether you're buying upholstery fabric, selecting a patterned sport shirt, or deciding the pattern of your sunroom floor tiles.

Form, Light, and Color

Color and light accentuate a form, bringing it to life, transforming it from an ordinary household object to one of fascination. When you bring a blue bottle of mineral water to the table, use a white tablecloth so you accentuate the cobalt blue; you will also have a high contrast of dark and light so you see and appreciate the full shape of the bottle. Serve the water in stemmed crystal so you see some of the sensation of blue color, energy, and light on the white cloth and around the stem of your glass. Your glass has a round base. Move it around, watching how it overlaps the blue reflection on the white cloth. (You can create this same effect using a cobalt-blue water pitcher.)

As soon as you notice the slightest sign of indifference, the moment you become aware of the loss of a certain seriousness, of longing, of enthusiasm and zest, take it as a warning.

ALBERT SCHWEITZER

If you have a fluted or grooved stemmed glass, place it near the bottle and enjoy moving it around. Now look at the shadow cast by the glass and the reflection of the blue bottle on the tablecloth. Do you see a dramatic fan design with light and shadow in a half circle, almost like a scallop shell? Stare at the shadow. The rays of white light extend beyond the form, rays of divine light.

If you have some cut crystal, bring a piece to the table. I like to experiment with a small cut crystal salt dish. Move the bottle near the crystal until the blue light becomes part of the crystal. Now move the bottle away. The blue is the most dramatic contrast against the white. A white wine or champagne bottle will impart a sea-foam-green color. Don't be discouraged if you don't see the green as well. Clearly it is more subtle.

Hold a white napkin next to the blue water bottle. Move it until you see the light-blue form of the bottle in the napkin. Fold the napkin in different directions so the blue light dances. Look at your hand. It, too, is under the spell of this light. You are seeing beyond the object itself. You are seeing its effect on its surroundings. In reality, you never see objects in isolation. Everything is seen in different degrees and character of light, and from different vantage points because we are always moving about.

I have some blue glasses that were hand-blown in Biot, France. I find them especially wonderful for water, because in the glass are hundreds of bubbles that resemble drops of sparkling water. Their reflections on the white tablecloth and napkin are pale blue with lots of light points that look like stars. Later, I'll show you how they are used in a subtle composition of light and blue-and-white colors.

• If you have a clear marble in a strong color—say, purple—roll it around on your white tablecloth and discover the brilliant pinkish-purple light rolling underneath the marble, turning the white tablecloth a beautiful crushed-raspberry color. You can find handmade marbles at craft shows as well as in museum shops. The more vibrant the color, the more wavelengths of light energy they possess. A clear green glass marble has the same brilliant light but the color is paler. Placed in front of the purple glass marble, the green marble is swirled with the intense crushed-raspberry color.

I have some heavy stemmed glasses with swirls of different colors—one purple, one green, one pink, and one blue. Often I drink my coffee from one of these glasses. The white tablecloth picks up the color of the swirl. The light shining through the black coffee makes pinkish-red light sensations on the base of the glass. Because each colored glass creates a different experience, there is good reason to have a variety of different shapes and colors to stimulate and delight the eye.

• Put some red mouthwash in a clear glass decanter and rest it on the ledge of your sink where the light illuminates it.

Integration of Form and Decoration

If you have a variety of different-shaped dishes, look at them on a white tablecloth, then turn them upside down. Hold them up in front of you. You may have some oval plates as well as round. I have square plates and even a set of naturalistic green leaf-shaped dishes. Many plates are round in outline but the painted border or relief pattern consists of leaves, fooling your eye into thinking the outline is irregular.

This exercise in form also leads you to see pattern better, and observe how the two often go hand in hand. Form should follow function as well as the pattern. Judge what forms are ideal for their pattern, color, and decoration. Rate your plates from one to ten based on how the shape and pattern work together. When a potter decides on the shapes of a vase or pitcher, the painted decoration and colors are integral to and just as important as the form of the object.

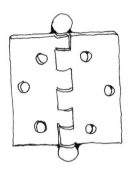

Look for examples of this wholeness where form and ornamentation are one. Consider a tulip—the blossom, the graceful curves of the stem and leaves, and even the flowerpot. You don't want to separate the form from the decoration of the container. If a pot is too large for the delicacy of the tulips, it will overwhelm them. If a container is too small for tulips in blossom, reaching out in all directions, it will look unstable, top heavy, and spindly.

Color Contrast Emphasizes Form

You should have clear contrasts of color in the forms in your home. The red of apples is intensified when they are combined with limes in a green bowl. Red tomatoes served on a round green dish with relief work that looks like a leaf are visually exciting because red and green are complementary colors. If you add mozzarella cheese, the white pops out like a ray of sun.

If you put a piece of spinach and a piece of chartreuse-colored Bibb lettuce on a white plate, what is your eye drawn to? It is probably drawn to the spinach leaf, because the deeper green has more wavelengths of energy and therefore more visual weight. Shut your eyes. Visualize the outline of the spinach on the plate. Do the same with the Bibb lettuce. You see the spinach far better because there is higher contrast between the dark green and the white plate. A mixture of the two colors is lively against white porcelain. The varied lacy forms of the leaves excite the eye, while the solid pure shape of the plate grounds your composition. Together, color and form enhance and dance.

Form and Function

There is no need to have ugly things underfoot. If you believe that your life can become a work of art, let all the objects in your immediate surroundings be as pleasing to the eye as possible.

Even when selecting an iron or a thermos or a flashlight, be guided by your eye before you know the cost. You are going to use an iron, for example, for hundreds of hours, holding the handle in your hand. You should feel the object is attractively designed as well as functional, even if that means you pay a little more for it. I've never understood why most manufacturers put brown cords on irons when they will be used in a light-colored room. I've never seen a brown laundry space. Maybe this is so we won't trip over it or otherwise knock the iron over. Nonetheless, the brown cord is an eyesore.

Even jobs that are repugnant or dull or tedious tend to be quite satisfying, once you get right down to them. This happens when we just do what we have to do.

THOMAS MERTON

Some utilitarian objects are sold at museum gift shops and housewares stores. These stores are excellent places to find superb contemporary designs from all over the world. Whether a knife sharpener, a Scotch tape dispenser, a staple gun, or scissors, these are functional objects not only seen every day but touched by you and your family. The way they look matters as much as the way they function. Often when utilitarian objects are well designed for their function, they don't need any ornamentation to improve their appearance. Look around and see for yourself.

Examine different chair designs. The purpose of a chair is to provide a comfortable and stable seat. You can find many different styles that meet this criterion without pleasing the eye. There are some chairs that are so ugly, they actually block the eye from any pleasure no matter how functional they are as seats. Look around, sit down, and evaluate what chairs can serve the purpose of being a practical sturdy seat as well as being an aesthetically pleasing form that satisfies the eye. Rate the chairs from one to ten for function and one to ten for aesthetic appeal.

Walk around your house. Everyone owns a few uncomfortable, unstable chairs. We also have some extremely comfortable ones. How many chairs do you have that are extremely comfortable as well as very attractive to look at? We often see chairs from the back because they are pulled up to a table or desk. Upholstered chairs may "float" in the middle of a room. Look at the front, the profile, and the back. Wooden chairs can be graceful as well as comfortable. Study the shapes you like, look at the lines, the curves, the splay of the legs. Some of my favorite chairs are Windsors, French Provincial ladderbacks, and French Regency, because of their shape, curves, carving, and sensuous comfort.

Time plays a part in our understanding of a form. We don't see an object once. We see it in different lights, at different times of day, in different seasons, and from different vantage points. Some forms you were attracted to at one stage in your life you now have outgrown. If forms are our visual vocabulary, expressing us, we should be sensitive to what they communicate and surround ourselves only with the forms that speak to us. In this way seeing better translates into living better.

When you go out to paint, try to forget what objects you have before you, a tree, a house, a field, or whatever. Merely think, here is a little square of blue, here an oblong of pink, here a streak of yellow, and paint it just as it looks to you.

CLAUDE MONET

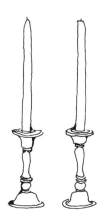

Material

Our world is made up of materials, both organic and synthetic, existing in their pure form as well as made by man or machine. To see with depth the diversity of materials in our immediate environment, it is crucial to understand the characteristic properties of different materials, experience their texture, and study how they are transformed from their raw state into art or functional objects. Once we become intimate with materials in this way, we can make the most of them in our home as well as appreciate what we see wherever we are.

Characteristics of Individual Materials

Material beauty has a great hold on our senses. Consider the impressiveness of the stained glass in a cathedral, the gold of a king's crown, the marble of the Parthenon, the fire of the stars. Every object is composed of matter, of a substance or substances that have solidity and weight. There is no form that can't be enhanced by an appropriate sensuous material.

When you lose simplicity, you lose drama.

ANDREW WYETH

Appreciating any object or scene requires seeing the materials and having some knowledge of where they came from, how malleable they are, their color variations, whether they are opaque or translucent, their textures, and even their temperature. For example, marble is cool, cork is room temperature, and glass can be cool but also becomes hot when exposed to heat.

The Artist and the Material

Because Michelangelo understood the nature of marble, he was able to chip away at the solid mass until he revealed the figure inside. He understood marble was a brittle material; he couldn't have lots of elements jutting out or they would break. His marble sculptures could be rolled down a hill without any part breaking off. This image of a marble sculpture by Michelangelo tumbling down a hill unharmed helps you to understand his genius in carving life into rock. At the same time, the stubborn nature of materials is that they impose their own limits. Even a genius must deal with the limitations of the materials he chooses. Michelangelo developed a relationship with marble, artist to material, where he knew the marble's properties intimately. He was aware of how to get the material to work with him: it is precisely the cold brittleness of marble that made Michelangelo's lifelike sculptures miraculous and fascinating.

Similarly, it is exactly the hardness of a diamond that makes a cut diamond interesting and such an achievement; the spectrum of light gleams from every facet. Gold is a soft metal with a sensuous untarnished feel, while platinum is harder. I designed a diamond ring using yellow gold, but the diamonds had to be set in platinum for strength. The visible outside areas were a golden-yellow tone.

The secret of ugliness consists not in irregularity, but in being uninteresting.

EMERSON

Knowing the malleability of materials is essential to the process of molding and shaping them. A carpenter knows what wood is best for different uses. A wood carver prefers softwood so as to carve the intricacies and delicacies of a work of art. A quilter works with cotton material; a rug hooker uses wool.

A potter needs to know the appropriate temperature for firing in a kiln or the piece of work could explode. Even the powdered minerals glazed over clay to produce specific colors are affected by the temperature of the kiln. The potter also needs to be aware of what minerals respond best in certain temperatures to produce desired colors.

Observing other artists, experimenting and studying the results, can turn an amateur potter into a knowing professional. Understanding the nature of the material similarly heightens the seer's appreciation for different types of pottery or ceramics. You learn that majolica, faïence, and delft earthenware is created by the potter's method of mixing sand and clay together with water, molding the material to a desired form, and finally glazing it with an opaque white glaze containing tin. This method is called tin glaze.

You discover that earthenware is porous unless it is glazed, and that articles made of clay are fired at lower temperatures than porcelain; thus you appreciate the difference between clay and porcelain. Porcelain is an extremely hard, translucent ceramic fired at high temperatures, first produced in China in the seventh or eighth century; the method of manufacturing it wasn't mastered in Europe until the Meissen factory's discovery of the technique in the early eighteenth century. Because porcelain withstands more heat in the firing process, it is more refined and more durable than earthenware, and therefore more desirable.

A Hierarchy of Materials

All materials are not equal. A stone bridge may be considered more beautiful than a wooden one, although Claude Monet's wooden Japanese bridge in Giverny has extraordinary charm and simplicity in the perfect setting he created from an ugly gully. Clay does not have the substantial weight, interest, character, and presence inherent in marble. The character of marble is fixed from the moment it exists, whereas clay must be molded and fired to become useful and beautiful. If it weren't for the hard, sturdy marble of Greek sculpture and architecture, we would have no surviving examples of the Golden Age of the third and fourth centuries B.C. If the pyramids weren't made of stone, they wouldn't be with us today.

Wooden historic monuments are rare because fire often destroys them. The "three little pigs" built three houses, one of straw, one of wood, and one of stone, and we all know what material lasted.

How is it possible that so many of the fragile clay vases of Greek antiquity have survived? Certainly they weren't found in a perfect state. Archeologists had to find the fragments and put the pieces together. Through the study of ancient art we can learn about the endurance of materials and the role they played in ancient cultures. We can also gain insight into contemporary cultures by observing the materials they use in everyday life.

All natural or organic materials have a life force. The more authentic the materials in your immediate surroundings, the greater vitality and satisfaction you will feel. The natural world is composed of organic materials. Most man-made materials are less satisfying than natural ones. More and more fake materials are available, but they can't replace the real thing when it comes to seeing. How do you react when you look and see plastic or silk flowers, originally believing them to be cut flowers from a garden? When you travel through New England and see frame houses, how do you respond when you discover the "wood" is vinyl or aluminum? Seasoned seers can detect the artificiality from a distance.

Every authentic seeing experience requires you to draw near to the subject.

When you use plastic, be sure you aren't trying to pass it off as leather or wood. Plastics that are colorful and aren't trying to be something they're not are a different matter entirely. Plastic is a wonderful material in many ways. It is inexpensive, comes in bright colors, and can add pleasure in strictly utilitarian places. You can have a fun, brightly colored dustpan and brush, wastebasket, tote bag, plates, glasses, knives, forks, and spoons for picnics at the beach, and wonderful, playful trays, place mats, and aprons, all made from plastic. Materials should be appropriate for their use, not trying to fool your eye unless in a whimsical way. Jewelry even comes in plastic. A colorful plastic ring shimmers, reflecting light, and only costs a few dollars. A similar ring made of crystal is not only fragile but costs considerably more. In this case, your eye is happy to be fooled. Eyeglass lenses used to be made of breakable glass. Now they are made of colorful plastics that are attractive, tinted in many colors, and practical because they don't shatter.

Plastic doesn't break easily and is more flexible than glass. Years ago, we made crystal curtain poles; now we make them out of clear plastic. We used to have white glass towel bars, but they are now made of white plastic. Plastic water glasses in a bathroom or around a swimming pool make sense. The clear cylindrical legs that hold up our bathroom counter look like glass but are actually Lucite. The old-fashioned legs were always made of glass.

As a rule, any material seen and experienced should enhance our emotional involvement, not detract from it. Using colorful plastics in utilitarian areas adds vitality to the space and can make you enjoy your work more.

A natural beauty is a beautiful thing; artificial beauty is a beautiful representation of a thing.

IMMANUEL KANT

When a material is not the real thing, it is usually designed to look too perfect to be true. Artificial ivy is *too* spring green, flowers are unnaturally perfect, the clapboard never peels. Whereas when observing a New England stone wall, each stone beautifully fitted in place, you feel the weight of the stones supporting the dry wall, through wind and hurricanes. Likewise, for authenticity, Formica countertops should not be marbleized. Choose white or a solid color. We all fall short of being purists, but whenever possible, we should select authentic organic materials. For a flower to move your soul, it must come from nature and not be man-made.

Materials add sensual enjoyment to our lives. Being able to see the inherent value of certain materials over others brings additional positive meaning to the hours we spend at home each day. The value of a material depends not only on its intrinsic value but also on how the material has been shaped into an object, how well the design has been executed. The beautiful patina of an old wooden table is charming, nourishing your soul. You see the imprint of the tree in the antique wood grain and enjoy the shine from the years of being waxed and rubbed by human hands. Though an antique table may be extremely valuable, it is not pretentious, because the old wood gives it authenticity, charm, and warmth. The fact that the table was made from a tree by an artisan adds to your appreciation of bringing nature into your home. Perhaps that's why we love wood floors so much.

It is possible to use valuable materials inappropriately, creating a more negative than positive feeling. For example, marble in the wrong place has a negative value. If you are trying to create a French country living room,

Living Room

Since we live in a tiny eighteenth-century cottage, we wanted to bring in lots of light and open up the space. White walls, simple unlined curtains, and repeated flowering chintz allowed us to unify two small rooms, giving the illusion of doubling the space.

(All photographs except for those of the Kips Bay Atelier by Andreas Von Einsiedel)

Our Bedroom

ABOVE: When we bought our cottage, the fireplace didn't work, but Peter and a master mason devised a way for us to have a fire in our bedroom. We use the fireplace morning and night, from September through June, because of the cool sea air. We sit by the fire for hours, to read and write.

LEFT: The view of the harbor is from the window to the left of the mantel. By moving the bed three feet off center, both Peter and I can sit in bed and watch the boats come and go. My favorite fabric, "Joy," is casually draped on the bedposts, self-lined and puddled on the floor, requiring no sewing.

LEFT: At home, the kitchen is the center of our family life. When we bought the house, there was a huge Formica island in the center of the space. Once we ripped it out, we were liberated to put a favorite old farm table in its place, surrounded by carefree painted folding chairs. All of the cooking equipment is on one wall elevation, allowing the space to be a sitting area for conversation and enjoyment. Good ventilation gave us the luxury of hanging a favorite painting nearby.

ABOVE: This unique space on the north side of the house provides ample room for our collection of pottery, pitchers, and platters. There is a window at the north end, with pink geraniums peeking through. After removing eight layers of awful flooring and finally unearthing the original wood floor, I wanted to celebrate by painting white and blue stripes to coordinate with the color scheme of the kitchen. Because we love this space so much, we keep the door open, except in harsh winter freezes.

Kips Bay Atelier

ABOVE: On the twenty-fifth anniversary of one of my favorite charities, Kips
Bay Boys and Girls Club, I was invited to design a room along with the ten
original designers who had decorated the first showhouse. Rather than
selecting a grand room, I chose two converted maids' rooms in the attic.
Inspired by Gertrude Stein's atelier in Paris, where I had stayed, I wanted to
create my own private haven where I could write.

LEFT: I simply filled the room with my favorite things: Everything is
immensely personal, including my journals, books, favorite art, porcelain,
and objects. I love hearing the clanging bells of the church across the street,
and the sunlight streaming into the room intensifies the vibrant colors.

(Kips Bay Atelier photographs by Jason Schmidt)

Bathroom   There is nothing more wonderful than natural light permeating a bathroom. We installed a simple, classic white pedestal sink, replacing a modern one with a chunky cabinet below. By enlarging the storage space behind the beveled mirror, everything that was stored below the sink is now behind the reflective glass. Leaning our heads back in the high, old-fashioned tub, we can watch the sailboats swirl in the harbor.

you would select a carved, curving wood mantel instead of marble, because marble would be too hard, too strong. However, to add shine and color, you could select a Vermont verde marble for the facing. You may select marble for the bathroom countertop and tub surround, but refrain from putting it on the walls. Marble is an excellent material for window ledges because it is easy to clean and maintain. In a white room, white marble window ledges will not attract your eye. Window ledges, unlike the flowering plants that adorn them, should never be focal points.

As my eyes search the prairie I feel the summer in the spring.

C H I P P E W A   S O N G

If you have money to spare, you can secretly have your hardware gold-plated. It will still look like brass but will require no maintenance. If you want ornate hardware gold-plated to show off your wealth, it will still look like brass.

White porcelain knobs are more appropriate on white cabinets if you need several dozen, because brass would look too busy. But if you choose horizontal pulls for your cabinets and need only a few, brass will look handsome.

Surface Materials

By becoming more aware of the substance of a surface, you recognize more materials and will be more adept at selecting suitable ones for your home. Surfaces are made up of a multitude of materials, from paper to stone. Look around you at some of the surfaces in your house and yard. Begin with the floor and work your way up. What different materials are used underfoot? The sidewalk could be brick or stone. What is the material of the path to your front door? The hall floor? Walk around, noticing all the different materials that comprise the floors inside the house as well as the garden. Grass is a surface. The pebbles in our Zen garden are a surface. The brick of a patio is a surface. If you have a brick patio, study what type of brickwork is on the floor and identify the pattern. You could have a brick driveway and extend the brick right into the floor of the garage. In a client's dining room, we used old terra-cotta tiles on the floor, running the tiles right up to the fireplace. Because they're fireproof, we didn't need to use a different material for the hearth and so create a visual disruption.

Look at all floor surfaces with a critical eye. If there is a step up or down in a garden, for example, there should be different-colored stone or other material to indicate the surface transition so people won't fall. If you have a wood floor in the living room, examine how the floorboards are laid. If you have a rug, what material is it made of? How is it woven? What texture does it have? Is it flat and tightly woven? Or is it a high-cut pile? Are there wooden saddles separating carpeting from a wood floor? Brass strips are never as attractive as wooden saddles. All saddles should match in color and should be the width of the door frame. After you've examined each material, add them up. How many different ones do you have on your property? You will be amazed at the variety, especially in the natural, organic materials.

Nothing odd will last long.

SAMUEL JOHNSON

Now look at your wall surfaces, including your baseboards. If you have a tile floor in your kitchen, use a wooden baseboard. A plastic core molding cheapens the appearance of the whole room. Plastic moldings may be easy to maintain, but they look it, disappointing the eye. Why do you like the look of rough stucco walls in your kitchen?

Now examine the top surfaces of the window ledges, tables, and appliances in your home. By isolating the different surface areas, you can examine the materials from painted wood to painted metal, from porcelain to stainless steel, from copper to marble. How appropriate is the material for its use? How well integrated is it with the room? Does it work in concert with the other materials? A white Formica countertop surrounding a white porcelain sink in a small kitchen, for example, looks more expansive than a dark Formica countertop surrounding a stainless steel sink.

This surface adventure will teach you a great deal about the diversity of materials and how they work together. You will smile as your hand touches the antique wood desktop. You touch cork, then marble, and feel warmth, then coolness. Perhaps you've grown not to like your glass-top table because it always looks dusty and cold. This surface analysis can save you from making costly mistakes in the future. You will observe what materials are the most sensuous to you, the ones you truly love seeing and touching, and you can admit that certain ones do not inspire you. A drab taupe Formica surface could easily be replaced with energizing white. Or maybe you prefer wood and are willing to maintain it because it nourishes you and reflects your love of trees and nature. I've often mentioned my love affair with my butcher-block counters. Despite the care they demand, they warm my heart with their naturalness, honesty, and earthy beauty. Sometimes the caring is part of why we love something.

Now think broadly of all surfaces, even the exterior of your house, doors, or windows. Some things appeal to us because of their covering. The exterior of a box can be so attractive you don't care much about its contents. I adore pretty soap packages, for example, and save them as special gifts for my bathroom and kitchen sinks. They look inviting before you see, smell, and use the actual bar of soap. For me, the same allure is true with perfume. Companies spend a great deal of money on packaging as well as on the container, not just the essence or scent of the perfume. The beauty of the material often stands out best when the form is simple. Visualize a Chanel perfume bottle. The simple form in clear glass is so alluring. All I have to do is look at a Tiffany box and I sense luxury and beautiful design. The robin's-egg-blue box has become a symbol of that luxurious feeling.

What are some of your favorite materials? Do you like wood, paper, stone, tile, porcelain, silver, gold, crystal, copper, marble, silk, cotton, wool, or leather? Do you have any material in your home, garden, clothes, or linens you do not like? How do you feel about rugs made of synthetic fabrics versus organic materials? Whenever possible, use wool, silk, or cotton for the fabrics and rugs in your home, because these organic materials breathe, wear well, are easier to clean, and look better.

There are times when you want to buy clothes made of synthetic materials. For example, I have many wool and silk suits, but when I'm traveling I'm happy to wear polyester because it doesn't show wrinkles. But I can't imagine having anything but 100 percent cotton bath towels and always prefer 100 percent cotton sheets. We have napkins that are 100 percent cotton, linen, even silk. Those in our linen drawer made of a synthetic material may look attractive, but they feel sleazy to the hand and stains are nearly impossible to get out, especially lipstick stains or chocolate. If linen wrinkles, so what? Many people prefer seeing wrinkles in table linens and bedsheets to settling for synthetics.

Earth's the right place for love: I don't know where it's likely to get better.

ROBERT FROST

The Intimacy of Textiles

Of all the materials that we bring home and live with each day, textiles are my favorite because we wear them, we sleep in them, we sit on them, and they add color, pattern, comfort, and sensual pleasure to life. We are able to express our spontaneous spirit in hundreds of little ways with fabric that we can't do in the weightiness of more permanent materials. Fabrics are the most flexible material, allowing us daily variety, something we can't say of tiles, stone, wood, or marble.

While some cotton prints can cost as much as silk taffeta, we're able to find inexpensive fabrics if we're willing to look around. Become a collector of odd bits of fabric. For example, I bought a cotton blue-patterned napkin, the only one left, for one dollar, about twenty years ago. At the time, I was not concerned about where I would use it. How odd to have only one napkin of a particular pattern, one might think, as a reason not to buy it. Wrong. This twelve-inch-square textile became the inspiration for the color scheme of a beach house. I also tuck it inside a basket to keep bread warm. Sometimes I place it on top of a twelve-inch-square wicker table in the bathroom when I use blue and white towels. I've served Peter breakfast in bed using this napkin, and when I was asked by Fieldcrest Cannon to add colors to their Royal Velvet towel line, one of the five blues in the napkin became "iris," the most heavenly towel color. We always find uses for the things we are attracted to, and these sensuous fabrics become softer and more comforting the more we use them.

Properly understood as a question of focus, unconditional love is the creative process.

PETER ROGERS

When you see place mats, napkins, guest hand towels, kitchen towels, or embroidered pillowcases that speak to your heart, don't pass them up if they are reasonably priced. I bought four white square pillow shams in Madeira, Portugal, in 1980, that we use every day. I love to iron them so I can appreciate the fine handwork and intricate detail of the embroidery. Ironing can be a form of visual meditation. I have moments of sweet reflection when I put the freshly ironed, crisply starched pillow shams on the bed.

When I went to work for Mrs. Brown in 1963, I was introduced to the French company Porthault Linen, which has a limited line of 100 percent cotton items for the bed and bath. I couldn't afford to buy from this store for myself, but I enjoyed taking my clients there to shop for their houses. In 1967, when Alexandra was born, I splurged and bought a multicolored-pastel, flowered-print baby pillowcase with pink, hand-bound scalloped borders. I used it in her carriage and it adorned her nursery. Although that pillowcase has now disintegrated from repeated washings, the pattern is still available, and I now use a similar pillowcase on our bed.

A blanket can be so appealing your eye doesn't want it hidden under a coverlet. Blankets made from lamb's wool and cashmere with fringed ends look great folded at the foot of your bed or placed folded on a footstool and are available in many mouthwatering colors. Because large retail chain stores buy in such quantity, they can sell these items at reasonable prices.

A blanket should not be considered strictly utilitarian, because your eye experiences it so frequently. Most children have a favorite blanket that always makes them feel cozy and loved. I have one in lilac that is the same color as the moldings on the four white doors in our bedroom. In the

Genius can be bounded in a nutshell and yet embrace the whole fullness of life.

THOMAS MANN

summer, it is a welcome addition to the new Zen linen closet. Always keep in mind that seeing is constant, inside closed spaces as well as outside. You can see beauty in a stack of colored blankets or cotton throw rugs.

Words have rhythm and personality, and the same is true of textiles. The personality of a fabric depends largely on what culture inspired it. These fabrics, in turn, express you because they reflect your love of a certain culture's art. If you love Provence, there are Soliado provincial geometric prints that echo the spirit of place. Something as simple as place mats and napkins can set the mood, making you feel you've been transported to the South of France. Whenever I wear intensely bright fuchsia silk, I'm carried back to 1959, when I was a teenager in India, wearing this chromatically intense color in a sari. Just as each culture has its own traditional cuisine, so it has unique textiles in weave, colors, and dyeing methods. Whenever I see Thai silk, I recall its origin. I have photographed women weaving complicated ikat designs while children played underfoot, shaded from brilliant sun and heat by the swaying silk on the loom. We have references from wherever our life's journey has brought us. All these materials that have meaning and memories are what infuse your home with energy, character, and soul.

When you travel and find fabrics you like, either sold by the yard or made into place mats, napkins, tablecloths, sheets, or pillowcases, bring them home to keep alive the memories of your experience in a foreign place. You don't have to travel far to see handsome textiles in local craft exhibitions and sales. A shelf in our linen closet holds a collection of fabric pieces gathered in my travels over forty years.

The Fabrics We Wear

Fabrics we wear closest to our skin can be soft and comfortable and sensuous, even colorful. Look at your pajamas, nightshirts, bathrobes, and underwear. Do you see a variety of colors and patterns? Do you have a combination of stripes, checks, and plaids? What colors do you see? Taking inventory of your intimate clothing is revealing, because it tells you a lot about yourself. These items are yours to wear and have no other purpose. You have obvious preferences beyond fit. You wear a certain style of sock or stocking and underwear. Do you care what you wear to bed at night? Do you like the way your robes feel and look?

Our lives are full of compromises. Nothing is ever perfect, but when you are particular about some of your intimate wardrobe, it makes a huge difference in how you feel as well as in how you feel about yourself. Having a variety of colors and patterns adds more spice and allure to our daily lives. Some people wear a uniform to bed, the same year in and year out, but I believe we should have a wide range to choose from. We should be able to match our mood to a color or pattern.

The day is coming when a single carrot, freshly observed, will set off a revolution.

Paul Cézanne

Even though others may not see you in your intimate materials, you feel good inside and your face radiates this. When you look in your closet, do you like the nightgown and underwear you see? We all get caught up in the demands of life, and there are times when we let these little things go. But take a hard look, and if you don't like what you see, maybe you should treat yourself to a few new intimate items that will make you feel good.

Creative Uses for Everyday Materials

See with the eye of an inventor. When you look at a kitchen towel, try to think of five different uses for it—kitchen curtains, guest towels, napkins for a bistro dinner. Whatever objects you use every day, look at them to see what other uses they can have for you.

- I use some pretty printed cotton guest towels with scalloped tops and bottoms for napkins. One day while I was ironing them before placing them back on the shelf, I saw their potential as bathroom curtains. I bought two brass spring rods (they also come in white) and installed one on the top and the other halfway down the bathroom window. I picked a one-quarter-inch-wide ribbon and cut 8-inch-long strips and sewed them to the curtain in the center of the ribbon (four inches from each end) on the top of every other scallop, using four pieces of ribbon per curtain panel, or eight per pair. After sewing the ribbon to the curtains, I tied little bows over the rod.

If you want to make some quick and easy curtains, guest towels or even kitchen towels work well and look great. No sewing is involved except for attaching ribbon tabs on the top. You can add a valance by folding a pair of hand towels in half, draping them over a third spring rod, and shirring them in place. Two-tier curtains made from cotton dish towels fit most standard-sized double-hung windows. If you need additional length, the ribbon tab can hang down an inch or two from the rod.

- Look through your favorite sheets and napkins. You might have some pretty guest towels that you rarely use. Perhaps they could be used as napkins.

- If you have a kitchen towel you especially like, you could make it into a small pillow cover. Buy an inexpensive baby pillow. Wrap the towel around it and sew the two sides on the machine. Put the pillow inside and hand-sew the end.

- Look at your napkin inventory. If you have some brightly colored napkins in rainbow colors—red, orange, yellow, blue, green, and violet—consider making each place setting a different color with primroses in a basket for the centerpiece.

- Make a ribbon tablecloth. If you have a plain-colored tablecloth, the next time you have a party buy some wide ribbon in a bright stripe or plaid. Cut four strips of ribbon the length of the cloth. Do the same for the width. Lay the cloth on the table you'll be using. Without sewing, place one ribbon panel at each edge of the length of the table. Evenly distribute the other two ribbons on the table. Do the same with the ribbons on the width of the table, but weave them over and under the ribbons already in place. After the party, remove the ribbons and roll them up to protect them from getting wrinkled.

I have more memories than if I were a thousand years old.
CHARLES BAUDELAIRE

- If you have only one pretty cotton napkin of a set, you may line a small drawer with it, or you can place it on top of a small wicker table in the bathroom.

- Similarly, line a larger drawer with a favorite place mat.

- In a bedroom, you can cover the lampshades in the same material as the curtains and upholstered chairs. The fabric looks nice when it is shirred from top to bottom.

- Use an old favorite sheet as a blanket cover.

- Cut up an old but loved towel—lime green or purple—into six-inch squares to use as fun cleansing rags. Or cut up an old but loved flannel nightgown for polishing rags.

- Stack checked or plaid kitchen towels in the bathroom as hand towels. They don't need to be ironed and can coordinate in color with your bath towels. They come in wonderful patterns and colors and become softer with every washing.

- Stock up on paper napkins of all colors and sizes. Using a variety of colored napkins for drinks and meals makes a sandwich and Coke festive. Patterned paper napkins are excellent for wrapping small gifts.

- Buy some round white paper doilies to line the bottoms of your wastebaskets.

- Treat yourself to some small decorative pillowcases that fit inexpensive baby pillows. When you have a variety, you can change them when you change the sheets. Men and children love them too. Add a few neckroll pillows to your inventory.

- Select four different-colored fat candles. Rest them on clear glass round ashtrays to put some cheer into a room.

Balancing Materials and Textures

Ideally, we want to use a variety of materials that the eye sees as being consistent in weight. Stone, marble, tile, and wood all seem to be substantially the same weight visually. If too much marble is used, however, it will upset the balance and symmetry of the composition of the parts. Marble might be the right material for a hallway, but if you ran it into the living room, it might look excessive. Marble bathrooms can be elegant, but there has to be some relief from the marble's heaviness. If you have a green marble floor and counter, for example, white walls would refine the richness of the marble.

I like to walk about amidst the beautiful things that adorn the world.

GEORGE SANTAYANA

You may want a marble-top table with a beautifully hand-carved fruitwood base. The warmth of the wood softens the hardness of the marble. A table with a tabletop and a base both made of marble will not only look too rigid, it will be too heavy to move. Certain marble and granite countertops in a kitchen can be practical and look wonderful, but should be softened by an old sugarpine or cork floor.

There should be a balance between the hard materials in your house—

marble, tile, stone, iron, steel, wood, porcelain, crystal, brass, chrome, and silver—and the soft materials—fabrics, pillows, and rugs. Evaluate the balance of materials in each room in your house. If a bathroom has too many hard materials, you may want to add a soft curtain, perhaps with a ruffle or a ruffled valance or a scalloped edge. You can add cotton area rugs and stack extra towels on an antique wicker table. You may want to place some folded washcloths in a basket on a counter. Rather than having a glass bath and shower enclosure, you can hang a pair of curtains on the outside of the tub with a plastic lining inside. If you want a pinch-pleated shower curtain heading, hang two separate rods, one for the curtains and one for the plastic lining.

A superior vessel takes a long time to complete.

ZEN SAYING

- In a bathroom where waterproof materials are a practical necessity, use hand-painted tiles to soften the hardness of tile floors and counters. For example, if 25 percent of the tiles are decorated with delicate flowers in several different colors and a variety of designs, these decorative tiles will soften the composition. The best way to place the patterned tiles is to eyeball them. Let your eye be the judge, elevation by elevation, of where they'll look best. Three blank tiles to one decorative tile is usually a general rhythm that works. The rest is up to your eye. There will be far more rhythm and interest if you balance them without being symmetrical. When tiling around a tub, anchor the four corners directly above the bathtub with a decorative tile, not of the same design necessarily but of similar pattern, to ground the whole composition.

  In your plan, draw in your tub where it is positioned in your bathroom in relation to where you enter. Assuming your tub is rectangular, number the three elevations where the tub is against the wall as one, two, and three, left to right. Pretend the walls are dropped down so they are level with the floor. Draw the lines for each of the three elevations. How high do you want the tiles to go? Measure. Usually they should go up as high as the showerhead if you don't carry them

up to the ceiling. The decorative tiles should be placed from left to right, one on the bottom left corner on elevation one, one on the bottom left corner of elevation two (the long elevation in the center), one on the bottom right of elevation two, and one on the bottom right of elevation three. Repeat this same pattern of tile placement above, either where the tiles end or where the wall joins the ceiling. The rest is up to your eye to see what looks best. When setting tiles, as when hanging pictures, you are dealing with more than a measurement. Always trust your eye.

- To soften the angles of a room, "puddle" the curtains on the floor by having them made two to four inches too long. To add more softness, make a draped table balloon on the floor by tucking under the skirt with ten to fourteen inches of extra material. This requires no sewing. Cut the material with pinking shears.

- Use a colorful cotton area rug in your closet over tiles to soften the look and feel warm underfoot. Place a small cotton rug in front of the sink in the kitchen and bathroom. To warm up the hardness of a laundry room, place a cotton rug on the floor.

Light and Material

Understanding the influence of light and color is integral to appreciating material. Different types and colors of matter reflect wavelengths of light to varying degrees.

- Matte, fuzzy, or glossy surfaces alter the way you see light. A matte finish absorbs light, a fuzzy finish traps light, and a glossy finish reflects light.

- To see light flowing through a translucent object, place a votive candle behind the object so it is illuminated without revealing the light source. On a serving table in the dining room, for example, place some candles behind decanters or bottles of wine. You can also place a candle behind a vase of flowers on a table.

♦ Hold a piece of material up to the light so you can appreciate the weave, color, and pattern. Look for the inner light. Many fabrics, especially silks and cottons, look best unlined as bed hangings or when hung as curtains. This way the light gets trapped inside the material and it glows. White eyelet or dotted Swiss bed hangings are refreshingly crisp and sun-drenched, reminding you of the foam on a wave. Using unlined printed cotton for a bed hanging requires no sewing if you drape the fabric over the top rail, self-lining the hanging. What you see from the inside is as pretty as what others see from the outside.

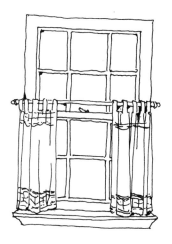

Appreciating the abundance of materials provided by nature, their distinct properties, how they are used to create art, and the purpose they serve in our daily lives is essential to bringing more beauty into our lives. When you increase your knowledge about the different types of wood used for furniture and floors, how difficult it is to sculpt marble, the process of making porcelain, the characteristics of precious metals, and the character of the fabrics you use and wear, you are developing your eye and on the path to seeing better.

Composition

Look around you—everything is a composition. The artistic arrangement of parts to form a united whole, whether within a single object, a furnished room, or one of nature's landscapes, is composition. To really see a composition, and to create a harmonious one, the eye of the observer must be sensitive to more than the individual parts that make up the whole. Special attention must be paid to how the elements are interconnected. What role does the space between the elements play? What is the meaning of the specific arrangement? In a furnished room, how is the art of placement expressed?

Everything that pleases is pleasant because it pleases.

IMMANUEL KANT

A composition is influenced by diverse forces. Nature presents you with endless scenes where all elements of visual perception are involved. When you look at nature, you can study these dynamic elements of composition. Investigate a seascape. First, observe the fundamental elements—the water, the sand, the rocks, the sky. Then observe the direction of the lines, motion, shapes, light and shadows, the relationship between objects and space, the colors and the energy you feel from the encounter. Study a sunset as a composition. How many hues and tints do you see in a sunset? How different are the colors in a sunrise from those of a sunset?

Artists and Composition

Artists, whatever their discipline, learn their craft by combining the essence of what they want to express with their artwork. How each artist interprets what is before him determines the composition. As you look at the natural world, you see thousands of things at once. You compose in your mind's eye through your sense of sight, combined with your own interpretation of what you see. You become a visual composer. You don't have to be a professional artist to visually experience a full life. Seeing through an aesthetic prism, learning what is harmonious and what is not, being able to add and take away and, as designers call it, to "style" a scene, a room, or a tablescape, is a great benefit to your daily life.

All artists compose their own vision of nature. Anthony Ashley Cooper, third Earl of Shaftesbury, wrote about the philosophy of art and aesthetic values:

A painter, if he has any genius, understands the truth and unity of design; and knows he is even then unnatural when he follows nature too close, and strictly copies Life. For his art allows him not to bring all nature into his piece, but a part only. However, his piece, if it be beautiful, and carries truth, must be a whole, by itself, complete and independent.

One easy way to teach yourself about composition is to take some still life pictures. First, you see something that sparks your interest, then you look through the camera's eye. Immediately you see you have a lens with boundaries that limits what you can include in the picture. You must select a portion of the scene, cut it out from the rest of the background, and frame it. The process of determining what to include in your frame is composition in action. If you are pho- 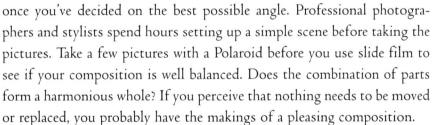 tographing a picnic table, for example, what side of the table do you want the lens to land on? Will you select an end view? How high will the viewing point be? If you are on your knees, you see one thing; if you're on a ladder, you see something else. In real life, you can walk around the table and look up and down at it, but when you take a picture, you have to capture the essence of the scene with a limited view or vantage point. Move the objects around so they look most appealing through the camera's lens once you've decided on the best possible angle. Professional photogra- phers and stylists spend hours setting up a simple scene before taking the pictures. Take a few pictures with a Polaroid before you use slide film to see if your composition is well balanced. Does the combination of parts form a harmonious whole? If you perceive that nothing needs to be moved or replaced, you probably have the makings of a pleasing composition.

Nature's beauty is fleeting. One of the sad sides of nature's beauty is the impermanence of its compositions. We see the old stone wall, the cows in the pasture, and the flock of birds in the pink-and-blue-ribbon sky of the sunset differently each time. The turning of the leaves in autumn and the rays of sunlight breaking through the forest canopy are also examples of nature's impermanent compositions. Being able to record these compositions as a permanent visual memory is easy on film or with a camera, but difficult on canvas. Claude Monet not only worked on his composition but would wait for the drama of changing light and shadow to emphasize the mood of the atmosphere.

Man's sense of place in the universe is due to a judgment about the beautiful.

ANTHONY ASHLEY COOPER, THIRD EARL OF SHAFTESBURY

In our own way, since early childhood, we have composed our visions from what we literally see and experience as well as what we envision, imagine, and dream.

When we're fortunate, all the diverse, rich resources in our daily life become the elements and forces that inspire a wealth of compositions. When we stand back and look at life with an eye to the overall perspective, we see ourselves expressed in all these infinite, varied, and wondrous compositions. We see something beautiful and learn to envision ourselves as being part of the scene we compose. We see a wicker basket and imagine a picnic with the grandchildren at the beach. We see an old bench in an antique shop and envision ourselves sitting on the bench in a garden meditating. We see a suit in the window of a department store and are able to visualize it on our body with a certain shirt and shoes.

Matisse as Master of Color and Composition

Henri Matisse showed us that life should be vivid and vibrant, never dull or colorless. His compositions are marvelous. His paintings and his later cutouts speak of intensifying the moment, awakening us to open up and greet each encounter with a more playful spirit. He is a genius as a colorist, placing stop-red next to go-green to make both colors pop if not explode. You look at three red goldfish in a large clear bowl; you know it is clear because you see the red fish so well through the water. They're not orange, but flaming red, and they are swimming in sea-foam-green water, the color of the waves in the Caribbean. And next to a naked woman are three flame-red flowers in a green vase resting on the table, completing this balanced, joyous composition.

Matisse's cutouts contain treelike leaves as outstretched fingers of color; he has them dancing in the air. There are no dreary browns, no musty, dusty, dull colors. Everything is vivacious and appealing. I line drawers with Matisse postcards so I see these orange, magenta, and yellow swiggles against green in the haphazard shapes and forms that bring pleasure. He calls out: Come hold hands, let's dance, let's sing—and you feel a sudden lightness of being. There's rhythm, harmony, and stimulation in his compositions. He draws you near the window or into his happy studio space, inviting you to see yourself in a better light as well as see more colorfully what is around you, inspiring you to surround yourself with a playful mélange of objects artistically arranged.

Look for the distinctive characteristics of objects that attract you. Identify salient features. Focus on one object at a time.

Because he simplified his shapes and forms and boldly brings us into this exotic, spicy life, Matisse helps us to clarify what we want, to let down our guard and add more energy and joy to the scenes around us. Lining drawers with Matisse postcards is a love pat, confirming my passion for clear exhilarating colors, encouraging me to skip rather than walk, to dance, and reminding me to celebrate being alive.

The Element of Passion in Composition

When you carefully select and organize materials so the parts hang together in a congruous way, you feel order and arrangement. When you add emotion, something intensely interesting results. When something is stirring to one person, it will be felt by someone else. Wordsworth explained that there should be some distance from the emotion in the time of expression—"emotion recollected in tranquillity." If you compose a room or a meal or a garden without passion, you may create a proper composition but one without the warmth that echoes the creator. Only after you discover your passion should you apply knowledge of form, material, and composition, literally shaping the moment so others can see and share your joys.

The right elements come together with ideal proportion, color, and unity when accompanied by emotions of passion and sentiment. Everything in your rooms should have meaning so you feel comforted emotionally, feeling love, not fear. We don't see cold-bloodedly. We see with our emotions and instincts. We want to be excited about our personal place, feeling that its aura is a loving one. We want to have strong feelings about what we see in order not to glaze over objects in indifference. We see with all our inner resources. When we wander through a flower garden, we have an immediate experience of life's mysteries and are touched and moved by the sheer beauty of the flowers in bloom, the warmth of the sun, the birds, butterflies, and bees dancing on air. If there is a serpentine path, it adds mystery and intensity to our aesthetic experience, because there is that wonderful element of surprise and intimacy ideal for contemplation in the privacy of perfect natural beauty.

Emphasizing What Is Important in Composition

Jennifer, an editor for a book publishing firm, came home from work one evening and was immediately drawn to the end table next to her living room sofa. There in all its glory was a framed picture of Jennifer and her husband after they became engaged. This object was of great significance. How could she heighten the photograph's impact in the room? What could she put next to it to please the eye? She was alone because her husband hadn't returned from work. So in love, she wanted this picture to glow with all the energy she shared with her husband. On the end table were also a lamp, some coasters, a red lacquer box, and the framed picture. What could she do to create a more powerful visual impact from this two-dimensional picture that was so symbolic of her life with her other half, her soul mate? What would you put on that tabletop?

I'd probably add a shiny brass clock to the table, one that was decorative and had a nice ring to the bongs. A clock, its ticks like breathing, can act as a very important reminder in life: Time is precious. (I have an old English porcelain cup with an elaborate leaf decoration surrounding the three words *Time Is Precious.* I keep it on my desk filled with colorful paperclips.) If Jennifer placed a dish with three lemons next to the framed picture, one's eye would be attracted to the life force and the intensity of that "touch of yellow," something Mrs. Brown advised should be in every room. Any cut flowers in a small vase will make you feel the tenderness of affection. Before her husband came home, she lit a candle next to the frame. He noticed it immediately. With outstretched arms he walked toward her and they had a sweet embrace. The table becomes an altar, the photograph the focal point.

See as if for the first time a beautiful person or an ordinary object.

SHIVA

The Focal Point

Every composition should have a focal point where energy is concentrated. A crackling fire in a fireplace, for example, arrests your attention. A newborn baby in a cradle draws your eye, not the antique cradle. Walk around your house and locate the concentration of energy in inanimate objects room by room. A high armoire could be a focal point, or a favorite painting, or a writer's desk. If you have a fireplace that is not in use, put a colorful floral screen in front of it. A mantel and hearth are strong symbols of the sweetness of home. The focal point shouldn't be a dark hole giving off negative energy.

If you put an object of great significance on a surface with space around it, it will command a presence, give significance to one form without competition. On an old wood table behind a sofa, one blue-and-white Canton vase can be dramatic as a focal point.

Create Artistic Still Lifes

A great way to improve what you see at home is to go room by room, editing objects from tables, bookcases, and other surfaces, and creating artistic still lifes in their place. Study favorite artists' still lifes. What attracts your eye? Is it the bowl of fruit? Is it the arrangement of flowers? Is it the way a table is set? Is it the juxtaposition of objects? One of my favorite Pierre Bonnard paintings, *Table Set in a Garden*, hangs in the National Gallery of Art in Washington, D.C. I selected it for the newly designed paperback edition of *Living a Beautiful Life*. (The eye-catching tablecloth, white with wide bands of pink ribbons, also appears in a painting of Bonnard's terrace and lawn in the Phillips Collection in Washington.) Artists are people, like us, and the Impressionists and Post-Impressionists tended to paint the intimacy of their domestic life when they weren't out in the country actively looking for painting locations. Like Bonnard's humble table, there are many objects in your home that can be focal points; you do not need to spend money to achieve dramatic and tasteful compositions.

No great thing is created suddenly.

EPICTETUS

Objects should be moved around regularly. Think of your possessions as inventory—while you're displaying some of them, you need to store others. A client in Texas calls this process "putting up." When a surface begins to look crowded, she "puts up" several items. In time, they'll resurface.

The best way to see your tabletops with a new eye is to remove everything and clean and wax or polish the table or mantel shelf or window ledge. Polish and clean each item. If you do this in an entire room, you immediately see how crowded the surfaces are. Rather than having a lot of things, too much for the eye to digest, select a few objects you love. On the coffee table, fresh flowers or a bowl of fruit will become a focal point. What are some of the things you love in a room? Books, flowers, framed pictures of loved ones, some porcelain, brass, and silver objects?

By moving things around, including furniture and art, you are breathing new life and vital energy into your rooms. There are thousands of ways, not one absolute way, for editing and rearranging still lifes in your rooms. To draw your eye to a pitcher of flowers, place it off center on a table with nothing else. Polish all your brass objects and place them in a collection on a shiny waxed surface. Place a chair in front of a table with a center drawer and arrange the tabletop with letter-writing paraphernalia, including an inkwell, a letter opener, a letter box, some pens, stationery, stamps, and a bud vase.

You will find that family and friends on the whole won't notice what you've done to change the atmosphere of your home. They might sense you've made some alterations, but they most likely won't be able to identify them. Enjoy these changes as your own sweetly private renaissance.

Test your visual memory and see if you can remember what is on your desk and on your end table in your bedroom. Your desk could be crowded with files and papers and your end table could be stacked with books, but in your living room, on the average, you should have no more than a half dozen or so items per table. There should be surface space to put down a drink, a book, a plate of cookies, or a bowl of candy.

Think of every surface as the basis for a still life that can be elevated into an artistic arrangement. Look at your desk, the dining room cabinet, the open shelf in your bathroom, the living room coffee table. See what you can do to rearrange the objects in order to see them in a better way. Move things around. Stand back and look. Examine one area at a time in order to completely focus. If a piece of glass on a picture frame is cracked, have it replaced. If the brown back of a frame shows in a mirror, put it on a surface where there is no mirror. If a stack of books has become messy, remove them all and put them back artistically. Do as Jennifer did: Place a candle next to a favorite object. When you light the candle, the treasured possession will be seen in a glow of light.

Use objects you love as symbols. I keep a dish of old pens in a variety of colors—red, orange, yellow, green, and blue—on my writing desk. They are rarely used but I like to look at them. The things you collect should tell a story about you. Try to have personal treasures shine forth in your still lifes, representing you well. When you love your objects they smile back at you. Try not to have random knick-knacks litter a table. Every visible object becomes a design element whether you like the object or not. Remember, seeing is democratic. One sees everything when one is focused. I've seen other-

wise attractive rooms ruined by ugly wastebaskets, dowdy lampshades, and cutesy gift store objects with no meaning. Objects have a tone of voice and speak to your eyes and brain. When we see how every detail adds up to a more inviting, gracious room that sings our unique song, we are inspired to attend to each detail carefully.

- Place a large round plate on the back of a ledge on a wooden or brass stand or secure it with a brad, a fine, headless nail. In front of the decorative plate, place some favorite objects. The round shape will frame the forms you want to be seen in composition.

- When resting photographs, paintings, drawings, or other items on a mantel, you can put some objects in front of others. Overlapping exists in nature. You look at a tree and the leaves and branches in the front hide some of those in the back. You don't have to see everything about an object. Often we can't see the back of objects placed in a bookcase unless the back wall is mirrored. Overlapping provides mystery.

- If you choose to have a square or rectangular see-through glass top on a coffee table, be sure the four edges are rounded so they are not dangerously sharp. Place some books and decorative objects near the edge of the surface to alert others to see the transparent glass and avoid hurting themselves.

Open Cabinet Displays

When displaying decorative china in open cabinets, consider having matching pairs on plate racks on each side of a single plate, dish, platter, or vase in the center. Layer them, putting some plates in the back of the shelf and others overlapping them in the front. Keep in mind that the eye doesn't have to see the entire shape because the brain is informed, and harmony results. Angle the plates on either side inward slightly to create a cozy feeling, bringing the eye back to the center of the composition.

If you want to add a framed print to a group of china pieces, rest it on the shelf, and place a small plate on a rack in front of it. This adds a bit of mystery, and people can come close to examine the print in detail.

Simplicity in Composition

Simple shapes are enhanced when they are separated from other objects of more complexity, because they have a different character and tell another story. A bulbous white plaster bean-pot lamp on a simple round pine table is more dramatic and pleasing to the eye when there aren't a lot of ornamented, fussy, small objects around it. A few pears on a plain dish would look better than a collection of crystal animals, for example. The simplicity refreshes the eye.

You and the object or scene you observe must establish an emotional connection. The richness of your seeing experience depends on it.

If you are placing fruit in a bowl, the less decoration on the bowl, the better. Let the eye appreciate the composition of the simple shapes of apples, oranges, lemons, and limes without visual competition. If, however, you want to display a favorite decorated bowl, select one fruit category—say, lemons—and put only lemons in the patterned bowl.

When you have several options of different things that can fit together in a composition, remember the principle of economy: Choose the simplest composition. Never go beyond what is necessary. Use nature as your teacher. Make everything count. Look at a tree or a daisy. Nothing is excessive. If you have a simple white porcelain pedestal sink, an appropriate faucet set is one that is unadorned. Your eye sees the clean lines, the straightforward appearance, and is satisfied. Nothing more is needed, therefore nothing more should be added.

Look at a patchwork quilt. What do you see? Simple shapes and forms can be arranged in highly sophisticated designs, and when used abundantly with subtle distinctions that can create optical illusions, become visually complex without being busy or jangled. Recently, I saw a large ebony console table with four objects on it that made an impression in my visual memory. Three of the objects were white vases, all shaped differently, and the remaining object was a white square wooden flat of baby grass. The dark surface of the table made the white shapes stand out. The twelve-inch square of perfect one-inch-tall new grass was a feast for the eye.

A rock pile ceases to be a rock pile the moment a single man contemplates it, bearing within him the image of a cathedral.

ANTOINE DE SAINT-
EXUPÉRY

When you look at the overall composition, some things may appear too complex. Study the elements, the individual parts that make up the whole. Try to visualize the drama of the three white vases and the grass. Only a few features were prominent. Each part was relatively simple, but the whole was dynamic. The utter simplicity of the natural grass allowed you to be in awe of the graceful shapes of the vases. The shapes alone might have been too austere.

If you have an ornate piece of furniture, place a vase containing one kind of flower on it to simplify the composition.

Repetition in Composition

Homogeneous forms, made up of parts that fit together to make a whole, are as rare as a cloudless blue sky. Most objects are not composed of the same or similar nature. Look around. For the most part, wherever you look you see dissimilarities. The oak is different from the maple tree, but

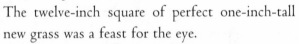

they are both trees. You see seams in carpeting, grouting between tiles, cracks between wood floorboards, mortar between bricks, spaces between wood bookcases and a plaster wall; they all vie for attention. Keep in mind that the eye wants stimulation and variety, but this needs to be balanced with repetition of other elements.

Because we live in a highly colorful world, the shapes that make up whole structures and compositions should be as simple as possible. Complexity should not be the goal; the visual world is complex enough. Repeating shapes wherever possible is soothing to the eye, brain, and nervous system.

In architecture and design, and even when planning a dinner party, planting a garden, buying clothes for your daughter, or decorating your sunroom, the more similarity, the more repetitious shapes and colors, the greater the impact. When you decorate a room, symmetry and repetition bring harmony through balance. Chairs can be slightly different if you are a collector of antiques, but they should have compatibility in shape, color, and style. One fabric should dominate a room. One color should be predominant. When there is too much going on, it is similar to weeds overgrowing a garden, choking the simple beauty of the day lilies.

When giving a dinner party, have a theme and a color scheme, and limit what you serve. Feature chicken or salmon, not both. Let everything else be part of the composition that creates the whole. When arranging flowers in a vase, consider the impact of one flower in abundance: a blue pitcher of white daisies; a purple glazed ceramic vase the shape of a mustard pot, filled with hyacinths in pinks, purple, and white. Envision three dozen yellow daffodils in a clear cylinder where you have twisted the stems, making them as graceful as ballerinas. The eye is refreshed by this crisp, clean, clear visual statement.

There is . . . something special in the essence of beauty, a special quality in art: the conviction carried by a genuine work of art is absolute and subdues even a resistant heart.

ALEXANDER
SOLZHENITSYN

Grouping and Displaying Collections

We are soothed by similarity because visually we prefer similarities to opposites. This can be called the law of grouping.

Look at the careful composition the fruit vendor makes with lemons, limes, apples, oranges, and grapefruit. You see the power of repetition, like with like, apples with apples, grapes with grapes, carrots with carrots. He makes a great effort to arrange them, but it obviously gives him pleasure for us to see them looking their best. When you go to a flower store, notice how intense the colors appear when you see dozens and dozens of the same-colored flower. Because flower arrangers get paid for creating unusual floral bouquets, they rarely plop two dozen peach roses in a clear glass vase and say *voilà*, yet two dozen purple irises, peonies, or anemones look sensational, as do two dozen yellow tulips. Simplicity has power. Compositionally, it is more interesting and dramatic to achieve a balance of elements asymmetrically. In the law of grouping, objects either harmonize or fight for attention in their visual relationships. The closer they are in their specific category, the more freedom you have in composition.

When grouping objects, keep in mind the companion law of simplicity. Some parts belong together in close proximity while others do not. Look at each object, each form, for an echo of the shape of another. The cobalt-blue poison bottles on the window ledge are all rectilinear in shape: fluted blue bottles with wide, slightly rounded shoulders and a small opening. Because they are old, each one is slightly different in design as well as size. Some warn, in glass relief, "Not To Be Taken," while others state, "Poison. Not To Be Taken." But they are all poison bottles, all the same cobalt blue, all of similar design and proportions. Grouped together in size sequence, they are attractive. However, if they were randomly placed throughout the room on different table-tops and window ledges, they would confuse the eye, and we would miss both the charm of their similarities and the details of their differences.

Think of all the different ways you can

group parts together to create a cohesive whole. You can place similar shapes together, as in the example of the poison bottles. You can display objects together that are made of the same material—all brass, all glass, all jade, or all silver. Color is another way to group forms. If you have certain things that are in the same color family or of the same color intensity, these objects will look good together. I have a client who collects china. Each pattern belongs together in a grouping and looks unattractive when jumbled with other patterns. In the dining room glass cabinet, we were able to house each set in its own space, creating a harmonious composition made up of different but well-arranged parts. When you have several variations of a certain type of object—for example, paperweights—they will be extremely harmonious when placed together in the same composition. Small oval and round enamel pillboxes have repetition of shape, as well as a close range of scale and similar colors, and look better when grouped together than when scattered randomly among objects of a larger scale with less intricate detail.

I've been thinking about seeing. There are lots of things to see, unwrapped gifts and free surprises.

ANNIE DILLARD

When people dance, there is a similarity of direction. They move at the same speed to the same music; dancers belong together. What objects do you have that seem to dance together? What groupings seem to be natural pairs? Look for objects that are reciprocal, that complement each other. In cooking, salt and pepper, oil and vinegar, and bread and butter go hand in hand. With visual objects, the more strictly similar each form is to the others, the more unified the elements, the more harmoniously they will exist side by side. When birds fly together in the same direction, their speed and movement in synchrony, they go together compositionally. Look for consistencies in shapes, color, brightness, movement, material, and personality, remembering the principles of simplicity and similarity. Avoid having brightly colored pieces in the same arrangement with drab earth colors. When you repeat the material, you can group many different shapes together and they will be attractive: Consider a festive array of intensely colored silk pillows in various shapes and sizes, tossed in the corners of your sofa.

Each object in your house has a personality, a mood. Some pieces are sweet, some are whimsical, and others can be aesthetically sublime. While it is always good to mix and match objects of different qualities in a composition, let your eye judge to be sure something cute doesn't water down something of great artistic merit. I would never place my chartreuse plastic Slinky next to my collection of porcelain fruits and vegetables, but it might be a perfect playful note in my office, amid the brightly colored boxes I use for filing photos and papers.

Think of grouping things together where there is a theme, an intrinsic nature that connects them. What are the essential characteristics that bind two objects together? Because of our experiences, the brain and the eye will enjoy seeing a pen next to paper, eyeglasses next to a book, a watering can in a garden, soap next to fluffy towels. These are familiar references that tell a story.

Objects placed together as a collection should have at least one thing in common. For example, they could all be the same color or they could all have handles and spouts—teapots, coffeepots, and pitchers. They could also be the same shape but in different colors and patterns. Visualize all your objects with at least one thing in common. Look around. Can you spot some that have two or three or more? Photographs in frames, botanical watercolors, still life paintings, paperweights, crystal decanters, inkwells, carriage clocks, and fruit in a bowl have a common theme because they are the same kinds of objects. If you collect porcelain fruits and vegetables as I do, the fact that they are all porcelain and inspired by the garden makes them look good together.

- A collection of many objects of the same color and a similar design when grouped together do not look busy. To create a rich display, don't forget to place some in front of others rather than lining them up.

- When grouping your objects in a cupboard, begin by putting the plates, platters, and dishes right up against the back of the shelf. Secure them with a tack if there isn't a groove in the shelf. Next, place different-shaped pieces of the same family. As long as the color scheme is the same and the patterns are compatible, the shape variations will look harmonious, adding interest to the composition. The back area should be higher and larger in scale than the items you place up front. What you place in the front should never upstage the back or it will appear heavy and hodgepodge.

- An arrangement of several different-shaped porcelain vases in a variety of sizes in colorful solid hues is eye-catching as well as harmonious. If you had the same composition in a bunch of different patterns, it would look awful.

- If you have several objects of the same material and shape, line them up from large to small. The repetition of form and material will be relieved by the order of the graduating sizes. You can do this with baskets or boxes, bottles or bowls.

- When hanging objects on a wall, one over another, three is better than two. You can hang five, but not four. The eye wants to focus on something interesting, not the lines created by the negative space between the objects at eye level. If you have one large object, place it in the center, with the two smaller ones on top and on the bottom. When hanging an entire wall of photographs or watercolors in a variety of different-sized frames, don't line them up in any rigid, mathematical arrangement. Use your eye. If hanging three prints over a shaped headboard, the middle print can be several inches higher than those on either side. If the prints are the same size, you should use strict measurement, hanging them at the same height and distance from each other.

- When displaying objects in a collection, place the largest object in the center.

Simple Hints to Add Drama to Your Compositions at Home

Often all you have to do to bring vitality to a room is add something a little unusual, or do something out of the ordinary with your own flair and spirit.

- Place a lily plant in your bathroom so you can examine the buds as they open. Study the polka dots on the curled leaves.

- If you have some favorite colored glasses, display them on the back of the kitchen counter. They'll be ready for use and will provide a feast for your eye.

From so simple a beginning endless forms most beautiful and most wonderful have been and are being evolved.

CHARLES DARWIN

- Put a lemon on an end table near the lamp as a decorative object. Notice that people will touch it to see if it's real.

- If you want to make a small watercolor or design appear larger, use clear glass around it rather than an opaque mat. This way the object is suspended in air, drawing your attention to its features.

- Buy clear plastic shoe boxes so you can see your shoes displayed in your closet.

- Not all paintings have to be hung on a wall. They look less formal and permanent if you rest them on a horizontal surface. For example, place a small painting on the back of a table or on the back of a sofa. You can even rest several paintings against a wall on the floor. There's something relaxed about not having everything flat against a wall. Use plate racks as easels to rest small paintings on a ledge or on a table.

- Don't overlook the floor as a potential surface for compositions. Place baskets or a collection of wooden boxes underneath tables. Stack an assortment of marbleized boxes against a wall or at the end of a desk. Rest some prints or botanical watercolors on the floor against a wall. Place a basket filled with logs at one side of a fireplace and a set of polished brass fire tools on the other for balance and shine.

- If you have a pleasing composition on one wall that you love to look at, place a mirror directly opposite the favorite composition so the eye can enjoy its echo as well.

- The best way to call attention to a composition is to put one live flower in a vase. Our eye is naturally drawn to living things, and a flower never fails to delight us.

- When stacking books on a table, don't line the books up with the lines of the table. Place them on an angle to make them active and immediate. Have part of the stack hang over the edge of the table to add dynamism. Even a paperback book takes on energy when it is deliberately placed so a portion overhangs the edge of the tabletop.

Limits are an aspect of form, and are thus one aspect of beauty.

ROLLO MAY

Don't be too neat or too rigidly proper; the spirit enjoys loosening up rather than lining up. Often you see a composition that has all the right elements but somehow makes you feel uncomfortable. By placing the objects more dynamically, you make everything look and feel so much better.

- Some bottles are so attractive you won't want to recycle them. You can refill a pretty oil or vinegar bottle with less expensive brands in the future. Whether a bottle is inside a cabinet or in the refrigerator or on a shelf in the bathroom, your eye is experiencing the shape, color, and design. Some bottles have relief work on them. Look for attractive bottles wherever you are, and find ways to put them to practical and decorative use.

- Open a favorite picture book to a scene that especially appeals to your eye. Keep it open on a table. Every day, open the book to a different photograph. This will focus your attention, helping you to see one image well at a time.

- Take one favorite plate from a cabinet and hang it on a wall in the kitchen with a plate hanger. Every week, change the plate to a new design for a breath of fresh air. You'll notice the difference. See if anyone else does. Plate hangers come in seven sizes from two to twenty-four inches. Buy several different sizes—they are inexpensive, and in the future you can use them in any room.

- If you place a mirror across from a window, the design of the windowpanes will reflect in the decorative mirror, creating energy and greatly increasing the light.

- Place a tray on the back of a kitchen counter to hide the duplex outlet in the backsplash. Look under each table in your house to see if the electrical outlet shows. If you can see the outlet, try to hide it with a stack of decorative boxes or baskets. No matter how pretty or graceful the table may be, no matter how fine the decorative objects displayed on its surface, the eye will immediately be drawn to the ugly outlet.

  Look as well for any lamp cords that disturb the setting. Can you live with a brown cord hanging down a white wall? If you place a lamp to one side of the table you can tape the cord to the back of the table leg to hide it from view.

- When hanging paintings on walls, the center of the picture should be at eye level as you enter the room. Table lamps with shades, flower arrangements, and objects bridge the space between the tabletops and the paintings. Use this as a guide, but trust your eye in making subtle changes.

- A work of art should always be viewed against a solid color wall. The walls may have several paintings, making the wall composition complete.

Color Hints

- In dark-colored rooms, avoid white or off-white upholstery, because the outline of the furniture will dominate the space. The contrast is too high and the richness of the dark background makes the fabric look thin, as if it were muslin waiting to be covered. Generally, when you have dark-colored walls, a printed fabric with a dark-colored background looks best. In a hunter-green room, for example, a hunter-green plaid or floral print will look good.

- If you have white or pastel-colored walls, an upholstery fabric with a white (or pastel) background looks good, because it adds to the light, open feeling of the space. For example, you can have pale pink walls, white trim, and a pale blue–background print with some pink in the design. Or you could have a yellow wall color with a yellow background chintz, though a white background chintz with lots of yellow in the pattern would be equally successful. I once decorated a guest room with jonquil yellow walls, white trim, blue ceilings, and a white-glazed cotton jonquil chintz. You could almost smell springtime.

- Whether bookcases are the same color as the walls or a contrasting color makes an enormous difference to the composition. If you have solid-colored walls, the best way to integrate the bookcases is to paint them the same color as the walls. If you have pastel-colored walls, you can contrast the bookcases, perhaps painting them white to match the woodwork in the room so they blend in nicely.

If you have dark walls with woodwork in the same color, natural or stained wood bookcases will look awkward. They will appear to be free-floating rather than built in. The composition will look disharmonious. But when they are painted "out" to match the walls, they disappear in depth and structural form and simply become the receivers of books.

- If you have a fireplace, look at the interior fire brick. You can paint the brick black using fireproof paint in order to recess it and provide high contrast to the flame and embers.

- Dark green is a good color to put behind a display of crystal glasses or decanters because it is such a strong contrast to the light-filled crystal.

- If you have a white piece of linen with open-work embroidery, place it over a brightly colored cloth so the openwork is seen in a pretty hue that adds richness to the composition.

Colors have strong affinities to our emotions.

- Paint the back wall of bookcases a color contrasting to that of the sides and shelves to give depth and a subtle addition of color. Pale green, yellow, or blue is pretty against white bookcases.

- If you have a brown cabinet, paint the inside a pretty color so your objects will show well. If it is a valuable antique, you can stretch silk instead, in order not to hurt the value of the piece. Choose a color that will complement your objects. A yellow interior would be pretty with blue and white porcelain, for example, but if you have green rugs, pale green would be attractive also.

- Place exotic seashells on a dark surface in order for their form to be most visible.

- If you place some lemon and lime wedges on a richly colored dish—cobalt blue or Chinese lacquer red—on a white tablecloth, they will stand out. The same fruit placed on a clear dish would not be as eye-catching.

Creating an Indoor Garden

Create an indoor garden by filling a sunny window ledge with flowering plants, including hydrangeas, African violets, and daisies. Place a pot of English ivy on each side and build a 10-inch-wide × 6-inch-deep ledge above the window in the center. Put a small copper fish poacher on the ledge filled with trailing ivy. Train the ivy in the pots to grow up to join the ivy above the window by using transparent tape.

All creation or passage of nonbeing into being is poetry or making, and the processes of all art are creative; and the masters of arts are all poets or makers.

PLATO

- Geraniums look charming in a basket, as though they were just brought in from the garden.

- Look at your old watering cans as ideal containers for cut flowers, placed at a seating area in your garden or sunroom.

- Terra-cotta pots look best when they have been outside, in use, growing moss on the exterior. They are understatedly elegant when you use them indoors for orchids and ivy. Always place a glass or porcelain dish underneath them so they won't ruin the tabletop. When you see terra-cotta pots without a dish under them in a decorating magazine, you know they have been plunked there for the picture only. In this case, your eye is not pleased when it is being fooled. The best photographs are the ones that capture reality. The dishes make sense, and as a result, the eye and the brain feel at ease.

What kinds of gardens do you like best? Japanese, English, or French?

Why? To me, the English garden seems to thrive on neglect. Japanese gardens are meticulously designed and maintained. I always find them spiritual places for soulful contemplation. Many formal French gardens are too rigidly clipped for my taste.

Balancing the Hard and Soft Edges in a Room

The emotional quality of a room is made up of many elements, with line being a major factor in how the room feels. One exercise I find helpful with clients is to take inventory of all the furniture in a room that is angular with hard-edged straight lines versus curvilinear shapes and forms. Usually there is more of one kind than another. Add up all your straight lines and curves. What do you see? Are your rooms dominated by squares and rectangles with hard right angles, that make the space feel rigid? If you want a softer look, you can pull up a chair with curved legs and a shaped apron to a desk as angular as a Parsons table, and it will make the room feel cozier and more sensuous. Spaces are usually more attractive when they contain a combination of shapes. A room could have hard-edged ledges, contemporary and clean lined, and look good with antiques that are hand-carved and curvilinear. The contrast shows one off well against the other, just as a tree seen against the sky shows up better than when seen next to similar trees.

- Look at all the shapes in your living room. Study the direction of the lines and forms. Look for curves. When you see lots of curves, you feel greater warmth than when everything is too straight. Study the legs of tables and chairs. Examine the fireplace. Are there some curves on the apron of a table or in the mantel design? Ideally, you should have a combination of curved and straight lines because it's best to have a balance.

- Curves add rhythm. French Provincial style is a good way to train your eye to the rhythm of form. If you have a cabinet with straight lines, display some round porcelain dishes in it, or on the walls on either side of it, to add curves that will provide rhythm. What are some objects in your house that have great rhythm? Are they well balanced or symmetrical?

- Enjoy the way a square tablecloth draped over a square table has a triangular drape that softens the edges and creates a more romantic surface for dining. Think of Venus' flowing garments.

Balancing Positive and Negative Space

In architecture and design, we often refer to what we call negative and positive space. If you have something rich in drama, you may want to contrast its positive energy with some negative space. Negative space is not wrong or harmful but a way to allow the eye to focus on something important. For example, if you have a great painting you love, perhaps you could place a mirror on the opposite wall so you see the painting again in the reflection. This is preferable to hanging a second painting, because the eye won't know what elevation to look at. When you want an object to make a positive impression, make it easy for the eye to see and appreciate it.

Look for originality in every object. Feel the authenticity and sensitivity of a well-made form.

If you hang a colorful bold quilt on a wall over a bed, you could place another bold geometric quilt on the bed and the eye will see the two quilts in compositional harmony. If, however, you have a bold quilt hung over a sofa covered in a bright-colored chintz, the eye receives mixed signals and does not know whether to look at the sofa or the quilt. Looking at them together could cause dis-ease.

Look around your rooms and see if there are areas where two positive spaces compete with each other in the same composition. When you compose your outfit for the day, you don't choose two different patterns that will compete with each other. A plaid needs to be surrounded by negative space (solid colors), not paisley.

Composition Exercises

To help further train your eye, here are some fun and useful exercises that you can relate to your life every day.

- Observe others in a crowd. Watch their eyes. When a composition contains too many competing elements, our eyes dart from one item to another and we don't see anything well.

- When you hear a Beethoven symphony, you don't talk. You listen to the music, and in order to hear it well you have to feel it. When you face a natural landscape, a field, forest, or desert, or a seascape, the ocean, or a lake, understand it also as a symphony that must be heard as well as seen to appreciate it fully. As a daily meditation, go out and hear and see for yourself, alone and silent. Listen to the rustle of the leaves in the wind, the birds, the waves, and the rain.

    Open up to let an object speak to you as you look at it.

- The lower half of the visual field is dominant because it causes less stress to look down than to look up. The eye also favors the left hand, and because of strong conditioning in the way we learn to read and write, from left to right. In cultures where people write from top to bottom and left to right, they tend to be right-handed.

    The next time you go to the theater, notice that the lead actor enters stage left and often exits to the left, where the audience automatically looks. Observe this at the ballet and movies. When you look around your house, where do you look first? Most people will scan your living room from left to right. Take this fact into account in arranging your compositions.

- Go outside. Look inside through your windows at your kitchen, living room, and sunroom. Go inside and look at each space from the entrance door as well as from different locations in the rooms. Where does your eye go? Are your rooms pleasing to the eye?

- Learn to be a detached spectator in order to observe with a perspective that reveals the essence of what is before you. Step back and take it all in. Get a feeling for what you are seeing. Look at the big forms, the direction of the lines. Now look at the details. Feel their personality and character. Identify a variety of different forms. Look at the space between each solid mass. What's the overall feeling? Structure? Freedom? Softness? Formality? Too much variety? Too "matchy-matchy"?

- Study what is strong and positive when you look at a composition. What would you change? What do you like most and what do you like least? You can do this exercise at the supermarket while looking at displays of merchandise as well as at shoppers.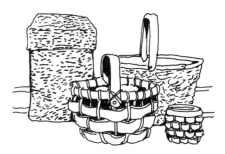

- Make a habit of trying to see three to ten new things when you return to the same scene regularly, say, once a week. Whether the composition is a coffee shop, supermarket, gas station, church, or favorite restaurant, gaze around. Be as detached as possible, free from emotional involvement, in order to see with new eyes. You will never see all the thousands of details at one glance, one visit. The scene in front of you is not static. Everything is always in flux. In nature, there is continuous change. Light is never constant. Look for the subtle as well as the bold differences, always recalling how things looked to you last week and last year.

This exercise can also be done four times a year, when the seasons change. If you live in a climate where there aren't dramatic seasonal changes, look for the subtle changes as light plays on the environment throughout the year.

◆ Observing a natural landscape requires keen discrimination, because it is indeterminate, not fixed or exact. Your eye needs to have the tools to see well in order to fully take in nature's stimulus. First, let your eyes deliberately sweep the landscape from lower left to lower right. Next slowly let your eye move counterclockwise until it alights on something that attracts your attention. Focus in on the color, the light and shadows, the shapes, the scale, and the symmetry. Is the scene harmonious and balanced? Keep your eye on this specific portion of the landscape until you feel you could envision it with your eyes closed. Now, sit down and close your eyes. Try to visualize the scene in front of you. Relax your body and concentrate your full attention. Do not peek. Remember that you first saw the scene from left to right, then counterclockwise. Spend approximately five minutes with your eyes shut, then open your eyes. How much did you recall?

An outward form makes a beautiful idea accessible.

To help train your eye, if you were unable to remember some of the major forms, do this exercise again. Concentrate on what you didn't visualize the last time. To be able to refer to this landscape in years to come, photograph it, adding what you've experienced to your visual memory bank. The more you're able to recall what appeals to you visually, the more wealth of thought you'll experience.

Studying Composition in the Home

View everything as a composition, even parts of the whole. For example, some of the most wonderful art you see is often reproduced in details rather than in its entirety. You see a detail of a Claude Monet garden or a

Fantin-Latour still life. Some parts of a whole composition are visually strong and are more arresting to your eye than the whole scene. When I lecture, for example, I show the whole composition of a house, garden, room, or table setting, and next to it I show a close-up detail of one rose in an antique tea caddie, or a chair with the light creating a dramatic shadow on the antique sugarpine floorboards. Look for the simplicity of the detail that is a true part of the whole. If you were to take pictures of fifty details of a room and scatter all the photographs on a table, they should all be compatible, pieces to be drawn back together to make the composition.

Light is the largest gem in the crown of beauty, and has the most marked influence on the knowledge of every beautiful object.

ARTHUR SCHOPENHAUER

Each part of a whole becomes its own individual self-contained whole. A chair, vase, and lamp are all complete in themselves, and when they are part of a room, they either add to or detract from the composition by their own integrity of design. A simple lamp made from a beautifully shaped vase has integrity and will not drag down a composition. A large cut crystal lamp with an enormous drum-shaped shade can seem out of place and may overwhelm the subtle details of the composition.

Photograph each room in your house from a series of angles. Stand in the doorway looking toward the windows. Stand with your back to the windows and photograph the doorway view. Stand in front of the closet (or fireplace) and photograph what is straight in front of you. By doing this, you see the depth of the space as well as the different ways the room is actually seen.

Don't try to take flattering pictures. Take in what you actually see as you move around. The camera doesn't lie; it merely records what you see through the lens. Of course, you don't experience space day to day looking through a lens. Your eye takes in the whole. But by breaking it up into smaller parts, certain elevations, you see the parts that compose the whole.

These are called "scouting shots." Often they turn into "before shots." You will see some eyesores in these pictures that you had never noticed before. Investigate what can be improved, where the parts can be put together in a more attractive arrangement. Remember, every room, regardless of its shape or size, can always look more inviting, fresh, gracious, and charming.

Changing Your Compositions at Home

When you see the same pictures on the wall month after month, year after year, the eye has no surprises and the paintings eventually disappear because the eye loses interest. There are so many distractions, noise, family events; it's important to move your art around from wall to wall as well as from room to room. Stimulate your eye to see new compositions. Switch your end tables from one end of the sofa to the other.

There should never be only one location for an object. When all the

elements that make up a composition are in proportion and of similar scale, there should be great flexibility in the arrangement of the parts. If you were moving, everything would have to be located in its new home. Imagining how you might rearrange things is a great exercise in opening your eyes. All change arouses heightened seeing excitement. If you change one thing, you should re-see and rethink everything. Remember, every whole is composed of integrated parts. Use your house as a seeing labora-

tory. Put a different chair in front of a desk. Move a love seat near a window. Put it at an angle in the corner so you can sit there and see a favorite tree outside. Now create a composition by adding a small tray table and an open-arm chair. See your living room anew.

Visual Editing: Focus on the Positive

Every scene, inside and outside our house, has some negative energy, elements we can't do anything about. This necessitates a form of visual editing where you focus on what is positive. Your living room might have an awkward radiator that you can visually ignore because you love the furniture so much, in the same way a friend might have a scar on his face that you no longer notice because you love that person. I could describe my view as beautiful, but you see it more objectively—the telephone wires, the cars, the houses that allow only a sliver of harbor to be exposed. Some people would get stuck looking at the cars in the driveway rather than gazing beyond at the view of the boats in the harbor.

No one sees well all the time. Once in a while it is a good discipline to take off your blinders and see the eyesores as well as the treasures. People see with their whole personality. If you're an optimist, you'll tend to block out more than a pessimist. It is always best to open your eyes. Even if you look past the cars, you should be aware there are cars in the driveway. When you're able to really see well, there's a good chance you can do something about some of the ugliness, even if only within the borders of your own home. Perhaps you could repaint your radiator, or rest a windowpane mirror in front of it. Until you see the situation, you can't find a solution.

For judging of beautiful objects, taste is requisite; but for beautiful art, for the production of such objects, genius is requisite.

IMMANUEL KANT

Taking Inventory

Think of your possessions as inventory. You have a lot of things—some good, some not so good, some favorite treasures, and some that are so ugly your eye is offended. You grow into your taste. Generally, when you are young, you haven't opened your eyes and don't have a lot of money, so you may buy inexpensive, gaudy objects that you will eventually outgrow. Perhaps you have bought things that served a functional purpose, but over the years you see that it is time to edit them from your inventory. You are demonstrating you have opened your eyes and are developing a degree of discernment. You realize that it is better to sit on the floor than to sit on a chair that sends out bad karma. There is such a thing as one rotten apple spoiling the whole barrel. No matter how harmonious everything else is, if there is a real eyesore, the rest of the composition will suffer, because the eye's energy is dragged down by the negative element.

See if you can spot one irritating object in a room or on a table or in your front yard. This exercise isn't always enjoyable, but it brings positive results. It's better to let go of something that doesn't fit in with the other shapes and forms than to settle for the confusion it creates.

New things are made familiar, and familiar things are made new.

SAMUEL JOHNSON

Keep in mind that there is some seriously ugly furniture in fashion today, and manufacturers and marketing professionals may try to get you to go along with the hot "new retro" looks. If you're lucky, something you've grown to recognize as ugly can be passed on for a profit at a garage sale or at auction.

Correcting Flaws

Ten years ago, when renovating our cottage in Connecticut, I'd had enough of the contractor's expenses and decided to take a break. Whatever work wasn't completed on the cottage would be done eventually, but not then. The inside surround of the fan window over the door was not completed. At first, I saw it every time I walked down the stairs. I thought of it as the Islamic flaw. In Islamic art, artists make one deliberate flaw in order not to offend God with man-made perfection.

Years went by. The children would inquire, "Mom, when are you going to finish the door surround?" I'd smile and answer, "Someday." I'd really blinded out. Ten years later, a contractor was doing work in the house and the unfinished frame obviously bothered him, because he offered to complete the job. The pleasure I get from its being framed and painted is enormous. I can now open my eyes with great pleasure as I look at this sight. Every house has a few of these eyesores that can be corrected. Looking back, it was bad energy to have our front hall look as if it were under construction for a decade. I'm not alone, however. The largest cathedral in the world, St. John the Divine in New York City, has been under construction for over a century and is still unfinished on the outside and inside. People have become blind to the scaffolding. Most of the congregation doesn't notice, because they are so accustomed to this incomplete look.

I've found it useful to train my eye by cropping photographs and pictures. I do this with slides and photographs I've taken as well as with pictures in magazines and books. The former art director at Doubleday, Alex Gotfryd, showed me how to properly crop a picture. He used to place Post-it notes, preferably white, on all four sides of the picture. He'd move them around until he formed the ideal composition. You can also do this with pictures you have taken of home compositions to determine how to change them for the better. I'm always fascinated by what I end up cutting out of a picture.

Common Mistakes and Simple Solutions

Last September I was asked to appear on the *Today* show to illustrate common decorating mistakes and simple solutions. The producer wanted to split the set down the middle with the mistakes on the left side and the solutions on the right. The wrong half of the set looked as though it had been decorated in the forties, just barely coming out of the Great Depression. The heavy maroon curtains and taupe valance hid most of the window. The beige venetian blinds were closed, blocking out the morning light. The furniture was all dark mahogany, very matchy-matchy, with pedestal bases; in front of a window was a three-tiered whatnot table cluttered with random objects without distinction. On the top was a crystal vase containing no water, filled with dusty, faded pink silk roses. There was a high glass-fronted cabinet containing crystal glasses and china plates that looked as though they were being stored in the living room.

The high-backed open-arm chair was covered in a sad, drab brocade that felt dingy. Dark maroon wall-to-wall carpeting covered the hardwood floor, the walls were painted in shades of beige and taupe, and a musty beige lace place mat that seemed to have come straight from an attic box was draped over a dreary brown coffee table.

There were objects scattered everywhere. The only place the eye could glance without feeling melancholy was at a white cachepot on the mantel filled with fresh English ivy, the one symbol of freshness and energy. Of course, the problem side of the room even had its half of the mantel stained dark brown.

Beauty without grace is the hook without the bait.

EMERSON

Walking over to the solution side of the set, we felt as though we'd awakened from a terrible dream. We opened the window to expose the full foliage in the sunlight, and we opened the cabinet doors to bring life to the collection. The walls were painted a cheerful bright yellow with white moldings and woodwork. Yellow, a primary color, has lots of wavelengths of energy and is a color you associate with cheerful sunshine. The reason I am not an advocate of beige is that it is not a clear color and therefore doesn't give off vital energy. Beige absorbs light.

On the solution side, the autumn leaves glistened in the sunshine that streamed through clear windows with white trim and shiny brass hardware. The white translucent curtains that hung from white poles and rings didn't eclipse any sunlight, adding warmth and a touch of romance.

A charming painted French Provincial desk stood in front of the window with a small vase on its surface brimming with fresh flowers. On the mantel, painted white on this side of the set, was a green cachepot with ivy as well as two pieces of porcelain, a bunch of asparagus, and a large artichoke. Over the mantel hung a small square painting of a quaint village in southern France surrounded by blue sky and blue mountains. To the right of the windows was an antique Italian fruitwood commode, freshly waxed. On it stood a white porcelain lamp in the shape of a mini-vase with hand-painted flowers and a white opaque paper shade that was properly proportioned for the lamp.

A small flower painting was placed on an easel, along with a silver oval-framed picture, two brass carriage clocks, and a square glass plate with a dozen colorful antique pens. (Whenever you want to display many small objects such as pens, always put them on a plate or a small tray.) Over the commode hung a painting by Roger Mühl of rooftops in Provence.

A chair was covered in a clear clean yellow-and-blue brocade. In front of the chair was a small sweet footstool wrapped in a purple-and-green silk plaid. Half the coffee table was painted in a pretty hunter green to contrast with the drab brown of its other side. An art book and a vase of *fresh* bright yellow tulips sat on the coffee table to create a simple, colorful, attractive still life, the yellow flowers echoing the cheerful yellow walls.

The true function of art is to criticize, embellish and edit nature.

H. L. MENCKEN

On the solution side of the set, the hardwood of the floor was stained in a natural shade, so the atmosphere was light and airy. On top of this lovely wood floor, we placed a pale-green cotton dhurrie rug with a refined pattern that complemented the brocade on the chair.

The yellow side of the room felt uplifting. The furniture and objects had been selected lovingly over time, and you felt invigorated to be in this space, refreshed by the clean clear colors, the sunshine, the cheerful art by Mühl, the porcelain by Lady Anne Gordon (a gifted potter and friend from England), the fresh flowers all sang a happy tune. The solutions to the mistakes were straightforward—don't block the light from your windows; maximize the amount of natural sunlight that enters your space. Don't crowd a room with boring matching furniture. Select interesting pieces that complement each other. For example, the table next to the chair in the solution side of the room was an old knife box on a stand, ideal for holding a drinking glass, a book, and a small vase of flowers. Have hardwood floors and an area rug rather than claustrophobic wall-to-wall carpeting. Paint your coffee table an accent color, because too much brown furniture in a room tends to drag it down. Use a clear color for your walls; if you want it lighter, tint it up with white, don't tone it down with gray or brown. Remember, the walls set the tone for a room.

The Power of Visualization in Composition

When you see a pitcher or a glass dish or a tray in a store or at a friend's house, if it catches your eye and you like it, try to visualize how this object would look in your house. Envisioning doesn't cost money. You may decide you don't need another pitcher or set of glasses or that your tray collection is sufficient. But it helps train your brain to imagine where you'd place something you see if you were to have this item in your life.

To be able to see a vase in a store, and visualize how it would look if it were made into a lamp, prevents frustrating mistakes. The more often you see an object one place and mentally transport it to another, the quicker and more skilled you'll be at visualizing how various objects will look in your rooms without actually bringing them home. Flea markets don't allow you to return something if you get it home and don't like the way it looks.

Every time you see a lamp made from a vase that has been wired, study its details. Does it have a wooden base? A brass base? No base? Where was the vase drilled for the cord? How is it capped? By examining the elements you see how things come together.

You look at a hat. You try it on. You look at the hat on top of your head. You look at a lamp. You look at a shade. You now see the lamp and shade as one, as if you were trying on a hat. If you don't like the way a hat looks on you, you try on another. You should follow the same process with a lamp base and a shade. You think you can see the proper proportion and scale, but you can so easily be fooled. A hat might not fit and a lampshade could be too big or the wrong shape.

Mrs. Brown once told her designers at a monthly meeting, "If you are an architect, the building could collapse. If you are a doctor, you could kill a patient. But when you are arranging the things in your house, if you don't like what you see, you can correct it." I think of this wise advice often. Even the most tutored eye can't foresee everything.

Certainly it helps to use your eyes actively. What you focus on becomes part of your brain trust. Whatever seeing experiences you have on your journey are imprinted, sometimes indelibly, on your brain, to be retrieved from time to time, sometimes several decades later. In essence, memory itself is seeing.

Visualization Exercise: The Larder

Look in your larder. Take visual inventory of the cans, boxes, bottles, and other objects. Scan every shelf. Now close the door. What can you remember about the contents and layout? Don't try to remember quantities of things, just categories. Write down everything you remember seeing. Open the door. What do you see that you were unable to visualize with the doors closed?

Look at each shelf from left to right, starting with the top shelf and working your way down. When the door is closed, you will remember the contents more clearly if you mentally scan the space in the same way as you did when the door was open. This exercise will help you visualize images of things you have seen that are no longer in front of you. With practice, you can train your brain to look at empty shelves and envision your supplies lined up. You will be able to visualize ahead of time dishes in a cabinet, books in bookshelves, linens in the closet, as well as where you want your appliances placed in your new house.

Genius is the talent (or natural gift) . . . the innate mental disposition through which nature gives the rule to art.

IMMANUEL KANT

Practice this exercise with a room in your house. Walk into the living room. Look at all four elevations. Look down at the floor space. Leave the room and go to another space. Sit at a table with a large sheet of paper. Draw a floor plan of the room. First locate the windows and doors, then draw in the furniture, trying to recall every piece. Go back into the room and see what you missed.

Mealtime Compositions: Eating with Your Eyes

Eating is one of the most sensuous, delicious, colorful, fragrant, stimulating, happy experiences in all our lives. I admittedly love food and I've always, since early childhood, liked sitting at a table that is set attractively, using linen napkins and pretty china and crystal. I sympathize with Claude Monet, who got up at four o'clock in the morning in order to capture the changing light, but got grumpy if his lunch wasn't delivered at eleven thirty, piping hot. I enjoy a beautifully served meal and try to eat leisurely, without rush or controversy.

Mealtimes are important to restore you (thus we have the word *restaurant*). Dining shouldn't be fast. I think the time spent eating a nutritious meal brings necessary restorative powers vital to our overall well-being.

Throughout my childhood, we ate our breakfast at a round table in a sunroom off the kitchen and always, without exception, we dined at the dining room table. We had large, white, monogrammed damask napkins with silver napkin rings. I don't know what happened to the rings, but I still have these napkins and use them with great pleasure. Some of the best seeing happens "at table" with loved ones or alone. You don't have to go to a museum to see an artist's painting of a table setting and wish you were there. You can set your own and walk into the scene and be at the banquet. You can see and touch your silver and crystal. If you don't have silver flatware, you can use brightly colored bistroware that is just as pretty in its own way. I love colorful glass plates and glasses at each meal, even if I'm alone. I get out a tray, put a place setting on it with some flowers and the food, and I go into the living room, light candles, play music, dim the lights, and have a rich seeing experience.

◆ When you go to a friend's house for dinner, examine the way the table is set. Imitation is the greatest form of flattery. Look around. Are there some ideas you can take home and incorporate immediately? If you keep a seeing notebook, write them down so you won't forget them. Everything you are attracted to somewhere else can in some way be incorporated into your own life. Once I noticed that a friend sets her table with the prongs of the large dinner fork facing down. I thought it looked charming, and now I often do the same when I create a table setting. I've always liked large-scaled forks, even for eating salads. When Peter and I ordered our sterling flatware, we specified twelve serving forks to use as dinner forks. Turning the fork prongs down looks handsome and feels European.

Table Accessories

I sometimes like to use fork rests. I found some in Provence made of pottery that look like peas in a pod. Simple crystal rests are more elegant. You can find inexpensive "chopstick rests" in oriental stores in a wide variety of colors and designs. Another tabletop accessory I enjoyed as a child are napkin rings. They add a festive look to the setting. You can find attractive napkin rings wherever linen napkins are sold.

A Restaurant Seeing Adventure

Do you have a favorite restaurant you go to regularly? Can you remember how they serve the butter? Are they butter balls, scoops, or squares? Is the butter triangular? Is there a sprig of parsley on top? Is the butter in a mold? Ask a friend or lover about the butter. Can you remember how the bread or rolls are served? By remembering their shape, you recall the pleasure of the taste. Are the small baguettes served in a wire cylinder on the table, or placed on a butter plate? What shape are the rolls or bread slices? One restaurant places two half circles of butter, one sweet and the other salted, to form a circle on a small dish. The salted half circle is garnished with a sprig of parsley to highlight the difference. An Italian restaurant might serve olive oil on a plate for dipping, while a Thai restaurant might serve a peanut dip.

The ear tends to be lazy, craves the familiar and is shocked by the unexpected; the eye, on the other hand, tends to be impatient, craves the novel and is bored by repetition.

W. H. AUDEN

Visual memory is essential to reliving pleasurable, sensuous experiences and translating them into your own home. What you see that you like outside your home should be stored in a visual perception bank for instant withdrawal.

Relive where you were last seated for a meal at a restaurant. What shape was the table? Do you remember the shape of the glasses? Were there flowers on the table? If so, what kind were they? Try to describe them, including their container.

What color were the napkins? How were they folded? Were there napkin rings? Were they elegant and refined or a funky paper or plastic design? Describe the way your food looked when it was presented. What did you have? Can you remember what decoration, if any, was on the plate? Can you re-see the decoration of the dining room? What style chair did you sit on? If you sat on a banquette, what color material was it covered in? Can you recall the weave? How did it feel to your hand? Was there a pillow? Can you remember the lighting? Was there a pink glow? Many restaurants decorate with red to stimulate the appetite. They often put a pink tone in the lighting for the same reason.

If you jot down a few answers to these questions, the next time you go to this restaurant compare your notes with what you literally see in front of you. How accurate were you? How well were you able to re-see what you had experienced?

This exercise can be extremely helpful in all settings to increase your visual perception. When you make a deliberate effort to see details, including graceful proportions as well as awkward ones, you are training your eye and brain to see more and more and more and more everywhere you look. You'll eventually  be able to take in a room in a sweeping glance. You'll absorb all the details that make up the room's composition. Remember, in every composition there is repetition of form, material, and color. If there are one hundred chairs in a restaurant and they are all alike, all you have to do is focus on one chair. Study how it looks from the front, side, and back. Is it comfortable? Is it compatible with the decor?

Whenever you see a detail you like, write it down or make a simple drawing of it to use in deciding whether you can use it in your own home in the future. I remember seeing some olive-knuckle hinges in a palace in Portugal that I was immediately drawn to. The shape appealed to me, and there wasn't anything like them available in the United States. I sketched, measured, and photographed them and later had replicas made for the indoor shutters of our New York apartment.

By seeing the minute details, you will deepen your vision to absorb more and more detail, eventually being able to see and feel the total composition well. But always remember to first focus on one thing at a time, so your eye and brain work together for accurate perception.

Arranging and Placing Flower Bouquets and Table Settings

Keep in mind that the entire home is a composition made up of smaller compositions. We create new compositions every day when we arrange flowers, prepare meals, and set the table. The morning we were to open our house to the public as part of the Stonington Kitchen Tour—an annual event that invites people to view the kitchens of eight houses to raise funds for a local charity—Peter polished some brass and silver at the table and I went outside to make flower bouquets for all the rooms. Everyone who comes in the front door of our small cottage is able to see the entire first floor. I wanted the repeated shapes of flowers everywhere, to please our visitors' eyes. The dahlias were so brilliantly colored, all I had to do was to put them in containers; they arranged themselves. The sheer profusion of flowers with their inordinate sizes and their intense colors—fuchsia, yellow, pink, orange—created a stunning overall effect.

I made bouquets using blue hydrangeas from the garden—they had turned to a purple-and-green coloration with the approach of fall—and sprinkled them around the house. For the library, I made a bouquet of white lilies and yellow snapdragons. Since this small cozy room off the living room has a good view of the water, we have two desks there, both facing the window, so we can work while watching the boats come and go. This is the room where we decided to put a large yellow still life painting after it was restored, because we have a yellow chintz love seat and ottoman that complement it well.

We gain in knowledge and truth by pleasing our eye through beauty because the beautiful inspires love.

As I placed the white lilies among the yellow snapdragons, I was thinking about the purity of my blue-and-white kitchen at the back of the house. What flowers would I put on the kitchen table? Would a white pitcher of dahlias of mixed colors be pretty? White and yellow snapdragons would also look sweet.

What table setting would I use? Soon Peter would be finished with the brass and silver polishing, and I could wax the old wood and set the round French farm table. Would I use blue-and-white place mats and napkins or bring in more color? One composition decision leads to the next. I love envisioning a table setting where everything is harmoniously compatible.

We had risen before six to start our preparations, so we had plenty of time and were enjoying ourselves. It was pleasant to go around the cottage seeing what finishing touches we could make to improve the way things looked. The best way to enhance your seeing sensitivity is not to rush.

Peter went around the cottage that sunny, happy morning and polished all the brass knobs and hardware on our antique tables. Whenever Peter polishes any object or piece of furniture, he likes to recall where and when we bought it and the features that attracted us to it in the first place. This regular examination intensifies his ability to see and appreciate the object's refinement. When you polish a treasured possession, you are expressing your love for it and adding to its energy.

What is it that attracts the eyes of those to whom a beautiful object is presented, and calls them, lures them, toward it, and fills them with joy at the sight?

PLOTINUS

After I'd placed flowers in all the rooms, I spread some French blue-and-white-striped tablecloths over the garden tables and made some flower arrangements for them. I put the cushions on the chair seats and on the bench, feeling grateful we'd be able to enjoy the garden. The sun felt warm at eight o'clock in the morning, and the humidity was low. Who could ask for anything more?

Peter came outside to have a look around and we sat together for a minute. Looking up, we saw not a single cloud in the sky. Everything looked so lush and pretty. We both anticipated a fun day. When Peter went upstairs to bathe and dress, I looked once more at the kitchen table. White. I saw it set in white with a touch of blue. It would look so quietly elegant. I inhaled deeply to take in the wonderful smell of simmering fruit and herbal tea. I had cut up some apples, pears, and oranges and heated them up in some water with several teaspoons of different teas—black currant, strawberry, and lemon.

I selected white, fine-cotton place mats with tiny, pale-blue French knots and blue cross-stitch borders. They reminded me of the smocked dresses Alexandra and Brooke wore on Peter's and my wedding day. To keep everything simple, I used the matching napkins. I selected white porcelain bowls with delicate hand-painted flowers, remembering I'd bought them in Chantilly, France, when I was there decorating a seventeenth-century house. For silverware, I used chrome with handles the same color blue as the walls' blue trim. I picked out some handblown glasses with blue polka dots and a narrow yellow band around the rim, but when I put them down on this delicate table, I saw immediately they appeared to be too much for the table's simplicity. I'd have to keep everything pure. I selected clear glasses like the blue ones I adore, with tiny bubbles in the glass made in a glass factory in Biot, a town in the South of France above Nice. We'd traveled there with the children when they were young and watched the glasses being blown before wrapping them up and bringing them home.

As I arranged some white lilies in a vase, I remembered buying the vase at the same factory on a different trip to France. The glass has a tint of blue and looked so lovely with the translucence of the white flowers. The display of white on the table was dramatic. I'd set only two places at the table to make it feel romantic and also to leave lots of room for the lilies to spread their wings gracefully in all directions. Looking down on the natural circle of the flowers, I noticed how prettily the freshly waxed round table framed the arrangement. Mrs. Brown had loved vases of the same shape where the mouth of the vase splays out, allowing the stems to hold their place and the flowers to find their natural flowing position. She also adored white lilies. Because she passionately loved flowers, I associate certain ones with her, very much the same way certain smells can recall a friend or loved one.

As the sunlight from a south window fell strongly on the table, the petals of the lilies looked like white dotted-Swiss cotton, revealing hundreds of tiny dots that recalled the bubbles in the blue-tinted glass vase and the clear drinking glasses. I hated to leave the kitchen. Walking out backward, I felt light as air. The whole space was blue and white with one yellow dahlia mixed in with some hydrangeas on the butcher-block table. I mused how right Mrs. Brown was when she told me, "Every room needs a touch of yellow."

Because of a burst pipe weeks before the tour, we had been forced to re-do the kitchen. Even though the blue paint color was identical to that before the renovation, and the only changes we made to the kitchen were to tint the ceiling blue, bleach and pickle the floor, repaint the walls, and install a gooseneck faucet, the transformation was dramatic. The gradual accumulation of favorite things over the decade had turned into too much stuff. The contractor had photographed the walls before starting his work so that he could be sure to put everything back in its exact previous place. Bill was delighted when I announced that I would put things back myself because I wanted to change the look entirely. Sitting and looking at those "before" pictures one morning at breakfast made me see myself more clearly and made me more aware of Peter's inclinations. We both love objects. We're both collectors. Once we discover we have gathered two or three things of the same character,

I think you have to be very quiet within yourself to be creative. You have to be away from noise and listen.

SYBIL CONNOLLY

we continue to add to it, creating a collection. Everything grows to become a bunch. Whether it's our collection of pottery, trompe l'oeil dishes, framed pictures of family and friends, antique wooden boxes, teapots, baskets, blue English medicine bottles, or brass boxes, the tendency always slants toward acquiring more. Over time the amount of possessions tilts toward the unbearable, creating an environment cluttered with odds and ends.

When you live in a house with a full basement and attic, you can store your overflow and remain in denial. I know we're not alone, but it took a burst pipe to force me to see I was choking our lovely kitchen with too many objects. Under and around the butcher-block table were dozens of baskets, collected from my travels since 1959. I love baskets so much I once wanted to write a book entitled *Baskets Full of Ambience.* I'd placed baskets on top of all the white cabinets. I usually like these areas to have space to breathe the way the Japanese taught me, but, over time, I forget. I love clear, uncluttered counters, but eventually they end up with colorful handblown glasses covering their surface because I collect handmade glasses and find them too pretty to hide away in a closed cabinet. Since the tour I've been so inspired by the purity of the way the space looks, I think I'll keep a watchful eye to be sure I don't destroy its serenity.

Become a Critic

One of the ways I've helped train my eye is that from time to time I become a critic, as I finally did with my beloved kitchen. There is a distinction between what is universally considered beautiful and what is ugly. No object is insignificant or below notice, because every object has a purpose as well as a design. Restaurant critics have six different ratings—extraordinary, excellent, very good, good, satisfactory, and poor. Go to a familiar place that you visit frequently. Pretend you are paid to evaluate how it looks and feels to you. Do this exercise at a coffee shop, a newsstand, a dentist's waiting room, a restaurant, your child's classroom, a flower shop, or the dry cleaner. What do you see? Make it a vigorous habit to pay attention. Look at the colors, the lighting, the cleanliness, the maintenance, the style, the furniture. Feel the energy. What do you see that is original, that has character?

To copy the objects in a still life is nothing; one must render the emotion they awaken in him. The emotion of the ensemble, the interrelation of the objects . . . all interlaced like a cord or a serpent.

MATISSE

You can also do this with one object at a time by really focusing on its form, the material, the proportions and scale, the composition of the elements. I am fascinated by teapots, because I love handles and spouts. I like watering cans for the same reason. Some are better designed than others. Look at a pot or pan, knife, apron, candlestick, or print on the wall. No one needs to know your rating, but assigning one will sharpen your eye and train your brain. Through training and perseverance, you will immediately detect objects that are visually offensive and recognize forms that please your eye.

Today, identify one object in your home that bothers you. You've lived with it long enough. It's ugly and you never want to see it again. It could be old, worn out, broken down, dingy, grimy, or just plain vulgar. What item is it? What are you going to do with it? While on book tour I became friends with a young mother who had a huge, ugly chair in her living room that was such an eyesore she hated the room. She never went in there and didn't want her friends to see it. When I pointed with my thumb and said, "Out," everyone spontaneously clapped and cheered. Her face suddenly looked like an angel's. She was liberated. The room looked 60 to 70 percent better, she later wrote me, without the chair.

Be Highly Opinionated

In order to see your own style emerge, you have to be highly opinionated about everything. Consider your home off limits to etiquette, to conventional rules of correctness. When you are concerned about a code of behavior or a particular "look," you will never feel relaxed in your own home. Most people who are worried or concerned about social expectations buy things they're told to buy rather than surrounding themselves with things they love. Trying to be "proper" is enervating and drains the vitality of a house. Any form of trying to keep up appearances is draining. Every home is different from every other home because each object is personally selected, speaking to and for those who live there. The shapes you have around you represent your personality, spirit, and enthusiasm. Be sure you see yourself in each composition in your home. Seeing requires using your own eyes. You can't play by other people's rules if you intend to train your eye.

Try to avoid having objects that advertise a designer. You pay for a product. It is now yours. No one wants to see what in fact is simply the maker's label. When selecting a silk scarf, pass it up if it promotes the company as part of the design. The most important part of a silk scarf you are going to wear around your neck is the border. The center won't show unless you frame it and hang it on the wall.

People who sell china, crystal, and glass have a vested interest in labeling everything for a specific use. There is a proper plate for one thing and another plate for something else, they'll tell you. But you can decide for yourself what you prefer under specific circumstances. People are never happy being told what to do, but all too often they let themselves be told because they feel insecure about their own taste. You don't have to follow

other people's directions once you have the tools to see and use them wisely. We should want to train people to open their eyes and see for themselves. There is no art in living through others' eyes and expectations.

Consider your wineglasses. How many different shapes and sizes do you have? Do you have champagne glasses or flutes? Put one of each form on the

kitchen or pantry counter. Study their differences. Look at the height in relationship to the width. Look at the base, the stem, and the vessel. Hold up one glass at a time so the top of the stem is at eye level. Examine the form of the cup, the tapering of the stem, and the curve of the base. You will see fine points, certain details, that make one a better design than another, not based on cost but on form. Some stems are fluted, as are some cups. Look at each glass. Are some cut crystal? Are any hand-etched? Feel the thickness of the rim, where your lips touch. Is the stem tall enough for you to hold it comfortably? By engaging in this exercise, you are training your eye and honing your taste. Before you put the glasses back in the cabinet, rate them based purely on how they please your eye, not on how expensive or inexpensive they are. What is your pure pleasure in the glasses in your inventory? You might like them all for different reasons, for different occasions. See for yourself, but don't be talked into buying "proper" wineglasses. Buy what is pleasing to your eye.

Composition is everywhere. You compose when you plan a meal. You compose when you set a table. You compose when you build a house. All buildings have tone, form, shape, texture, scale, and dimension that comprise its composition. Each room in a house needs to be composed from all the elements that bring it into harmony. Every tabletop can be an aesthetically pleasing composition. Arranging flowers in a vase becomes a composition. The way you lay out a garden is a composition. Even when you wrap a present, you are composing. Remember Matisse, who taught how vividly we can live when we pay attention to all the compositions in our daily lives.

FIVE

Transforming the Ordinary

Pattern and Rhythm

It is the eye that brings us into wider relations
with our actual environment, and gives us the
quickest warning of approaching impressions.
Sight has a prophetic function. We are less
interested in it for itself than for the suggestion
it brings of what may follow after.
— GEORGE SANTAYANA

Once you can see what you can do to transform the ordinary into the extraordinary, your spirit soars. Dignifying your daily life, expressing yourself creatively, and adding embellishments is a great human achievement and a sign of civilization. Honoring each moment with a meaningful ritual and celebrating big

Is that what they call a vocation, what you do with joy as if you had fire in your heart?

JOSEPHINE BAKER

You're able to discover a visual stimulus that challenges you mentally, uplifting you to feel exhilarated.

and small events with spirit and vitality is so simple, but few people go through life with this perspective. There seems to be a survival, or coping, mentality rather than a thriving of transcendent, ebullient energy.

Through adding pattern to the plain, by refining the crude, we add to the sanctity of life. When you plan, arrange, decorate, and ornament your surroundings, you create a sanctuary at home as well as wherever else you are.

All people who see well can vastly improve their lives. We see with our eyes and our brain and also with our soul and spirit. By improving what we have, whatever our circumstances, by adding pattern and rhythm to the moments of our day, we open up to a larger capacity to penetrate life's riches more deeply, more soulfully, more lovingly.

This chapter illustrates how to bring more pattern, design, and livelier rhythm into your daily life. Everything has movement. Nothing is static. We move about in our spaces, seeing and experiencing things differently all the time. We can think of our life as an upbeat musical, not a dreary drama. We can clap hands, sing out in praise, smile, and rejoice in all the glory we see, always transforming what is ordinary to elevate life to an art.

Pattern

Pattern is the primary ornamentation of life and perhaps the most ancient method of decoration (even Stone Age man put intricate patterns on his early tools). Look around you. Everything has a pattern, from a picket fence to the shadows of trees; from a flock of birds in flight to an old cobblestone street; from the fabric on an upholstered chair to

The eyes would be offended if the movements were not graceful.

SAINT AUGUSTINE

the grain of a wooden table. Woven baskets have pattern, a ceiling (whether coffered or painted) has pattern, and so do banisters, gates, and doors, as well as their hardware. The eye responds favorably to pattern

because of its inherent order, rhythm, repetition, symmetry, and unity. Without pattern, our environment, both inside and out, would be lifeless and depressing.

Patterns can vary in character from the most simple brick patterns to the most intricate painting on eighteenth-century porcelain from the Sèvres factory that supplied Louis XV. You see pattern and ornamentation in all architecture as well as in every aspect of

nature. How can we learn to better discern and appreciate patterns that surround us every day? How can we use pattern more thoughtfully in our homes to make our living environment more alive and intimate?

Seeing Nature's Patterns

To learn about the variety of patterns in our midst, we need only to walk outside. Nature is full of patterns. Examine the patterns on leaves, stones, seashells, pinecones. Study the contours in the sand formed by the waves. Observe the shape and pattern of a tulip petal. Hold it up to the light to see the fine design. Examine some variegated varieties where you see the pattern of another color on the petal. Notice how there are no hard edges or solid colors but fine brushing of lines and color. In a yellow-and-green variegated tulip, see if you notice a fine line of red.

Have you ever closely inspected the pattern of a spider web? One morning, as I was pouring coffee in the kitchen in our Stonington cottage, I spotted a perfectly intact spider web taking up the entire bottom half of the open east window overlooking our Zen garden. I looked through a magnifying glass and had a good, long, close-up view of the mysterious spider (whom we named Charlotte) and her web. How could anything, appearing so suddenly, be so geometrically perfect? At first, I didn't understand how the spider could trap other insects without being caught in its own tender trap. By careful observation the secret was revealed. The spider's web is composed of spiral strands that are sticky as glue and radial strands that are traversable by the predatory spider, allowing access to the victim caught on a sticky strand.

In nature, some patterns are constantly changing—the waves coming to shore, the patterns created on the sand, the wash of seashells on the beach, the light and shadow of the palm trees, the ribbon stripes of colors and clouds in the sky, the puddles of water during a rainstorm, the striped pattern from the lawn mower in freshly mowed grass, the pattern of light on the side of the house with the shadow of a row of birch trees—these patterns, in the same manner as sunrises and sunsets, are forever changing, alive, and profoundly beautiful.

Go to an art supply store and buy a small 5 × 7-inch spiral watercolor notebook with plain white paper and a roll of transparent tape. On a sunny day, go on a pattern adventure outside. Gather samples of leaves, ferns, grass, and flowers. Tape these findings in your notebook. Examine the intricacy of the designs.

When you walk in the woods, see how many different trees you can identify by pattern. If you like to sketch, do a simple line drawing of the leaves of a maple tree, an oak, a cherry, and an elm. At home, notice and identify the kinds of wood around you. What tree is your kitchen table made from? Look at the direction of the grain. Your pleasure from a piece of furniture is enhanced when you can visualize the tree the wood is from. If you have favorite trees, do you tend to like the wood that makes up furniture from these trees?

When you see a brilliantly vivid sunset, when the blue sky is a flame of hot pinks and vermilions, get out some colored pencils or paint swatches and try to find similar colors. Your eye will be amazed at the intensity of the hues. Minutes later, as the earth turns, the fireball sky becomes blue gray.

Most man-made patterns are inspired by nature. You see leaves on the capitals of Corinthian columns as well as on the relief work on buildings. Similar patterns are carved in marble, stone, and wood, etched in glass, painted on porcelain and ceramics, printed and woven on textiles and rugs. Wood furniture is often decorated with patterns from nature using inlaid pieces of wood, an ancient art known as marquetry (the equivalent in wood floors is called parquetry).

Seeing Pattern

Dr. Sheila Danko, a professor of design at Cornell University, teaches her design students how to think flexibly and use their creative vision to search beyond the obvious in her course Making a Difference: By Design. For example, she asks them to create a visual alphabet of found objects in a problem-solving exercise on learning to see: Find the letter S in an iron fence. Notice the letter H in a brass hinge. See O in a doughnut. Look for I in a key escutcheon. Look at floorboards laid in a chevron pattern and see V.

Each student took colored pictures to capture the twenty-six letters of the alphabet. In Danko's words, "Students learned to look beyond the obvious to discover hidden potential in everyday life and to develop a critical eye for the world around them. At first it was hard to see any letters; now most students say they have trouble not seeing them."

Her students created a poster printed with the directive "See things as they might be, not as they are," available at the Cooper-Hewitt National Design Museum in New York City and the Smithsonian Institution in Washington, D.C. Proceeds from sales of the poster go to support youth programs that put the arts and design into education to encourage students' creativity.

There is a great pleasure in the effort to invent the exact thing which is needed. Use it. Break it down. Begin again. It is a great thing to be able to see. Seeing is without limit.

ROBERT HENRI

Professor Danko told me how challenging it was for her students to find the more complex letters. They called on friends and family for help. Laughing, Danko said, "Rather than having one hundred forty students, we're really reaching about five more people per student because they engage everyone around them in the project."

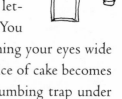

Do Danko's "learning to see" exercise with a spouse, a lover, or a child. Give yourself three weeks. Take pictures to record what you see. Use uppercase or lowercase letters. Remember to look at shadows as well as objects. You will become intensely stimulated by this project, opening your eyes wide to a range of seeing adventures you won't forget. A slice of cake becomes a V, a dented water drain a K, and the ubiquitous plumbing trap under the sink a J.

It is not necessary to hunt for the alphabet whenever you see an object, but you will notice that you are seeing more intensely, finding animals in the clouds and patterns in the grain of wood. Once you can look at one object and see something else, you will see into the depth of things. You feel more excited about the objects you saw well, and you will have the potential to see amazing things from now on through very different eyes.

Our Natural Attraction to Pattern

Because of our biological aversion to chaos, man perpetually tries to create order and unity through the repetition of pattern. We create patterns for our own pleasure, both instinctively and as an artistic form of self-expression. Whatever you do, consciously or unconsciously, you are continuously creating patterns. Even lining up a series of colorful boxes creates a neat pattern, and placing a bunch of pencils in a cup creates a pattern. The pattern on the hand mitt you use to wash your face, the weave and stripe of the cotton rug, the floral

Surprise is important.

GEORGE BALANCHINE

decoration etched on the glass mouthwash decanter, the pattern on your silver flatware, all are forms of ornamentation. The human desire to decorate, adorn, and create embellishments is deeply rooted in our pleasure at seeing—and creating—beauty.

All cultures throughout history have been uplifted by refinements, using bold, subtle, and intricate designs and ornamentation to embellish the rituals of daily living. The more closely you examine everything in your immediate surroundings, the more beauty you will see. You dry your hands on a cotton kitchen towel and see a beautiful woven design. You sip tea and discover some flowers painted on the inside of the teacup. The weave of your suit has a pattern. All textiles have a weave or a print. There are so many thousands of patterns that bring you pleasure, enrich the moment, and feast your eye. Go on a pattern hunt in your home, including your closet, and you'll be in awe of all the beauty you see.

Open a drawer and look at the dovetailing, a functional and most beautiful pattern. Look down at the floor and admire the herringbone pattern of the wood. I usually suggest that people look up in order to open themselves to the world above eye level, but there are so many beautiful floor designs, from intricate marble inlays to patterned tiles to patterned rugs. Look at all the colorful patterns on the clothes in your closet, from scarves to shirts and ties; look in the linen closet for the textures, prints, and weaves of your sheets and terry-cloth towels, blankets and comforters. Look at your tablecloths, place mats, and napkins for a variety of weaves and patterns. Go from room to room admiring the bold as well as the subtle. Once you look around, you'll see delicate beauty everywhere.

Patterns are the embellishments that create order and refine the rituals in our daily lives. The patterns of lace and embroidery work, and even the patterns on buttons, add refinement and increase aesthetic perception. Patterns please us in meaningful ways in our public celebrations as well as in our intimate private moments, helping us to see life's riches and experience them more abundantly.

> *Every man, however much he may seem to be all logical, cherishes at the bottom of his heart his own private store of imagination and poetry.*
>
> BENEDETTO CROCE

Our early ancestors saw the interacting points of light of the stars as representational forms. We intuitively connect dots, supplying the missing links. We have an inherent need to make wholes from parts. This is a visual phenomenon. Put a dot at twelve o'clock. Put another dot at eight o'clock and one at four o'clock. What do you see? Do you envision a triangle?

Shadow Play

Because I've trained my eye and brain to look for the shadows of objects—ironwork, etched glass, trees—I intuitively see shadows in spaces. The south light streaming through my kitchen window is brilliant, now that we've cut down a huge maple tree. On the bleached wood floor, it makes a pattern of light and energy overlaid by the outline of the double-hung window. The radiator looks like a picket fence, and the shadow of steam rises from the shadow of the radiator.

Look for shadows. They will help you see and know your objects better, and in quiet moments of reflection, they will enhance your pleasure in the time spent in your spaces. If you told someone you spent a few minutes staring at the reflection of your window and radiator while stirring chicken soup on the stove, they might think you're quite daffy. Enjoy these private moments of reverie. Seeing well leads to musing.

- Whenever you look at the grillwork on a door or a fence, or the pattern on the back of a dining room chair, look for the echo of the design in the shadow. This shows you the silhouette and separates the pattern from the form, so you see it without the distraction of the material, color, and other embellishments. Then look back at the real object. This is fun to do wherever you have enough light. Looking in a puddle after a rainstorm, you can see the reflection of a pattern of birds in flight. To really appreciate the splendor of the design of trees, look at their shadows.

A certain blue enters my soul, a certain red affects my blood pressure, another color wakes me up. I don't cut the oranges and reds like the greens and blues.

MATISSE

- If you have a colored glass plate with an etched design, place it on a white surface. White is light, therefore it is preferable to do these experiments on a white background with strong lighting. Lift the patterned dish approximately one inch off the surface of the table or place a flat piece of glass—perhaps a glass ashtray—under the dish to elevate it. Look at the bright light under the dish. Now examine the etched pattern in the shadow. The surface is tinted with the color of the plate. Lift the plate up slowly, then lower it. Once you know to look for the pattern echoed in shadows, you double your seeing pleasure. At a candlelit dinner, as you pass this dish around, watch the pattern dance on the white tablecloth.

- Years ago, I found a Day-Glo chartreuse Slinky at a gas station on Lake Michigan that has proven to be a great source of amusement for me. By placing a white piece of paper in my left hand and holding the Slinky in my right hand, connecting the two ends like an accordion, I'm able to see moving stars on the paper. You can find truth and enlightenment everywhere. While it is fun to play with the Slinky on the stairs with a giddy four-year-old, I love being able to play with it in the light.

- For a few dollars, you can amuse yourself for endless hours with a colored Plexiglas ring found in most children's toy stores. Buy a multicolored ring. Hold it up to a sheet of white paper and move it around, creating undulating swirls of light, energy, and color. A man can tuck this in his pocket, experimenting with it at his desk at the office. Colored-glass rings work as well, but they are expensive and may break.

The masters painted for joy, and knew not that virtue had gone out of them. . . . It was a fine effluence of fine powers.

EMERSON

- If you have a faceted glass or gemstone ring, you will see the facets reflected in the shadow on nearby surfaces. The next time you place a piece of cut glass on a white tablecloth, light some candles and notice how pretty the patterns are when contrasted against the white.

Outline, Form, and Pattern

Ornamentation should emphasize the aesthetic quality of an object, making it more ideal. This enhancement of the intrinsic beauty of the lines of the form adds refinement and harmony.

If you have any dishes with scalloped edges, cut-out borders, or any other repetitious forms that are not simply round, bring one of each pattern to the table to look at them individually. Now look at their shadows. Each design's shadow will inform your eye clearly about the outline of the plate. If you have some dishes you like because of their pattern and colors, turn the plate over so you see only the outline of the form. It's perfectly possible you've never really seen the actual subtleties of the form before, because the pattern takes over. When you feel you know the form, turn the plate over and examine the decoration. Usually you will see a well-integrated design, where the pattern is influenced by the form and uses it to create a more intricate decoration. For example, if a plate has a repetition of pinched-in areas, much like a piecrust, the artist takes full advantage of this by creating a smaller design in the center of these impressions.

When something is well designed, you will be instinctively drawn to it, but your pleasure will be enhanced when you can appreciate why the decoration is so compelling. I was raised not to examine the undersides of dishes to see where they were made, but I often do so in order to see the pure form of a dish's outline without the embellishment of ornamentation as well as to learn where it was made.

When you find the ideal interplay between pattern and form, you appreciate greatness. When something looks right to you, zoom in on it for further examination. Is the pattern familiar to you, or is it something new? Study the artist's technique. When you see something that doesn't seem to work, observe the decoration, then examine the form. Trust your eye. You may be looking at two disparate ideas being put together. A graceful Ming-vase shape is often more lovely in a plain color or decorated in a small-scaled, delicate floral design. When this bulbous form is splashed with large-scaled flowers, it becomes disturbingly busy. You couldn't imagine putting flowers in the vase, because they would compete with the pattern. I've often said that more than 90 percent of man-made objects are not made by people with an aesthetic eye and my aesthetic friends think this figure is conservative. Don't be embarrassed when you don't like looking at something. It is a sign that your eye is improving.

Who are you going to believe, me or your own eyes?

GROUCHO MARX

The cutout is what I have found to be the simplest and most direct way of expressing myself.

MATISSE

Pattern and Scale

Pattern can change the appearance of scale. If you have a blue-and-white porcelain vase painted with houses, trees, bridges, and people, and you place this lamp in front of a blue-patterned curtain, the lamp will blend in with the curtain, and the scale of the lamp will be reduced. If the lamp base is a solid color that contrasts with the blue of the curtains, perhaps yellow or red, the lamp will appear much larger. If you have a pastel-patterned love seat set against a light-colored wall, it will look much smaller than if it were covered in a bright solid color. Small and subtle patterns reduce the apparent scale of an object. Large bold patterns make objects look bigger.

Pattern Direction

Some patterns are directional and others are not. With direction in mind, look at each design to determine how the pattern is laid out. Examine a rug, fabric you want to use on a sofa, the pattern of wallpaper you want to use on your walls and ceiling.

Just as appetite comes by eating, so work brings inspiration.

IGOR STRAVINSKY

Many salad and dinner plates have a directional pattern and should be placed as squarely upright as possible, as if you were hanging a picture on the wall.

If you have a small rug with a directional pattern, do you lay it so the pattern is right side up as you enter a room, or upside down? If you have a hooked rug with a directional pattern—tulips, for example—make sure the pattern is right side up as you enter the room. If you have a hooked rug showing a dog or another animal, the legs should be closer to your feet as you enter; an upside-down dog would be disturbing to the eye. The rug should invite you into the room. Once you're in the room, your brain makes allowances for the rug being upside down.

I have a white bone china coffee cup and saucer in a tulip medallion design made in England by Coalport. The design has been perfectly executed in order for the pattern to have rhythm. Tulips grow vertically, reaching straight up from the bulb to the blossom. How would you imagine using the tulip as a design for a round saucer and a cylindrical cup with a handle? Take a plain white cup and saucer from your cabinet and envision the design. On the border of the saucer, there are four undulating medallions with one tulip in each decorative panel, located north, south, east, and west. What is the direction of each individual tulip? See the tulips in your mind. Do they grow from the bottom of the saucer to the edge of the rim? Do they go around clockwise or counterclockwise? The tulip located on the north has the blossom facing west with the stem and leaves facing east. The tulip located on the east has the blossom facing south with the stem vertically facing north. It's upside down. The tulip on the south faces east and the one on the west grows north. In the center of the saucer is a medallion, where there are four tulips that appear to dance with all blossoms reaching out toward the raised rim, one at two o'clock, one at four o'clock, one at eight o'clock, and one at ten o'clock. The leaves and stems are painted in a playful pattern, almost as though they were ribbons. This medallion with four tulips is repeated on the north and south side of the cups with the handle facing east. The tulips face the four directions.

This sweet cup and saucer show how to use a directional subject, in this case a tulip, in a nondirectional way. I can look at the saucer, turn it in all directions, and the tulips are always dancing, tossed around in perfect harmony and rhythm, echoing the curve of the saucer. By moving the saucer clockwise, you relocate the direction of the tulips. Maybe some of you have a cup and saucer with the same pattern and know the tulips are purple, yellow, red, and orange. The raised rim is brown. The true magic of this cup and saucer is how wonderful they look when the cup is filled with black coffee.

The center medallion on the saucer is not seen when the cup is in place. But when you sip your coffee, you see this pretty dish and appreciate the rhythmic echoes of the design.

Seeing requires looking beyond the surface of things into the depth of things. By taking the time to work out the pattern of the tulips, you see how much more you appreciate any good design. It's fun to know how to work out patterns as well as to know how they were created. When you commit yourself to seeing one thing well, you can transport this visual knowledge into all other areas of your life. My goal is to challenge you not merely to look but to see. At times you will feel frustrated because you want to see better, but once you catch on, you'll have the power to create visual statements that are echoes of who you are.

The Power of Stripes

Stripes can add drama to a room, especially where there are no competing patterns. In a bedroom, for example, bold blue-and-white-striped sheets would be most effective when accompanied by white curtains and a white quilt. Stripes are tigers. Leave them alone.

- Stripes are attention-getters. When there are too many parallel lines, vertical or horizontal, our visual system is upset. Stripes are rigid, forced, not natural.

- If you have a long, narrow room, a striped rug running the room's width will create the illusion of a better-proportioned room, more gracious in width. This same rule applies to a wood floor in a narrow room. Laying floorboards widthwise will give the room better proportions.

- Striped patterns on walls should be limited to entrance halls and powder rooms because they are repeated on all four elevations. Because of their rigidity and vertical strength, they are more distracting than soothing in rooms where you might want to read or admire art on the walls. Striped curtains are attractive and striped pillows can be an appealing accent in a room.

- Stripes are the most obvious directional pattern. If you are using a stripe pattern on a bench, it can run vertically with the selvage on the left and right. If you choose to use the same stripe on a sofa, first study how the stripes will run. You may decide it would be too busy with the stripes going in different directions.

Stripes on the Diagonal

Avoid using diagonal stripes on furniture, because the absence of vertical symmetry is unsettling to the eye. However, a wood floor laid on the diagonal has added interest and depth because the eye follows the line, causing the room to appear larger.

I learned of the power of the diagonal line years ago when I bought a red, white, and blue dress. I was drawn to this dress the moment I saw it on a hanger—and soon discovered how dramatic it felt to wear it. The diagonal stripes had energy, tension, and excitement. I never went unnoticed when I wore that dress.

Think about a man's necktie. When you see a stripe, it is usually on the diagonal. There's a punch to stripes on an oblique angle. The excitement is in the angle of the stripes coupled with the color combination.

Visualize a red-and-white candy cane. The red-and-white stripes on the diagonal are attention-getting. On trains, diagonal stripes are used to alert you to the railing of the steep steps to the station platform. When you put a striped tablecloth on a table, you will see the stripes on the diagonal because of where you are sitting or standing. When stripes are perceived on an oblique angle, they have a powerful impact on the space.

* If you are upholstering or slipcovering a sofa or chair in a stripe, consider using a welting (a fabric-covered cord that fills in the seams) in a solid color found in one of the stripes. If you use a self-welt (made of the same fabric as the upholstery), the stripe

is cut on the bias, or diagonal, so it looks like candy-cane stripes and is disturbing to the eye. But when used on a chintz-covered chair or sofa, self-welt blends in harmoniously.

If you want to add drama to a pair of striped curtains, you can make a one-and-a-half-inch cuff using the same fabric on the diagonal. The treatment is energetic without being busy.

- ◆ A zigzag pattern always attracts the eye and can be cause for uneasiness; if it is too strong the eye will look away. The combination of zigzags and stripes is unsettling as well.

Pattern Combinations

Look at patterns on fabric, wallpaper, and rugs, and notice the variety of shapes and geometry. When something is well designed, you see the pattern as a whole unit, a cohesive design. If a pattern is not well balanced, certain areas will pop out at you, disturbing the harmony. Different patterns can coordinate with each other if they repeat colors. When 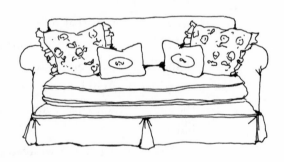 using a large-scaled pattern, select small patterns to go with it so that the eye can focus on the dominant design. In our living room, we have a floral chintz on the upholstered furniture. The cushions on the open-arm chairs are covered in a small, geometric, snowflake pattern.

- ◆ Several simple and complex patterns and details combined create a whole design built up from the simple to the complex form. Simple checks, plaids, pinstripes, and small geometric designs can be used with large floral designs as well as with Chinese patterns containing figures, as long as the colors coordinate closely and there is breathing space around each different fabric. Think of musical harmony, where instruments in the background support the main compositional theme.

- How many different fabric patterns do you have in your living room? How many solid colors do you have? Is there pattern in the weave of your fabrics? How many different colors do you see in a particular chintz? When selecting a print, often you see only the colors in tiny squares on the selvage, but a well-designed chintz could have as many as eighteen colors; some have even more. Usually a room has five or more colors besides the browns of wood. The more shades and tints of a color in a room, the softer the effect. Prints with a large number of colors create a richer, softer appearance than one with fewer, bolder colors.

- Do you have a pattern in your rug? If your furniture is upholstered in a printed fabric, and your furniture sits on a patterned rug, the upholstery should not have a white background—and preferably not even white in the design—because white is strong in a richly colored pattern and will compete with the rug design. An Oriental rug with a light background makes it difficult to use patterned fabrics on furniture that sits on it.

- If your room is monochromatic, you can use several small-scaled patterns in the space because the colors are all harmonious. A blue-and-white room can have plaids, checks, florals, and solids and not appear too busy as long as the patterns are in shades of blue with white.

- You can use different-patterned dinner plates; as long as the size and color scheme are similar, they will look harmonious.

- You can mix many china patterns together if the theme and colors are of the same family—for example, flowers or geometric patterns.

- When you place pattern on pattern, the colors and designs should echo each other. A linear print on a sofa that sits on an Oriental rug should have similar hues as well as flowing lines that are compatible. Squint to see how closely they relate. If you are using a printed material for curtains and have a patterned rug, the colors should be repeated in both the curtain material and the rug. To relieve the busyness of chintz upholstery, you may choose a rug with simple stripes or a small geometric design with a decorative border, for elegance.

- If one fabric pattern dominates a room, the other designs should be considerably smaller in scale and repeat at least one color of the main fabric.

Work and play are the same. When you're following your energy and doing what you want all the time, the distinction between work and play dissolves.

SHAKTI GAWAIN

Ornamentation Reveals Personality

Ornamentation sets the tone of an object, but there should always be a harmonious connection between the pattern and the form. The distinctive features of a form convey the essential character of an object, and its ornamentation should extend our understanding of its character. A delicately patterned teacup is functional, but it also serves a second purpose—it has been decorated to be used for social events and add to the appearance of a room. Often teacups and saucers are displayed on a rack or put in an open cupboard for viewing, not hidden away in a dark storage space. The ritual of tea is by definition social, and its utensils are ornamented for public use and pleasure.

The essence of a spoon, a ring, a piece of furniture, a silk tie, a napkin, a room, or a house is ornament working in tandem with form. Whether for one person or for a celebration, ornamentation makes things pleasing to the eye. All ornament has character. Ornament informs the eye of the character and nature of an object because it is specific. You feel harmony or discord. Patterns are part of the world's whole, making a statement about order and beauty in a detail—a floral design, a shell motif, stars, or angels.

Just as artists are not aware of their style because it is not separate from them but mirrors their personality, you reveal yourself in everything you see as well. Look for the connection between the pattern and the person. You'll be informed by what you see and be able to incorporate this awareness into your own surroundings. You may not be a stripe person. You might love chintzes because of your passion for gardening.

The aim of every artist is to arrest motion, which is life, by artificial means.

WILLIAM FAULKNER

We are all highly opinionated when we see acutely. By observing the various shapes and colors of ornamentation, you discover that you are drawn to certain forms and patterns while others do not attract you. Only by really observing what details you like and don't like will you be able to bring home the good and leave the visually bad outside your immediate environment. Open up to see everything. Be stimulated by what you see and like and what you see and don't like.

Seeing well leads to the self-knowledge that is translated visually in your home. One way to evaluate your appreciation of ornamentation is to walk around a city or town and look at the ornament on architecture. Notice that certain shapes appeal to you, while other patterns make you feel uncomfortable. While you may enjoy round shapes, an architectural frieze with circles broken up with vertical fluting may appear monotonous to you, whereas an egg-and-dart detail is more interesting. Does this realization lead you to conclude that you prefer an oval or egg shape to a circle or round form? Recall that the circle, when seen flat as on a frieze, is too strong, just as a series of round windows would be because it doesn't have any vertical-horizontal frame of reference to the building. Recall how eye-catching polka dots are—but how monotonous they can be, to some tastes.

Human beings ought to communicate and share all the gifts they have received.

MEISTER ECKHART

Pattern Associations and the Intimacy of Pattern

Ornament must have meaning and significance. What is the story behind the decoration? Ornament is always part of something else. When the girls were little, I put brightly colored plaid, striped, and polka-dot ribbons in their hair, just as my mother did in mine when I was young. I designed a ribbon tablecloth using these different-patterned ribbons that was later made into a fabric design. The emotional, warm story behind this whimsical geometric pattern makes the design young, fresh, and happy—and that is how I feel every time I see it. (To make your own ribbon design, use the same ribbon for the length as for the width. Whatever you do vertically, repeat horizontally. This will balance the pattern so it will be nondirectional, and the design will be pretty from all four sides.)

Patterns have a strong power of association and can transport you thousands of miles away. One of my favorite types of printed textile is a monotone, with one color—often red or blue—printed on a natural linen ground, often with a historical subject. Called *toile de Jouy* after a town in France, this fabric reminds me of France. It looks charming when used with French Provincial furniture.

◆ When you see one pattern or ornamentation you like, be on the lookout for more objects with the same ornamentation. You may have favorite dessert plates from Germany and delight in the delicacy of the hand-painted flowers, different on each plate. You may enjoy hunting for more like them, or for solid-color dishes or glasses to complement them. You may discover patterns you associate with happy times at your parents' or friends' houses. Patterns always have the power to recall pleasant memories. When your children grow up and live away from home, they return for visits with fresh appreciation of

It is extraordinary how extraordinary the ordinary person is.

GEORGE F. WILL

what they were exposed to growing up. Suddenly they see these patterns as pieces of their childhood, and all their collected memories open up. I grew up seeing my grandmother's butterfly quilt on my parents' bed. Every time I see it now, I recall my grandmother and can visualize my parents' bedroom in vivid detail. When Alexandra and Brooke left home to live in their own apartments, they took their antique patchwork quilts with them to put on their beds so they would always feel a connection to their childhoods.

- To revive a pleasure, buy a tablecloth or set of napkins from a favorite inn or restaurant. Every time you set the table you'll relive the memory, re-seeing it in all its detail. I bought a pastel floral tablecloth in a gift store in Provence in the early 1980s. Every time I use it, whether on the kitchen table or out in the garden, I visualize our enchanted breakfasts in the garden of the inn. The pattern keeps that memory vivid. One day Claude Monet noticed that the fish he had just purchased was being wrapped in colorful Japanese prints. He later came back to the market and purchased the whole stack of prints. Some still adorn his lovely house in Giverny.

- A blue-and-white, hand-painted porcelain inkwell can evoke strong memories of Provence. The scallops on the top may remind you of the apron on your French Provincial end table. But it is the flower pattern, hand-painted in shades of French blue, that adds to your pleasure, because you recognize this faïence as French Provincial, a favorite style.

- The more attention you pay to the ornamentation of an object, the more you are attracted to it and the more fixed it becomes in your mind. There are certain patterns your eye always delights in seeing— china patterns, etched crystal, marbleized end paper in a book.

- The ornamentation on an object adds intimacy to your private moments of contemplation. If you are drawn to an object because of its happy design, unity of pattern, and color, you will instinctively examine all of its intricate details. One of my favorite coffee cups and saucers is made of English Wedgwood bone china. The outside of the cup is all white with three fine bands of gold. The saucer is deep and white in the center with a gold band along the edge. If you put the cup and saucer on a high shelf, it looks plain, though you can see its simple and graceful form.

Art is a human activity having for its purpose the transmission to others of the highest and best feelings to which men have risen.

LEO TOLSTOY

When you bring the cup and saucer to eye level—as when serving or drinking—you are in for a delightful surprise. The pattern is all on the inside of the cup and saucer. A bold ivy-chain pattern decorates the white edge of both the cup and saucer. Below this border, a wide band of Wedgwood blue spatterware ends with two fine gold bands, leaving the middle portion of the saucer as well as the cup white. The ivy reminds me of the ivy climbing the trellis in our tiny walled-in garden.

When you are satisfied with the way the color and pattern are executed in an object, you become one with the unity, and you can't see how the artist could have conceived it any other way. If this ornamentation were on the outside of the cup, it would seem showy and redundant against the patterned saucer. Instead, the graceful form is white on the outside, with just enough gold banding to bind the cup and saucer together visually. The handle of this simple white cup is blue on the outside and gold inside, leading your eye into the blue inside the cup and curving down to connect to the blue of the saucer.

When an object is visually stimulating, you see everything better. Seeing is especially enjoyable when you are indulging in a moment's refreshment. The next time you sit down to tea in your home or elsewhere, pay attention to the patterns of the teacup, the saucer, and the other china. Eventually, you will have a large appreciation of different china patterns. Study favorites and try to visualize them as a fabric design or as wallpaper. A great deal of inspiration comes to artists from these intricate patterns.

Learning is movement from moment to moment.

KRISHNAMURTI

◆ The next time you're in a puttering mood, spend a half hour rearranging the cabinet where you store your teacups and saucers as well as demitasse cups and saucers. You probably have a variety of designs, colors, and shapes, many beautifully hand-painted. Touch each one and examine the proportions and the delicacy of ornamentation. Look at the details through a magnifying glass. Examine the fine brush strokes of the leaves, flowers, birds, butterflies, and other images. Pretend you have a fine brush in your hand and are painting on the decoration. Study how many different colors were used. Do you have some cups and saucers that you particularly like? Put your favorites on the kitchen counter. With a keen eye, analyze why you like these the best. How long have you had them? Where did they come from? Did you purchase them or were they gifts? Do you like them for sentimental reasons or because they are intrinsically beautiful? Is there a decoration to the design? Is there a border pattern? What are the colors? Do some have gold in the design? Is your selection varied in size and delicacy of detail? I think it is more fun to have

There is nothing in this world constant but inconstancy.

JONATHAN SWIFT

a variety of cups and saucers rather than one large set. That way you have a continual feast for the eyes.

Put everything back with a fresh, up-to-date evaluation of what patterns you currently like best and want to expose yourself and others to. Weed out the sets you no longer like. Every cup and saucer has a personality. There is a story behind what you see. You may find that you have lots of different ones that delight you and will give you pleasure when you are in different moods. You may be inspired by thinking of the different countries where the china was made. (If there is an Oriental pattern, you'll feel transported to Asia.) You may also find some disorganization that needs rearranging with a critical eye. To a tutored eye, it is unsettling to see mismatched cups and saucers. Each *set* can be different, but the eye is offended by random confusion and delighted by the beautiful discipline of matching patterned cups and saucers.

The Patterns of Mealtime Celebrations

So it has come at last, the distinguished thing.

HENRY JAMES

Every time you prepare and serve a meal, you are creating edible patterns, with the plate as the background or canvas.

When you plan a meal, draw a series of circles on a piece of paper representing different courses. (If you prefer square plates, draw squares.) Visualize the food on the plates from the salad, soup, and main course to the dessert course.

All patterns have a color scheme. The color scheme of your food is as important as the color scheme of the flowers, napkins, china, and tablecloth: Food creates both a composition and pattern.

Visualize what you are serving on a plate before selecting the plate. You don't want the pattern of the food to compete with the pattern on your china. Plates that have a border pattern and plain center are easy, because the border frames the food. String beans can be artistically arranged and "tied together" visually with a sliver of red pimiento or a curl of lemon or orange rind. The food groups need space between them to breathe, just like the items on your table or the objects in your rooms.

Zest is the secret of all beauty. There is no beauty that is attractive without zest.

CHRISTIAN DIOR

Pattern Tips

Here are some tricks of the trade that will help you envision how your patterns will look in your home.

- If you want to see what a carpeting or rug pattern will look like when multiplied in space, place the swatch or sample in a corner of a room with two perpendicular mirrors forming a right angle. You can inexpensively buy squares of mirror that will help you to visualize the pattern in the room's dimensions.

- When choosing a pattern for a sofa, chairs, or curtains, always look at as large a sample cutting as is available. Often a small cutting cannot indicate what the fabric will look like in a large amount. Again, put two mirrors at right angles in a corner, take your sample, and put it in front to observe how the fabric will look in a larger piece.

- When patterns are simple and regular, they give off a feeling of order. Geometry and symmetry in pattern nicely counterbalance the multiplicity of nature. For example, if your room has a view of a large natural landscape, the simpler the pattern you use for your furniture and curtain fabrics, the better. If the view from your windows doesn't include trees and other growing things, patterns inspired by nature will bring the natural world inside. There should be no competition between the real patterns outside and the fabric patterns inside.

- Cover an octagonal hatbox in a favorite fabric print. Leave it out in your bedroom or next to your desk, filled with letters from loved ones. Line the inside of the box in the same fabric or spray-paint it a color you find appealing. Let it be a surprise for your eyes only.

- Line up a selection of small, different-shaped bottles on a shelf in your bathroom and look at the pattern created by the variety of forms.

- If you use fabric with a vertical stripe on a sofa or chair, be meticulous to ensure that the stripes on the back of the sofa and chair line up with the cushions and with the front. Any wiggle to the left or right will give the eye an uneasy feeling.

Sometimes skiers will talk about having a physical experience that's sort of metaphysical. They might call it an out-of-body experience.

LES OTTEN

- Baskets add pattern and texture to a room. When not in use, they can be displayed under a long serving table.

- Checks and plaids create a country mood, especially when used in rooms with pine furniture. When combining checks and plaids, repeat the same colors to harmonize the different patterns.

- An oversized print will look spotty if upholstered on sofas and chairs because the design gets cut up. Consider a large pattern for curtains because the design can flow without interruption. Also, the folds of the curtains will visually reduce the appearance of the large scale, making it look more graceful. If you have a large-scaled botanical pattern you want to use for curtains, use less fullness in the gathering.

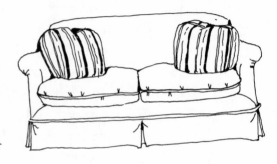

- Consider hanging a collection of

patterned plates on the wall next to the tub. Select three pairs and a single plate to place in the center. Hang the center plate first. Then place one pair above and below the center plate. The two pairs should divide the space on the sides of the center plate in order for the outer edges of all the plates to form a circle.

> *All human actions have one or more of these seven causes: chance, nature, compulsion, habit, reason, passion, desire.*
>
> ARISTOTLE

- When you display your objects, remember that any collection creates a pattern. Put like objects with like objects, and group objects of the same size together. The eye, remember, needs to focus on the center of a shelf, cabinet, wall, or mantel.

- Put a white paper doily on a dark-colored plate. You immediately see the doily's lacy openwork pattern. If you have a lace or eyelet blanket cover, place it over a colored blanket or sheet in order to see a contrast that will emphasize the pattern. Openwork linen has a pattern as pronounced as a printed design. Rather than its being red, white, blue, or yellow with the cutout work looking gray because of shadows, place a favorite color underneath to emphasize the design, thus adding warmth and sensuality.

- A patterned fabric on upholstered furniture breaks up the form and softens the lines, making the chair or sofa look smaller. If your sofa is too large in scale for the size of the chairs, use a chintz pattern on the sofa, and a solid fabric on the chairs that is the background color of the sofa; the chairs will look larger and the sofa smaller.

- When using a pattern in a room, use it in abundance. You can create the impression of an indoor garden by putting a floral chintz on the furniture, alternating the repeat so it doesn't fall in exactly the same place on each piece of furniture, thus preventing boring repetition.

- When considering a tile with a geometric pattern for a bathroom, kitchen, or bar sink surround, always look at four tiles together in a square, because the corner decorations on each tile will create a larger pattern when joined.

- If you have a strong plaid blanket, and you want to soften the colors, place a white sheet over it as a coverlet on the bed. You will see the plaid pattern filtered by the white.

- To add rhythm and pattern to a room, you can highlight your moldings by using a contrasting color or a deeper color in the same hue as the walls. If you have moldings under the chair rail attached to the wall space, you can paint them yellow, if the trim, including the wainscoting (the space below the chair rail), is all white and the walls above are yellow. The repetition of the yellow on this molding will integrate the upper walls and the lower area. If you want to add pattern and texture to a space, consider installing applied moldings on the flat wall space between the chair rail and the baseboard. This adds warmth and rhythm to an otherwise flat, dull, unadorned space.

Every day it is a new beach for me. I see it with new eyes.
EKNATH EASWARAN

- On a painted chest of drawers or a high cabinet, use a darker hue to articulate the moldings. The piece of furniture can be Brittany blue and the moldings on the drawers could be a blue several shades darker.

- Avoid decorative switch plates. Why call attention to an electrical outlet, something that is strictly utilitarian? Refrigerators and switch plates should be designed to do their jobs, to keep food cool and to turn a light on and off.

    On a white wall, the light switch should always be white. If you have brown switches, it is inexpensive to have them changed to white. If you have a fancy decorative switch plate, remove it, buy an inexpensive plain one at the hardware store, and paint it the same color as the wall. If the walls are covered in wallpaper, cover the switch plate with the same wallpaper. If the wallpaper has a design, be sure to match up the pattern exactly. Any variance will disturb the eye.

Think about the vital energy the Chinese call ch'i.

♦ Wallpaper is repetitious and static. I prefer seeing art on the walls because it can be moved around and added to and it expresses the personality and taste of the owners more than wallpaper can. Use pattern for your furniture, not your walls. Keep the walls simple and plain so you can have bookcases filled with the pattern of books and can hang prints, photographs, or paintings without worrying about their compatibility with the wallpaper pattern. Complex wallpaper patterns are too busy to hang art on because the design competes with the decorations.

Every soul is a melody which needs renewing.

STÉPHANE MALLARMÉ

Pattern Exercises

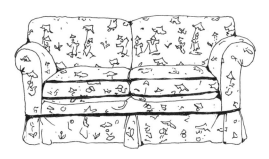

♦ When you walk on a sidewalk, patio, or garden path, notice the material and pattern of the surface. Examine the brickwork, the stonework, and the way the material is joined, especially the pattern.

♦ When you're taking a walk in the country, study the fences you come across. Notice the different types of white picket fences and iron fences. Count how many different patterns you find.

- Notice the steam in your coffee cup, the pattern it makes, and how similar it looks to a gray translucent version of fire. Hold your cup up to the light or a lamp. The fact that heat rises provides you with a few moments of quiet amusement, a seeing pleasure for its own sake, a Zen time to meditate.

- A stack of firewood is a pattern. If you have the space to create a square stack, rest four logs east to west. On top of this base, place four logs north to south. Repeat this pattern until you reach a desirable height. This nondirectional pattern is pleasing to the eye. Remember the example of string beans on a plate? You can arrange them the same way you stack your wood.

What I am after, above all, is expression.

MATISSE

- Draw a dot in the center of a piece of paper. Draw rays going out in a circle. Stare at these radiating lines. Do they tend to jump?

- Look at your furled umbrellas. What colors and patterns do you see? Look at a furled American flag. How does it appear?

- After you finish eating a salad, look at the pattern on the plate created by the oil and vinegar.

- For a few dollars, buy a small pyramid-shaped object called a "snapdragon" at a museum gift shop. Look through the small end to the multifaceted large end that repeats the image of a tiny square in multiples, each a separate image yet identical to all the others. If you twist this seeing device, you will see a whole series of different scenes. This is a great way to train your eye, because you may study the pattern isolated from everything else. You will see exciting images and designs. The snapdragon is very dif-

ferent from a kaleidoscope, because you see actual objects and parts of things in front of you. A kaleidoscope is merely a tube containing mirrors and pieces of colored glass that create bright, interesting patterns when rotated.

We should let our eye speak to us and sing to us.

With the snapdragon look at a rug on the floor. You will see the folds of cotton become a pattern when seen twenty-four times. A vase of red tulips becomes a beautiful series of tulip patterns: By rotating this object you see some straight on and some in profile. Whatever you look at, you will see it in all its detail. Carry a snapdragon around with you.

♦ Draw an arch. Now draw a sailboat centered under the arch. Draw another arch. Draw a sailboat on the right side of the arch. Look at the centered boat. It looks as though it's on an even plane, like the arch. Look at the sailboat that is off center. It looks nearer to you. The boat that is off center would crash into the arch if it were on the same plane. Well-designed patterns don't have this ambiguity. Your eye doesn't want to have to worry.

♦ Go to a store that sells antique wicker furniture. Study the different patterns, the weaving, the round balls, the circles, and the crisscrosses.

♦ Stare at a tile wall a few inches from your nose. The tiles in front of your left eye and right eye fuse, giving the impression of one large tile. The repetition gives the impression of one whole piece. But when you are not near the tiles, you see the pattern created by the outlines of each tile, repeated hundreds of times.

♦ Look down at the tile floors in banks, office buildings, entrance halls, and kitchens. When you look right in front of you, you can see the grouting around each square tile. Now look straight ahead, north to south, as far as the eye can see the floor. Notice that you see only the vertical grouting; it looks like converging lines. You see the horizontal grouting only when you are almost on top of it. Move to the east-west access. The same effect occurs. If you were setting tiles in a rectangular room, the vertical parallel grout lines would cause your space to look longer and narrower if you 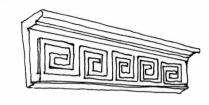 entered the space from either end, east or west. However, if you approached the room from a door opening north or south, the vertical grout lines would make the room appear wider. If you don't like this directional illusion, square tiles can be laid so one tile is set in the center under and above two tiles set side by side to break up the grout line.

- Go to a fine linen store and look at embroidered pillowcases, sheets, hand towels, napkins, and tablecloths. Examine the hem stitching, the French knots, and the openwork. Even on white linen you will find subtle patterns.

Appreciating pattern awakens us to a deeper awareness of all the depth of detail we experience each day. Identifying favorite designs and finding uses for them in our home brings continuous delight, adding refinement and grace to the objects we treasure.

Rhythm

I am certain of nothing but of the holiness of the heart's affections and the truth of the imagination.

JOHN KEATS

Everything we observe has rhythm, an inherent sense of movement, whether we are gazing at a still life of fruit or following a champion Olympic ice skater's measured motions. Rhythm of any movement or action is established by the regular recurrence of different qualities or conditions. Rhythm is measured motion flowing in a stream. Whenever you experience this harmonious flow, you feel like taking action. Rhythm can bring an object alive, but first you have to be sensitive to it. You must look for the movement in a still object. Developing the skills to identify and feel even the most subtle rhythm of objects is crucial to seeing the whole picture in the art of living.

Flowers are my music.

THOMAS ARNOLD

Rhythm stirs emotions and even physical sensations. We feel excited, calm, formal, casual, dramatic, refined. Our experiences are made up of a flow of sensations, fed by what we see. When your eye sweeps across the ocean, you feel a sense of movement, of being on a boat or of swimming. Your eye scans a valley and you feel physiologically as though you were running down through it. We either feel heavy and dragged down by what we see or delightfully buoyant. When you have rhythm, you have music, and you also have movement. Look at a singer or an entertainer playing an instrument, and notice the body language. Anytime an object has visual rhythm, it becomes animated, alive.

Movement as Life

Movement is a sign of life. The wind, the waves, a waterfall, seagulls gliding, the rustling of trees in the breeze, are stimulating to see and create rhythmic pulsations, inviting the eye to move with the scene. Think how charming it is to see white sheer curtains dancing to the wind on a crisp September morning.

The next time you go to a beach, sit at the water's edge and watch the waves tumble to shore. Surfers know when the surf is up. There is an observable rhythm to the ocean. The water is thrust forward to the shore, then it retreats. There is a mood to the water. It's calm, it's choppy, it's high tide and low tide. Rent a video of surfers in Hawaii. Notice their grace and ease as they glide along the curl of the wave. Study how they ride the wave, tuning their bodies to the ocean's inherent rhythms.

There are Six Essentials in painting. The first is called spirit; *the second,* rhythm; *the third,* thought; *the fourth,* scenery; *the fifth, the* brush; *and the last is the* ink.

CHING HAO

Watch a champion figure skater stroke the ice. The flow of the skater's movement makes him one with the ice, the air, and the music. His body seems to have no limits. Watch the rhythm of a gifted athlete. Michael Jordan makes basketball high performance look easy. He is as graceful as a cat. Notice a cantering horse whose jockey becomes one with his champion's rhythmic movements.

Movement is one of the most compelling visual forces in life. Think of the charm of an Alexander Calder mobile with the primary colors and basic shapes gently moving in rhythmic motion in the air. There is a public park in Waterford, Connecticut, on a peninsula where the winds blow in from the ocean. On a Sunday afternoon, you see dozens of colorful kites flying above the Harkness Memorial at Harkness State Park, undulating, soaring and swaying in the air. Sailboats move in rhythm. Dancing, the golf swing and tennis stroke, the horse's trot, music, a child's mobile countenance, an airplane gliding, a wind chime and the tinkle of a crystal chandelier moving gracefully in a breeze, all remind us that life is movement. Even the act of reading has a rhythmic movement from left to right.

The Rhythm of Music and Dance

The dancer, musician, and choreographer George Balanchine once said, "I never believe my ears. It always gives me the melody but sometimes forgets the rhythm." Hearing alone is not enough to grasp rhythm; to truly feel rhythm, we also have to witness it with our eyes. Dancing makes the rhythm of music a visual experience.

Go to the ballet. Observe the grace of the dancers moving through space. Listen to the music. See the bodies move in response to the music, creating images without words. Look for the interconnectedness between the dancers and the music. "The ballet is a purely female thing: it is a woman, a garden of beautiful flowers, and man is the gardener," Balanchine believed. "Ballet," he teaches us, "is not intellectual, it's visual. Ballet has to be *seen*. It's like a beautiful flower. What can you say about a beautiful flower? All you can say is that it's beautiful."

The Rhythm of Art

In art, a composition has inherent rhythms and tensions. While a work of art, photograph, or textile design is literally static, the creator's work implies movement, and your eye and body move with what you see.

When we look at a painting by the British artist Joseph M. W. Turner, we can sense the whirl of the wind. When you feel the motion created by the artist's brush, you envision his movements, rhythmically flowing across the canvas, energetically creating action, suspense, and change. Water, animals, people, and even the atmosphere seem to move. All paintings are a rhythmic organization of energies. The abstract expressionist artist Irving Kriesberg refers to this sensation: "In a work of art, there is always an underlying structure of energies. The structure is usually responsible for the vitality, the life of the painting." He urges us to look for energy patterns, the equilibrium of forces. Seeing rhythmic energy makes us more physically energetic.

The art of Edgar Degas lets us come backstage to see the dancers warming up. He brought us to the racetrack to witness the grace of a trotting horse. And when he painted a woman ironing, he made me want to iron the linen and use a pretty tablecloth and napkins at my next meal celebration. He turned these everyday scenes into an art form through his mastery of rhythm. You feel the energy and grace of these common movements.

Abraham Lincoln practiced and understood the importance of rhythmic pacing to the eloquence and inspirational energy of his speeches. The Gettysburg Address is an example. He had to find the proper rhythm for these immortal two hundred seventy-two words.

The Rhythms We See Every Day

We are always reawakening to visual rhythms and harmonies that delight us. The curve is a more natural rhythm than the straight line, triggering a series of rhythmic movements in the optic muscles. That is why I am so fond of French country furniture. I love the charm of the flowing, wavy lines. Someone once said of the straight line that we either bend it or leave it. As we noted in chapter I, that's what the ancient Greeks did when they curved the lines of the Parthenon ever so subtly, pleasing the eye with the rhythm of line.

As a breeze or an echo rebounds from the smooth rocks and returns whence it came, so does the stream of beauty, passing through the eyes which are the windows of the soul, come back to the beautiful one.

PLATO

Scalloped Edges

Movement in the form of an undulating line, wave, or scallop can have an enormous impact on the eye. Whether on a sheet, pillow, towel, tablecloth, quilt, or fabric design, curves soften an object more than do stripes or a series of straight lines, thus making the object more intimate and appeal-

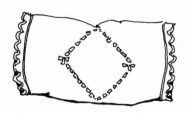

ing. A wavy line has more rhythm than a straight line, check, or plaid. For example, a scalloped edge on fabric has pattern and rhythm reminiscent of waves lapping against the shore or mountains seen from a distance. The deeper the scallop, the more expensive it is to create because of the hand labor involved. A half circle is the true scallop shape. Scallops can be small or large, deep or shallow, but almost always they are bound to give the fabric a finished, unfrayed edge, making it look refined.

Look at scalloped edges and examine the binding. Whenever a scallop is hand bound, it is usually done in a contrasting material for added detail and appeal. All fine handwork has integrity that your eyes appreciate.

When a scallop is bound by machine, the shape is different. It is called a running scallop, resembling waves more than half circles because a machine can't maneuver deep curves. I often use shirred valances with a running scallop to add rhythm to a window treatment.

When your eye learns to discern the difference between a hand-bound scalloped edge and one sewn by machine, you will probably feel it is worthwhile to pay the extra cost to have the work done by hand if it is affordable. Scalloped edges are a signature design feature of Porthault Linen, the French sheet and towel company. Their linens are mostly hand scalloped, but they also produce linens with machine-made bindings sold less expensively in department stores. In bathrooms where there are so many hard edges, colorful towels with scalloped edges, hand bound in a contrasting color, are a feast for the eye. Porthault Linen's sheets are the most luxurious imaginable, not only for their sweet small-scaled floral prints in pastel shades, but also for their scalloped edges. When I decorated a guest room in Florida, I used scalloped-edged sheets, unlined, as curtains, with the leading edges (the sides of the curtain that are drawn together) scalloped. The translucent curtains glowed, and the rhythmic edge echoed the waves of the water beyond.

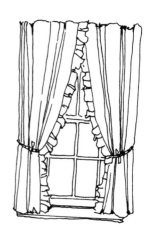

Ruffled Edges

Another pattern that gives rhythm to a fabric edge is a ruffle. Whether you ruffle a sheet and pillowcase, the skirt on a sofa or chair, a pair of curtains, or a seat cushion, this gathering softens the angularity of the straight edge or front. In a child's bedroom, I used pink-and-white polka-dot curtains with a double ruffle. The ruffle in the front was made from the polka-dot fabric, and the ruffle behind it was solid hot pink sewn one-quarter inch deeper in order to give the curtains a defined edge that arrested the eye. This detail made the curtains extra sassy.

Do you prefer a straight finish to a patterned edge? Do you like scallops? How do you feel about ruffles? If you have any quilts, examine whether they have straight edges or if they're scalloped or finished off in another pattern. I have a quilt edged in a series of rounded Vs. These have a different look than a rounded scallop because the lines are oblique, but the effect is full of energy. Some quilts have a rickrack—a sharp up-and-down edge. Any edge, whether of a tabletop or a bench, has rhythm when it is not straight.

Rhythm Everywhere

If you appreciate soothing, subtle rhythms in patterns, open your eyes and find them. Look at the weave of your blanket, the embroidery on your linen, the scalloped edge of the dust ruffle on your bed. Rhythm is seen in the folds of the sheets, the tie of a bow, the gathering of material.

How many rhythms can you see? Are there areas of your home that would benefit from some rhythm? A lace runner on a gleaming wood dressing table, scalloped place mats, scalloped hand towels on a marble bathroom sink; nature, plants, trailing ivy on a gleaming white windowsill, potted herbs clustered on the kitchen counter, a bouquet of pink peonies on the hall table, geraniums clustered in a rustic metal pail, shirred curtains, gathered corners on upholstery, a canopied bed, quilting on a bed, tracery on picture or mirror frames, patterned handles on china or on silverware, piping on the edge of chairs, curtains, and lamps. Look for opportunities to add rhythm to everything from drawer handles to lace tablecloths, napkins, hand towels, and pillow shams.

Sensuous Curves: The French Provincial Desk

Look for rhythm in the lines of furniture. Notice the outer edge of a tabletop. Next, look at the front and side. Nothing is static. Look for the energy, the harmony of lines. Identify a favorite piece of furniture. Describe why you are so drawn to it. What kind of personality does it have? Certain pieces have such rhythm and charm they seem to smile at you. One of my favorite pieces is a small French Provincial desk from the eighteenth century,

Imagination is the chief instrument of the good.

JOHN DEWEY

painted sea-foam green, with a center drawer. I smile whenever I see it because it has such a sweet appearance. There isn't a straight line to be seen. The top is painted brown to resemble marble. The top is wavy, soft and sensuous, with a bullnose edge that overhangs the base by three-quarters of an inch. Set two inches inside the edge of the top is a one-and-a-quarter-inch ochre band that is also wavy, echoing the outer shape. If this painted detail had been straight with right angles, it would have destroyed the softness and whimsy of the desk. The band is a trompe l'oeil inlay, and the corners are what I call "gubby"— rounded with a sensuous bullnose edge.

This little desk is a gem of proportion and rhythm. The generous five-inch apron accommodates a three-inch-high drawer with room underneath for a center scallop and graceful wavy lines leading the eye to a shaped tapered leg. The ochre color is repeated around the drawer and the shaped apron leads down the inside of the leg to ochre-painted hoof feet. The three-quarter-inch beautifully chased brass knob on the drawer looks like a daisy framed inside oblique lines. I've hung a cantaloupe-colored silk tassel on the knob to draw the eye to this small treasure.

The contrast in color between the brown faux-marble top and the sea-foam-green base illuminates the rhythmically graceful design. The profile of the desk is as beautiful as the front. Wherever we place this gem—at the foot of our bed, in front of a window, behind a love seat—it adds grace.

The essence of being alive is learning to see.

PETER MEGARGEE
BROWN

Look to see whether the same lines you like in one piece are repeated in another. My mother used to braid my sister Barbara's and my hair while seated at a fruitwood French Provincial dressing table the same scale and proportion as my sweet painted desk. When she died, I put it in our apartment bedroom, where I sat and braided Alexandra's and Brooke's hair. There is a mirror that folds down into a center well. I usually leave the mirror up, keeping in the well a square Porthault napkin in an impressionist design of rainbow colors scalloped in pink on all four sides. The scallops of the napkin complement the rhythm of the scallops and curves in the lines of the dressing table. The rhythm of the wood grain fuses with the scalloped lines and the scalloped fabric.

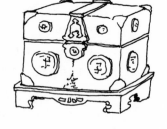

Rhythm, the miracle of ordered movement, is a most compelling, visual dynamic. Rhythm helps us to see what is energetic and beautiful in our daily perceptions. The next time you are in a car and it's raining hard, concentrate on the falling water and experience a Zen moment of seeing. All too often people complain about the rain. They don't see and appreciate the pattern of the rain cascading down their windshield. Recently a friend told me about a meaningful moment he had watching the rain while waiting in his car for his companion to pick up dinner at a Chinese restaurant. He real-

Then, as if no one had ever tried before, try to say what you see and feel and love and lose.

RAINER MARIA RILKE

ized it was more beautiful than the waterfall at a favorite vest pocket park in New York City. To see well you have to realign your attitude about what is important to you. The richness of a Zen seeing moment as you watch the rain splash down on your windshield could change your entire perspective, because it teaches you to look and really see whatever is in front of your nose moment by moment.

The process of seeing well involves action. There are certain "ah ha" moments when you will see *really* well. They can come out of the blue, as happened to my friend in his car. When you are engaged in pure seeing,

you make sense out of your life because you understand, as if for the first time, how individual our
vision is. And because you're able to enjoy such a
simple moment, available to everyone, you have no
need to tell anybody about it. Seeing is no big deal

The mind enjoys continuous change, surprising stimulations.

to someone else, but it makes all the difference in the world to you. Every
minute you are alive, you can see the energy of rhythm at every turn. Wash
your hands, feel the flow of water. Clap your hands, feel the rhythm of the
music. Open your eyes, watch the world's rhythms unfold.

In his wisdom, Plato understood the essential value of rhythm, teaching that "there is no difficulty in seeing that grace or the absence of grace
is an effect of good or bad rhythm."

SIX

Seeing for Yourself
Beauty and Appreciation

Yesterday is already a dream,
And tomorrow is only a vision;
But today, well lived, makes every yesterday
A dream of happiness, and every tomorrow
   a vision of hope.
Look well, therefore, to this day!
Such is the salutation of the dawn.
— SANSKRIT PROVERB

The world is a beautiful place, properly understood and pursued; it is one we can appreciate more and more the greater our vision. By preserving and revering beauty, we can, more often, avoid the ugly.

I send you my sincere best wishes for happy seeing days. I know you will go out and look at everything you see with fresh new eyes. Continue to focus on all the thousands of ways you can turn mere living into a unique, meaningful art form, seeing for yourself, through your own eyes, just how wonderful your life is, because you have now learned to open your eyes.

Beauty

Humans have a longing for beauty. The most valuable quality that delights our senses or mind is the beautiful. Beauty, from the Latin root *bellus,* meaning pretty, dignifies and enhances; it is brilliant and inspired. Beauty is true, tender, and exalting. The pursuit of beauty can be considered the quest for truth. The essence of beauty is to delight the world. The values beauty contains are *all* positive. The pleasure you feel when contemplating beauty reaches an intensity that speaks of the inner passion of the soul. In becoming absorbed in the beauty of the object in front of us, we discover the magic of life.

I first awakened to beauty in my mother's flower garden when I was three years old. This aesthetic moment taught me about my sensitivity to beauty, and I have been faithful to this little revelation ever since. My intimate childhood exposure to the wonders of natural beauty drew my eye outward, so I searched for beauty in all places, eventually beyond my childhood world. I have learned that the visible outward form of beauty expresses the mind, body, and spirit. Beauty always visually satisfies.

The Ancient Greek Precedent

The early Greeks thought the noble life to be the beautiful life. Beauty is of fundamental importance to my life, central to everything I value. My love of beauty increases and expands my love of life.

Beauty integrates us, gives us hope as well as joy in the serenity it brings. In the fifth century B.C., Athens, then a small Greek city-state, showed us a period of noble greatness based on strong belief in beauty. There is an underlying reason for the grandeur and glory of ancient Greece: Here were a number of city-states, especially Athens, devoted to beauty and willing to sacrifice for it. This elevated attitude may be why classical Greece has given us so many enduring principles of truth and beauty. In classical Greece, people talked openly about beauty, where everything fit together harmoniously, where nothing needed to be added or subtracted.

Painting is just another way of keeping a diary.

PABLO PICASSO

The Greek consciousness was that of highly attuned people, letting go of ordinary awareness. When looking at a scene or an object, they would study it until it was implanted in the inner mind and being. The Greek word *exstasis*, ecstasy, means to stand outside of or above. Centuries later, the French master painter Henri Matisse recognized this elevation of spirit: "I tend toward what I feel; toward a kind of ecstasy. And then I find tranquillity."

Through seeing beauty you enlarge yourself, you experience going beyond the limits of your body through a process of self-transcendence. This is how I felt when I had my first aesthetic experience and started on my path of devotion to beauty. What emerges from devotion to beauty is a sense of being empowered, uplifted, and aware.

Plato, the founder of philosophical aesthetics, was its foremost teacher. He saw the world as a beautiful place, and his beliefs were full of wonderful insights. He believed that all inspiration comes from a divine source and that "the divine is beautiful, wise and great." When you're nourished by beauty, your soul and mind soar. Plato's belief that beauty is truth was expressed eloquently: "the soul which has seen most of truth shall come to the birth as a philosopher, or artist, or some musical and loving nature . . . therefore the mind of the Beauty is ambrosia and nectar to the soul."

Let the beauty we love be what we do.

RUMI

Plato believed that a beautiful work of art

285

exists in its own right, not as an image of beauty but as reality itself. Beauty is, in effect, divine ordinariness, where the primary attention is really in the vision of the ideal, allowing the imagination to be liberated. What is beautiful should never be remote or elite. Beauty, in the best sense, is for everyone to experience and appreciate, not just the connoisseur. The public art and architecture of Rome and Athens are examples of the democratic nature of beauty. Then and now, beauty intensifies our sense of living in the moment and therefore is of primary importance. Beauty, shining in brightness, is the ultimate pleasure. We see, feel, and experience beauty through our sight and insight.

Work of sight is done.
Now do heart work
On the pictures within you.
RAINER MARIA RILKE

Domestic utensils, furniture, and all things for the house were once handmade with great care and satisfaction. Something well made and well designed is beautiful. Such objects, whether purely functional or embellished, delight us and uplift the rhythms and scenes of ordinary living experiences. Things of beauty should not be isolated in a museum but should be encompassed in our daily life.

We can foster a sense of everyday beauty, feeling it grounded and rooted in the objects we adore. Beauty is not vaguely ethereal, in the clouds, but is vital and real. Beauty is the keystone of living well.

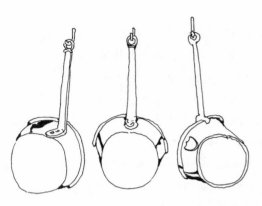

Beauty must be found, not brought to you on a breakfast tray, although that's a possibility. I remember several years ago bringing a friend breakfast in bed. She was so surprised by the beauty, she cried out, "This is too pretty to eat. I think I'll just sit here and feast my eye." In daily living, all too often, people operate on automatic pilot, mechanically crossing off chores on their "to do" list, blind to the beauty surrounding them. But unless you identify what is beautiful in your immediate environment, seeking, probing, and unveiling the thousands of little pleasures as you absorb the elements around you, life can become hollow and routine.

Beauty satisfies our deepest desires because beauty inspires love. True beauty is effervescent. There is a bubbling-up effect to inspire your eye. When you love what is beautiful, you are loving what is good, and you gain happiness.

Plato spoke to his teacher Socrates about love and beauty:

> For he who would proceed aright in this matter should begin in youth to visit beautiful forms; and first, if he be guided by his instructor aright, to love one such form only—out of that he should create fair thoughts and soon he will himself perceive that the beauty of one is akin to the beauty of another; and then if beauty in form in general is his pursuit, how foolish would he be not to recognize that the beauty in every form is one of the same . . . and he will become a lover of all beautiful forms; in the next stage he will consider that the beauty of the mind is more honorable than the beauty of the outward form.

We do not need to look for an explanation of our existence. . . . Our quest for an alternative is wholly unnecessary, for the real thing is before our eyes, if only we will open them.

FRANCIS THOMPSON

Ever since Plato's ideal of an aesthetic philosophy was expressed and absorbed throughout the world, we have come to understand that beauty can be experienced by sensitive people as an active goal and constant pleasure.

Once we're changed by beauty's enticing sensuality, we cannot go back to our unenlightened ways. Plato emphasized three ideas: Beauty, Truth, and Goodness. The Greek word for beauty *and* goodness is *kalon*. One word encompasses both beauty and the virtue of goodness: When you experience one, the other is present. Beauty is integral to honesty, ethics, and self-respect. In his enchanting prayer *Phaedrus*, Plato's teacher Socrates concluded, "Give me beauty in the inward person, and may the outward and inward person be at one."

Beauty elevates, inspires, exalts, and rises above the limits of a short life. All the accumulated beauty you see, feel, and envision is inspiring, flowing through your soul, lighting the dark shadows, providing a framework for contemplation of the great mysteries. The pursuit of beauty ultimately makes one wise, and the appreciation of the beautiful contributes to a more heroic life.

Appreciation

Always the seer is a sayer.

EMERSON

Come join me on this quest for beauty. Seeing is an art that can be learned by all of us over a lifetime of careful observation and study, as we come to recognize the fundamental universal principles. Beauty is the way and the goal of seeing the world. Beauty reinforces my love of the universe. Throughout our life we can be students of seeing. No one sees well all the time, but geniuses are known to make great contributions by sharing their personal vision, communicating whatever beauty they can see and experience. Something of magnificence is absorbed by them and they form it transcendentally into an image on paper, on canvas, or in marble. Michelangelo, for one, could take an inanimate block of cold marble and make an animate form burst forth from within, bringing the marble figuratively to life.

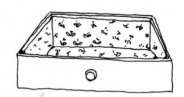

The psychologist Rollo May revealed that beauty saved his life. He came to the conclusion that "creativity gives us a grace in the sense that it is a balm for our anxiety and a relief from our alienation. It is grace by virtue of its power to reconcile us to our deepest selves, to lead us to our own depths where primary and secondary functions are unified. Here the right brain and the left brain work together in *seeing* the wholeness of the world."

When you look around, do you tend to see in all directions? The human eye has peripheral vision; it is not like a camera that captures images in only two dimensions. Do you go for walks and feel you are inside a painting, participating in the sensuous pleasures of becoming one with the mountains, the trees, the waves, the flowers, and

Ah, now I see with a new pair of eyes.

the sky? How long have you been aware of the powerful significance the visual sense exerts on your life? How affected is your sense of well-being by what you see? What is the disparity between what you see and what you want to see in your home, your yard, and your garden?

Right now a moment of time is fleeting by! . . . We must become the moment, make ourselves a sensitive recording plate . . . give the image of what we actually see, forgetting everything that has been seen before our time.

PAUL CÉZANNE

The ancients believed there was a god behind the eye. This is a mystery; could this god be the *brain* literally located behind the eyes? Seeing well sets us on the path to aesthetic experiences where we are more receptive to and appreciative of beauty. In order to actively pursue beauty, you must search for beauty everywhere. When you do, you will see a forest in a seed, an ocean in a shell, a house in a wooden frame, and an angel in a baby's face.

The Emotional Connection

The way things appear has a profound and surprising effect on our emotions. We look and we react viscerally. We all see physical things—a child's smile, the rustle of the blossoms and leaves on the dogwood tree, the patina on the lovingly waxed antique fruitwood table, the prism of colors in the bevel of a mirror. We pick up the vibrations of energy, opening our senses, feeling everything more acutely. These sensations of buoyancy and revelation are refreshing. As you train your eye, you see the immediate benefits of being able to understand and choose what uplifts your spirit and what depresses you. More and more, you're able to surround yourself with a harmonious atmosphere that makes you feel at peace and allows you to be more creative. There should be a strong correlation between what you *want* to see in your surroundings and what you do see. Appreciation for beauty gives you the motivation and energy to ensure that your house looks and feels inviting and attractive to you.

When your mind and eyes are tired, you can seek renewal in beauty. You have to rise above the anxiety you may be feeling and transcend your consciousness to an elevated awareness, recognizing that there is an organic whole, a source of unity and love. You have to become aware of things on a deeper level, open to new experiences and responses. You can visit a new town or city, you can move your pictures around. You can go to a concert in a church. You can camp by a beautiful lake and collect pinecones and colorful stones to bring the happy time back to your bedside table. Your eyes need continuous refreshment and stimulation. Whenever you put something tired in front of your eyes, your eyes echo the ennui, becoming tired as well. We need to deliberately stimulate our eyes with a variety of attractive sights. Your objective is more than visual stimulation; it is to expand toward your ultimate goal of living beautifully.

Aesthetics comes from the Greek *aisthētikos,* "sense perception"—in other words, seeing beauty. Aesthetic delight is felt immediately, since the process of seeing is instantaneous and spontaneous. If you have a high awareness of beauty, your dividend of happiness may derive from numerous simple things unnoticed by most people.

Seeing integrates your consciousness, producing a sense of order and leading to better mental health and a greater sense of well-being. You see that what is good is what expands the mind and soul. Do you believe that you can see your way to happiness? Do you believe certain design elements can unite in such harmony that they produce a spiritual experience?

It may be precisely because we are both nature and spirit that we conclude that beauty is a fundamental human need. We thirst for it. This has

> *Art is not an end in itself. It introduces the soul into a higher spiritual order, which it expresses and in some sense explains.*
>
> THOMAS MERTON

been true since the beginning and will probably continue to be the reality until the end of time. It is through beauty that we have hope for some window of happiness on earth. There's a poignant Persian saying, "If I have one penny, with half of it I buy some bread, and with the other half I buy a violet." I remember when the actress Sandy Duncan gave me a purple hyacinth and asked me to have the drum-shaped coffee tables, in her living room painted this heavenly color. When you see the tables, you feel you can smell the intoxicating scent of a hyacinth.

There is no large, no small;
Infinity lies before my eyes.

SENG-T'SAN

Religious differences and political ideology don't seem to deter our access to beauty. Beauty transcends religious and political boundaries, unifying all people. We join in a universal gratitude once we are exposed to beauty, be it a beautiful country or a marvelous object of art in a museum exhibition in a foreign land.

There is a yearning in all people to seek out whatever beauty there is, to be a part of a universe of beauty. At the same time, most people need to feel significant to give their life meaning. To feel this sense of signifi-

cance, we can create something beautiful ourselves that gives us delight. You can create a garden patch or brighten every corner in your home, looking for ways to make your surroundings more attractive, more inviting, more pleasurable. Whenever we create, we are searching for refinement of form out of chaos. Recent studies have found that highly creative people are sometimes drawn to chaos because disarray challenges them to find new ways to resolve and organize it into order and beauty. They are stimulated by the process of sorting out a new order from kaleidoscopic pieces of disorder.

Anytime you create beauty you are transformed internally. Your creativity is constantly unfolding, adding order to your life, rebuilding and re-forming you. You may think at the outset you don't have what it takes to create beauty; perhaps you don't think you have the strength or the courage to begin—until you experience a flash of inner vision, when you see what you can do to bring something forth from your core. Then the essential energy is there, and you are led to paint or dance or sing or write or decorate.

Seeking Beauty and Light over Darkness and Gloom

Consider the last lines of the nineteenth-century British poet John Keats's *Ode on a Grecian Urn:* " 'Beauty is truth, truth beauty'—that is all ye know on earth, and all ye need to know." Many people have not yet been touched by grace through beauty and are not aware that

I discovered the secret of the sea in meditation upon the dewdrop.

KAHLIL GIBRAN

they can transcend darkness to live in the light. Yet an integrated human being can understand that through the aesthetic experience you are healed; you may transcend the polarity of nature and spirit, freedom and destiny. The dilemmas of life are overcome by creating, by loving, in some cases by simply doing. Each individual makes a choice whether to emphasize despair or joy in life. Beethoven had a miserable childhood, but he found a way to grace through his music. He once exclaimed, "Whoever understands my music will henceforth be free of the misery of the world."

To the persistent explorer the world is beautiful. Each of us can seek out more beautiful forms that make us feel peaceful while meditating. Just before the year 1800, German idealist philosopher Friedrich von Schiller, then in his early twenties, wrote a wise discourse on beauty and aesthetics entitled "Letters Upon the Aesthetic Education of Man." He began, "Beauty is indeed the sphere of unfettered contemplation and reflection; beauty conducts us into the world of ideas, without however taking us from the world of sense. . . . By beauty the sensuous man is brought back to matter and restored to the world of sense."

Nikos Kazantzakis, a favorite author, loved to take long walks in his beloved Greece. During a period in his life when he was having a spiritual crisis, he'd take walks and talk with monks and other wise, holy men he'd find along his path, confessing his inner struggles. One ascetic admonished Kazantzakis, declaring, "Woe is you, woe is you, unfortunate boy. You shall be devoured by the mind; you shall be devoured by the ego—the 'me,' the self." Trembling with frustration, Kazantzakis yelled back, "Tell God it is not our fault but His—because He made the world so beautiful."

Just hearing, just seeing, just feeling. That's all there is.

CHARLOTTE JOKO BECK

Is it possible to have moments of infinitude where you feel perfect freedom, a sense of unbounded space and time? Have you ever had an out-of-body experience when outdoors, alone, in nature's paradise, when you lose all fear, including the fear of death? The beauty of blossoming lemon and lime trees, the glory of apples and pears ripening against a rich, blue sky, the shimmering silver grace of a grove of olive trees, the feeling of being caressed by a weeping willow undulating in the wind, have the power to touch us on a deeper level.

Why can't we sit in a field of Texas bluebonnets and feel touched by a divine spark? Why have many of us lost sight of the reality that heaven is along the way? Why can't we take more delight in what we have in front of our eyes? Are people too caught up in the rush, noise, and confusion of routine demands, to slow down and glimpse eternity through nature? Have we forgotten that real seeing and true living take time and contemplation?

Look at a cut flower. Gaze at the wonderful reality of its tenderness. A flower blooms, is cut at the stem, and is going to die. But the fact that a cut flower is on the way to death doesn't diminish, while alive, its potential to refresh our spirit. "Only when we confront death, in some form or another, only when we realize that life is fragile, do we create beauty," Rollo May teaches us. We learn to absorb the shadow into the light, always keeping in mind the greater the light, the deeper the shadow. Beauty can be considered the garment of our spiritual life.

Rollo May himself was experiencing some spiritual confusion in his early twenties and coincidentally was teaching school in Greece, a country where people tend, perhaps because of the powerfully beautiful environment,

to find themselves spiritually. He wrote about his aesthetic experience in a tender book entitled *My Quest for Beauty*. He describes having a breakdown because he suddenly recognized that he had, up until then, gone through his life being a good person but had failed to use his eyes to feast on beauty. "I realized," he confessed, "that I had not listened to my inner voice, which had tried to talk to me about beauty. I had been too hard-working, too 'principled' to spend time merely looking at flowers!"

Why do so many intelligent people so often suppress their emotional reactions to beauty? Is it because once you open yourself to see beauty, you will be moved, perhaps, to make some difficult changes in your life? If you are male, are you often afraid to expose your "feminine side"? Beauty has no gender. What are some of the most profound experiences where you've been surprised by beauty? Rollo May happened one day upon a field of poppies in Greece and had a moment of conversion. He looked and looked, opening up his heart, and sensitively sketched the flowers. What simple beauty inevitably stirs your whole being? I remember running barefoot in my childhood garden in the early morning light, seeing sparkling rainbows in the pearl drops of dew on the grass—the spectrum of red, orange, yellow, green, blue, and violet all reflecting the rising sun.

> *If enlightenment is not where you are standing, where will you look?*
>
> ZEN SAYING

I recall being five years old, taking a walk with friends, ending up at the top of our dead-end road in an open field. The sight of thousands of smiling yellow daffodils caught me off guard. I wasn't prepared for such ecstasy. Why are we adults so often *on* guard, narrowing our possibilities for these small epiphanies? My friends and I picked as many daffodils as we could carry down the hill to my house, where we tied ribbons around bunches, then went door-to-door selling the bouquets for a nickel each. It wasn't until I was in high school and read William Wordsworth that I realized how profoundly I had been affected by the daffodils that spring day:

I wandered lonely as a cloud
That floats on high o'er vales and hills,
When all at once I saw a crowd,
A host, . . . of golden daffodils.
Ten thousand saw I at a glance,
Tossing their heads in spritely dance.

I remember putting one unsold bunch in a water glass and placing it on a table next to my bed. Lying there in the dark, I smelled their scent of earth, fresh rain, and spring. One May afternoon years later, Peter took me to a friend's house on Long Island for tea. He knew about her famous gardens and it was daffodil time. Arriving, I immediately saw yellow, not the green grass I expected. Everywhere I looked, I saw great clusters of daffodils spreading as far as the eye could see. I went for several solitary walks that afternoon, wanting to be one with the daffodils and to have the freedom and spaciousness to remember back, half a century, when I saw my first host of golden daffodils. As the poet Wordsworth continued:

When one sees Eternity in things that pass away and Infinity in finite things, then one has pure knowledge.
BHAGAVAD GITA

For oft, when on my couch I lie
In vacant or in pensive mood,
They flash upon that inward eye,
Which is the bliss of solitude;
And then my heart with pleasure fills,
And dances with the daffodils.

"It is artists," Rollo May once commented, "the musicians, the poets, the dramatists that remind us that life *is* worth living." We are all supplied with beauty if we're willing to open our eyes and our hearts to embrace it. Beauty is serene, sometimes subtle and diffident, sometimes dynamic and as exhilarating as a bugle call. All our energy focuses on it, increases our sense of being alive. We become intoxicated by beauty's mysterious charm and greatly enjoy the feeling of wonder. As we stand in reverence of something beautiful, there is a timelessness that transcends limits; we come to see beauty as eternal. Once you've experienced a timeless moment of repose, you feel tranquil, relaxed, and paradoxically, at the same time, vibrant. You receive new vigor, new power. Beauty has a way of giving us both energy *and* serenity that can be delightful.

Seeing the Wind

"Before anything else," Kazantzakis remarked of his quest, "I wanted to find an answer, my answer, to the timeless questions." I believe beauty is *the* answer. Beauty has the capacity to turn a moment into an ultimate experience. The search for beauty is an active choice. It takes time to listen to the wind, to hear it speak to you; and when you see well, you can see the wind. Claude Monet saw it so keenly that he was able to paint the atmosphere most people don't see at all. If you walk home from work with your head down, you are not using your active powers to let beauty move you. Look up at the sunset, the birds, and the trees. You have to open up to the beauty of light and all the activity of nature that is always changing in order to be transported to a higher consciousness.

Nirvana is right here, before our eyes.

HAKUIN

When you look at nature, you find it always fresh and alive. Claude Monet once described painting his lily pond:

> The basic element of the motif is the mirror of water, whose appearance changes at every instant because of the way bits of the sky are reflected in it, giving it life and movement. The passing cloud, the fresh breeze, the threat or arrival of a rainstorm, the sudden fierce gust of wind, the fading or sudden refulgent light—all of these things, unnoticed by the untutored eye, create changes in color and alter the surface of the water. . . . I have taken up things which are impossible to do: water with grass

undulating in the bottom. . . . This is a wonderful thing to see but quite likely to drive crazy anyone trying to render it. It is with such things that I am always grappling!

How did you feel the last time you really saw a sunset, when you lost all track of time and space? The sunset awakens our soul to love. "The colors of the sunset have a brilliancy that attracts attention, and a softness and illusiveness that enchants the eye; while the many associations of the evening and of heaven gather about this kindred charm and deepen it," Santayana suggests.

Like a sword that cuts
but cannot cut itself
Like an eye that sees
but cannot see itself.

ZEN SAYING

Continue regularly to reach out to see the impermanent beauty in nature. When you see some-

thing that moves you, be open to receive its gifts. In nature everything changes so quickly; you learn to reach out to see what you love as well as to go outdoors to experience the surprise epiphanies: birds in flight, a magnificent rainbow, or light illuminating a forest.

Sometimes extraordinary images occur in nature and we're here to see them—a ring around the moon, a double rainbow, hundreds of birds in flight. When we're present, actively seeing, we feel calm and contained and, at the same time, we feel that all is well with the world. We feel we were meant to see and experience the event that moved us. Anything that awakens us to the unknown world expands our imagination and is usually a positive experience.

Communicate a sense of
affirmation, of wonder,
of trust.

SYLVIA SHAW JUDSON

Your eye knows true beauty. You are simply moved. Something stirs within you and you are touched by the hand of an angel. You feel a breeze, you feel peaceful, and you are reminded to focus on what's important. You're inspired to try to bring this majesty and grace with you wherever you are.

Nature's Changes and Society's Progress

I'm invigorated by nature's momentary movements and surprises, but I'm not sure that all the fast changes in the marketplace are good. I don't always believe that the new is necessarily better. Fashion and home furnishings have markets and seasons and what is hot soon becomes passé. We're a fickle bunch. Manufacturers and retailers wouldn't bring on the "new and improved" that makes us dissatisfied with what we have unless we, the consumer, bought into the concept of equating change with improvement.

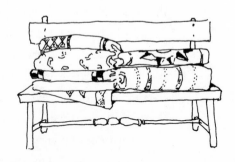

Beauty doesn't worship progress or objects that change their color and form just because there's a new selling season. It is wise to continue to train our eye to see the real beauty in contrast to the promised pleasures of advertising and marketing hype. What is new might be "improved" and yet it might be awful. Seeing better helps us to discern the true from the false, no matter where the public herd is headed. Few people would deny that the Parthenon is more beautiful than most examples of modern architecture. Whenever we experience a lessening of the quality and grace of harmony, no matter how popular a movement is, seeing things as they are is our most valuable asset.

The artists seek to overcome the boundaries of life.

ROLLO MAY

Annie Dillard, the Pulitzer Prize–winning author of *Pilgrim at Tinker Creek,* wrote a perceptive second chapter entitled "Seeing." She recalls her childhood near Pittsburgh, where she grew up: "It is still the first week in January, and I've got great plans. I've been thinking of seeing. There are lots of things to see, unwrapped gifts and free surprises." She continues, "What you see is what you get. . . . Unfortunately, nature is very much a now-you-see-it, now-you-don't affair. A fish flashes, then dissolves in the water before my eyes like so much salt. Deer apparently ascend bodily into heaven; the bright oriole fades into leaves. These disappearances stun me into stillness and concentration; they say of nature that it conceals with a grand nonchalance, and they say of vision that it is a deliberate gift. . . . For nature does reveal as well as conceal: now-you-don't-see-it, now-you-do." She goes on to observe, "The lover can see, and the knowledgeable." We do see better when we're focused and concentrating our energy in a specific direction.

How Artists Teach Us How to See

In his book *The Meanings of Modern Art,* art critic John Russell eloquently opens the first chapter, "The Secret Revolution":

> When art is made now, we are made new with it. . . . Art is there to tell us who we are. It gives pleasure, coincidentally, but primarily it is there to tell us the truth. . . . Art answered the great riddles, filled in the gaps in our general knowledge, and laid Eternity on the line. Above all, it gave reassurance; it told us what we wanted to hear—that experience was not formless and illegible, that man could speak to man without the obstructions of language, and that we were at home in the world, and with one another. That was long the function of art. Art restored to us the lost wholeness, the sensation of being one with Nature, and at one with society, which we crave from the moment of birth.

Marcel Proust, the nineteenth-century French writer and a five-star observer of the world around him, saw some still life paintings for the first time and wrote about the experience: "I never realized how much beauty lay around me in my parents' house, in the half-cleared table, in the corner of a tablecloth left awry, in the knife beside the empty oyster-shell."

Not all people or even artists aim to make others feel better about themselves and better about life. Everyone has to ultimately develop a personal

In a picture I want to say something comforting.
VINCENT VAN GOGH

299

See well, and a meaningful life unfolds.

attitude and perspective. My philosophy essentially is that beauty is truth and goodness.

The artists who love beauty and believe in it receive the gift of grace, and are able to reveal to us that beauty is divine. Matisse once expressed this mystical creative process: "When I make my drawings . . . the path traced by my pencil on the sheet of paper is, to some extent, analogous to the gesture of a man groping his way in the darkness. I mean there is nothing foreseen about my path: *I am led. I do not lead.*"

John Russell tells us that "every painting is a duet after all. If the man who is looking at it can't keep time with the man who painted it, then the painting is incomplete." Study not only the painting or building or sculpture but find out where and how the artist lived and what the social conditions were at the time. Until the arrival of Paul Gauguin, Paul Cézanne, Vincent van Gogh, and Claude Monet, few artists loaded their brush with pure color. Every era and region had its accepted colors, but these giants turned their backs to convention and let true feelings pour out. In the last five years of van Gogh's troubled, tragic life, he aroused all future art to the power of pure color to "set man free." This is a large order, of course, but his influence is found today on the walls of museums, galleries, and private homes.

The Impressionists and Post-Impressionists: Glorifying Everyday Living

Of all the artists I've grown to admire, the Impressionist and Post-Impressionist painters speak to my heart most directly. Ever since I was five and saw my first Claude Monet paintings along with works of art by Vincent van Gogh, Mary Cassatt, Berthe Morisot, Henri Fantin-Latour, Eugène Boudin, Edouard Vuillard, Gustave Caillebotte, Pierre Bonnard,

Edgar Degas, Pierre-Auguste Renoir, and Henri Matisse, I've been on a quest to see and learn to appreciate everyday life from these artists. Each one of them shows me the immediate life around them. I see their chairs, sofas, beds, lamps, wallpaper, fabrics, and colors. I see their spouses and children, their pets, their gardens, and their terraces.

They invite us to come sit at the breakfast table and break bread with them. We see what they eat and drink, and observe their china, crystal, and linen. I learn where their dining table is situated and I see the view from their window or French doors. These are men and women who also went outside, who painted in the natural light in clear, luminous colors. Vuillard was referred to as an "intimist" because you see in his work his mother, their house, their garden, and also the workshop that housed his mother's dressmaking business. He painted the bolts of fabric, the patterns, and everything else he saw in their intimate environment, including a woman napping or having a private moment of repose in her dressing room.

Another favorite artist whose work teaches us to see and appreciate domestic intimacy was Bonnard, who loved his home and his wife, Marta, whom he painted in the bathtub over and over. She loved to take baths and he loved to capture her vulnerability. You know what their bathroom tiles looked like as well as their living room curtains and the inside of the china cupboard. You even know what kind of dog they had. All of these images, including Marta in the tub, are not photographic but are impressions or interpretations of the artist—beauty is created by seeing life through his eyes.

John Russell put it well when he wrote about these artists: "Impressionist paintings of the top class have made so great a contribution to human happiness. Looking at them, we think better of life and better of ourselves." Who are these people who created these paintings? How could they individually and as a group make such an impact on the way we look at the world around us? The nineteenth-century French critic Edmond

Duranty explained, "It takes immense genius to represent, simply and sincerely, what we see in front of us." The greatest gift of the Impressionists is that they taught us to look around. They encouraged us to put our trust in our intuition and sensations. The ordinary experiences of everyday life had value and dignity. By first seeing life through their eyes, we learn to see through our own.

But beauty absolute, separate, simple and everlasting.

PLATO

Try to see your own life through the viewpoint of an Impressionist artist. This group of artists opened their windows and doors, let the sunlight dapple everything, making us see with refreshed eyes all the beauty, light, energy, and color that are there for the seeing in our immediate surroundings. In their passion for nature and their love of home, they open us up to wider visions of our own lives, enabling us to see things more beautifully. In order to do this, they had to break from the pictorial traditions of the past, going beyond their logical mind, so the eye could be free to concentrate on pure experience.

The Genius of Claude Monet

Who can rival Claude Monet in the art of seeing? He threw himself into seeing, then transformed his vision onto the canvas. Look where he set up his easel: in the ocean, on top of a mountain, in the middle of a train track, in a snowstorm. Treasure the sight of his lily pond, its mirrored image of the sky filled with pink clouds and the rhythmic swaying of the grass beneath its glasslike surface. What force drives a person to get up at four o'clock in the morning to examine the changing light?

Monet took it upon himself to show the intrinsic beauty in nature. He often spoke of nature as never standing still. "I can see more and more clearly," he said, "that I will have to work very hard to render what I am looking for: the instantaneous impression, particularly the envelope of things, the same all-pervading light."

He loved flowers so much he often told friends he was good for nothing except painting and gardening. Of all his gardens, his final home in Giverny is the one we've been invited to experience firsthand. He gracefully admitted, "I perhaps owe it to flowers for having become a painter." Whenever Monet was in his garden, he never felt lonely, since he was indeed surrounded by love and intoxicating beauty. "I have always loved the sky and the water, greenery, flowers," he said. "All these elements were to be found in abundance here on my little pond." He poured his energy, time, and money into his gardens and lily pond. "Everything I have earned has gone into these gardens. I do not deny that I am proud of them."

The goal of life is rapture. Art is the way we experience it.

JOSEPH CAMPBELL

Whenever you have a passion for something, you wish to concentrate on it in peace. I can remember my great sense of pride when my parents' friends would come over to our farmhouse to take a look at "Sandie's kitchen flower garden" and be impressed by its beauty. I didn't ask my young friends to help me weed, water, and prune because they weren't really interested in gardening. Because it was my special space, I preferred to spend time there alone. This was how I came early in my life to love contemplation, being free to think and experience lofty impressions in solitude.

Perhaps I owe being an interior designer to Claude Monet, because I felt that the interiors of most houses in the 1940s were stifling and morbid, just as he felt the Academy of Arts' old standard was sterile, mobilizing him to go out to the countryside to paint what immediately impressed his eye. He wanted to paint "the way a bird sings," not adhere to the artificiality of the French Academy's narrow judgment about what was good and what was not good. "I have no other wish than to mingle more closely with nature," he said, "and I aspire to no other destiny than to work and live in harmony with her laws."

Because of his vision and courage, he unwittingly started a movement that changed the way we see the world around us. He had to believe in himself and, through his daring nonconformity, rejections, and financial worries, carry on with his own vision. I owe a great debt to him as the artist who taught me not to look at the surface but to look *into* things, at the center of their being. He painted from the surface of the water-lily pond to the bottom, showing us all of what he saw and experienced. As an old man, he looked back at his point of view, quite humbly summing up his life: "I've always done what I saw without worrying too much about the process." Do what you see. Trust your unique eye. Make your environment your canvas that you fill with what you find beautiful.

Under the leaves
Of a morning glory:
Cat's eyes.

NATSUME SOSEKI

I have several photographs of Claude Monet taken by his son Michel. Seated on a garden bench at the edge of his lily pond, in dappling sunlight, he is wearing a wide-brimmed straw hat, his legs are crossed; his left hand is on the warm wood bench. I recall his poignant invitation: "Put your hand in mine and let us help one another to see things better." I imagine myself sitting next to him on that bench, holding hands, as we gaze out at his garden. I'm intrigued to follow his advice to "see things better." We must reach out, extending our eyes in order to see better. We have to thrust into the light, color, and energy to be open to the same enthusiasm and inspiration that nourished

We know that we are
creatures, limited by time
and space, but we also know
that truth, beauty and
tenderness are aspects of
the absolute.

SYLVIA SHAW JUDSON

Monet's work and spirit. When we see beyond the surface of things and are receptive to finding insights in the quiet of meditative moments, the harmony of beauty is revealed to us.

Few of us see as well as Claude Monet, and even fewer of us have a brush in our hand at four A.M., waiting for the sun. But what is remarkable about genius is the capacity of the talented soul to dedicate his life to his work, experiencing a transformation of the self as he creates some-

The sun and stars are mine:
if those I prize.

THOMAS TRAHERNE

thing in a form that expresses his feelings. There is a reverence in his expression; it is pure and full of integrity. This is why great creators have the power to take our hand and lead us on our own creative adventure. Through the instrument of their eyes we are inspired to see for ourselves.

With a tutored eye, the whole world can be changed in a flicker of sunlight. Monet painted the river Seine all his life, at all hours of the day, in every season. "I have never been bored with it," he said, "to me it is always different." When we open our eyes we, too, will never be bored.

Appreciating Two Artists:
Nicolas de Stael and Roger Mühl

My first meeting with my favorite contemporary artist, Roger Mühl, started with a question: Had he ever met the esteemed French artist Nicolas de Stael? It turned out that not only did he know de Stael; but he told me that in his initial encounter with the renowned painter, de Stael conveyed to him the beautiful constraint of simplicity, that is, what to *leave out* of the picture. This single idea provides startling insight to both artists' genius.

When I was a student at the New York School of Interior Design in 1959, I went to a retrospective exhibition of Nicolas de Stael's work at the Guggenheim Museum, a large circular building designed by Frank Lloyd Wright, located in Manhattan along Museum Mile at Fifth Avenue and Eighty-ninth Street. While Wright is not one of my masters, I found fascinating the experience of seeing art on the walls as I walked up the circular ramp, a new seeing experience.

I was alone when I went to see the de Staels, and as I walked farther up the ramp, I felt a lump in my throat. My lips quivered and I could feel my arms tightening up. There was something in his work that reached me in the center of my being. I have no idea how long I stayed at the museum. I seemed to enter the world of his paintings; their energy, colors, and passion spoke to me, urging me to focus and see more clearly.

Beauty adds immeasurably to our awareness, where we appreciate deeper, higher visions.

On my way down the same ramp I stopped before a small picture of a wooden salad bowl containing chartreuse baby Bibb lettuce—nothing more. I'd grown Bibb lettuce as a child gardener, and the tenderness of this painting with its humble subject matter arrested my attention. I stared at this picture, studying how simply he painted that lettuce; how with fast energetic strokes he expressed the essence of freshness in the least wasteful way. Not one extra stroke. He became a master for me right there, that day.

Tragically, Nicolas de Stael had committed suicide several years before this retrospective exhibition. As I headed toward the museum door, I threw some coins into the fountain on the ground floor; I made a wish

that I'd find a living artist whose paintings would move me so powerfully.

A year or so later, a young, unknown French artist, Roger Mühl, held his first exhibition in New York City. I went to see the exhibition on instructions from my firm to observe this new artist's paintings for a client in New Orleans. The same psychological experience I had at the de Stael retrospective happened to me again. But Mühl was alive, well, full of energy, and a strong lover of life. I thought about my wish at the fountain that rainy afternoon at the Guggenheim Museum and asked the gallery owner whether I could be notified when the artist came to New York again to exhibit. I wanted to meet the artist whose paintings had such a profound impact on my entire being. Within a year, I did.

I think you have to be ready to see wholeheartedly. I was ready for a living master. That was thirty-seven years ago, and my deep emotional bond with this artist's work grows daily. You have to trust your gut about

what moves and inspires you. I believe that the "less is more" lesson of Nicolas de Stael led me to be receptive to Mühl's extraordinary light, energy, color, and simplicity.

Whenever we go to Washington, D.C., we always pop into the Phillips Collection to pay our respects to some of our masters. There are several good de Staels there, as well as postcards and slides of his paintings. There is much mystery in this experience of coming into one's seeing. I am a colorist, loving fresh, alive, clear colors, yet many of the de Stael pictures contain lots of grays and blacks. The painting I was most passionate about in the first New York Mühl exhibition is a cool picture of snow and cold air, a dense atmosphere. At that time Mühl was living in Alsace on the border of France and Germany; all his early pictures from this era have a darker, more somber color palette than his later paintings.

Something internally drew me to Mühl's spirit. I'd follow him through his different "periods" and watch with great interest his development as an artist. Within a few years, he moved from Alsace to Grasse, the perfume center of the world, then to a small hill town in Provence near where Pablo Picasso lived, worked, and died. The brilliant light and palette of Provence brightened Mühl's palette; I began to feel that he was painting just for me.

The artist may be well advised to keep his work to himself till it is completed, because no one can readily help him or advise him with it.

GOETHE

When you select your masters, you are choosing an intimacy with the world the artist sees. Mühl's paintings are windows into sunny scenes in the South of France.

Mühl paints his life and all his years of becoming one with the beauty of Provence. His love of gardening is everywhere in his pictures. He has a healthy appetite for life, including a love of food, and all the splendor of being "at table" with family and friends is a favorite subject for him. He paints beaches and boats, garden gates and famous chef friends, always giving you the impression that you are moving into the picture, ready to sit down and participate in the conviviality. His images invigorate me, stretching me to live beautifully and appreciate the often overlooked beauty of living fully at home.

Could we teach taste or genius by rules, they would be no longer taste or genius.

JOSHUA REYNOLDS

After meeting Roger Mühl, I am further convinced that there are geniuses in our midst, and it is up to us to actively see well enough to seek them out. Mühl has committed himself to paint the beauty he feels and sees. He helps me stay committed to the beauty I can feel and see in my own life and environment.

How can you find and support your own sense of beauty? What does it feel like to exercise your power to know and understand what is beautiful to your eyes? What kinds of beauty lift you up, soften your heart, open your mind? What types of beauty exalt you, elevate you, and allow you to grow deeper?

The poet William Wordsworth suggested that beauty is "a virtue, by which pleasure is enhanced." Anytime you experience something that makes you value yourself more, you have found a form of beauty. The nineteenth-century British philosopher John Stuart Mill questioned whether all things beautiful were the same: "I cannot but feel . . . . considerable doubt whether the word *beautiful* connotes the same property when we speak of a *beautiful* color, a *beautiful* face, a *beautiful* scene, a *beautiful* character, and a *beautiful* poem." What is *your* definition of beauty?

If something is beautiful, it is handsome and lovely. It is elegant and graceful and, at the same time, it is spiritually uplifting. What is beautiful is appealing to our aesthetic tastes and instincts. What you love becomes beautiful, found in the eye of the beholder. And what is beautiful enhances you. It was Aristotle who believed in the realized state of potentialities—beauty inspires us to live up to our best, increasing our energy to act.

What are the beautiful experiences where you've been lifted on high, where you have felt an intensification of appreciation? Was there a phys-

A universal impulse toward beauty is enclosed in our common nature.

HEGEL

ical loveliness and charm to the senses appreciated through your sense of sight? Was there a sense of grace or appropriateness that excited moral pleasure as well as keen insightfulness? What was there about an encounter that increased your sense of mystery and faith?

What allows you to see the simple beauty in your midst? How often during a day do you see beauty? How often are you aware of its value to you? When you have an aesthetic experience, do you see it as an expression of the ideal, as a fleeting glimpse of divine perfection? Do you find common elements in beautiful objects and human experiences?

Do you sense the inner beauty in the objects you've selected that you consider beautiful? Do you read meaning into the things around you as symbols of the ideal? Whenever you live with things you really love and consider valuable, they become beautiful, and this connection is felt. You may have some objects around that are priceless because they were made lovingly by a child. What a shame it would be not to have these gifts on display for all to enjoy.

Beauty makes sadness bearable.

"Happy are those who sing with all their heart, from the bottom of their hearts. To find joy in the sky, the trees, the flowers," Matisse reminds us, "there are always flowers for those who want to see them."

Contemplation

Seeing well requires the introspection that leads to creativity. Seeing well requires time to consider and ponder things thoughtfully. Without valuing regular time to contemplate, we cannot open up enough to be receptive to appreciating beauty. Artists, poets, writers, and spiritual leaders all find ways to escape from the bustle of the world so they can have intensely personal experiences in a place where they can see without being seen.

Some people sit in a garden, others go for solo walks, still others retreat to the woods, a lake, a beach, or a mountain. At these quiet, soulful times, the mechanical, technological world has no value. We replace being "plugged in" with being connected to life's intangible mysteries. We are all starved for seeing with greater clarity as well as with a deeper consciousness. We begin on our path at one place and, step by step, we see more wisely, more compassionately, more lovingly.

During these deliberate seeing times when we make a commitment to be quiet, observing the beauty around us and also inside us, we feel our energy is happy. As we devote free time to pursuing our passions and pleasures, spontaneously at play, letting our imagination exhilarate our soul, we see with an expanded vision the overview of our life, not the nitty-gritty details that cause us to feel trapped by time. Many people seek happiness anywhere but in these private moments of reverie. Until we feel at one with ourselves, when we alone face the infinite mysteries, we will not see anything well. Become a sunrise and sunset appreciator. Often in the morning when we're at the cottage, I see the sunrise from the windows of my Zen Room. I throw them wide open, even in the winter, so I feel invigorated by the cold air. I'm completely alone to contemplate a new day. I've grown to need more and more this quiet time to muse. This reflective time shapes my attitude for the day, making me see with a larger vision, thinking loftier thoughts; before I concern myself with the business of life, I like to expose myself to my pure self, uninhibited by others.

We only need sight for visual understanding.

The eye is the best of artists.
EMERSON

Whenever you are mindful of the moment, wherever you literally are, you have the capability to be anywhere and everywhere you want to be. Fresh from your contemplative time, you visualize harmony and feel lighter and brighter because your awareness is wiser and more sublime. Contemplation, meditation, and introspection produce transcendent wisdom. Whether you tap into this inner state for a few seconds, several minutes, or hours, these epiphanies have a powerful effect on your faith, belief, and understanding.

All people are struggling to be creative in some way, and the artist is the one who has succeeded in this task of life.

ROLLO MAY

To see artistically, the way a poet, an artist, or a prophet does, you need to observe everything with keen appreciation. When we appreciate life fully, we open our eyes, our intellect, our heart, and our soul to pleasure and enjoyment of everyday rituals and celebrations. We need to appreciate what is good, because what is good is also good for us. Then we can value the good as truth as well as beauty. To know what you find beautiful and ideal is to give it value. You choose one thing over another because your unique consciousness finds certain things worthy. In order to discern good from bad, you have to know what is bad or wrong for you, therefore preferring what is good or right for you. Aesthetic consciousness required emotional consciousness. You have to believe in yourself wholeheartedly. We need to be conscious of our self-worth in order to give our life value and dignity. An increase in appreciative perception requires emotionally healthy persons to do their best under all circumstances.

Your feelings, desires, and pleasures mirror your values and appreciations. You are attracted to something because it makes you feel good. I value the worthiness of always living with fresh flowers because they make me feel a divine, spiritual connection. What are the elements in your own nature that make you receptive to beauty? Why are some people more susceptible to beauty than others? Those who have been blessed with early acute observation, who were exposed to beauty in both nature and man-made  objects at a young, impressionable age, and who have a strong desire to learn seem to be the ones whose excitement in seeing beauty is most vivid. They have come to understand the conditions that an object of beauty must fulfill: When something is beautiful you feel it viscerally—you feel pleasure and enjoyment.

Unless there is this quality of personal feeling, harmony is lacking. As the seventeenth-century Dutch philosopher and theologian Baruch Spinoza put it, "We desire nothing because it is good, but it is good only because we desire it."

You will, I am certain, appreciate all the infinite beauty in your midst once you open your eyes to see.

AFTERWORD

In these pages, I've given you, as best I can, a loving challenge. I've tried to help you open your eyes to a whole new
way of looking at your life at home and wherever you are each
day. It is my hope that you now have gained the essential
tools and training to help you continue to learn how to open
your eyes to see better and better, all the days of your life.

ACKNOWLEDGMENTS

*Deep appreciation to
my literary agent,
Carl Brandt, and
my editor, Toni Sciarra.*

INDEX